CIVIL RIGHTS

THE *1960s*

FREEDOM STRUGGLE

REVISED EDITION

SOCIAL MOVEMENTS PAST AND PRESENT

Irwin T. Sanders, Editor

CIVIL RIGHTS

T H E *1960s*

FREEDOM STRUGGLE

R E V I S E D   E D I T I O N

Rhoda Lois Blumberg

TWAYNE PUBLISHERS • BOSTON
A Division of G. K. Hall & Co.

Civil Rights: The 1960s Freedom Struggle, Revised Edition
Rhoda Lois Blumberg

Published by Twayne Publishers
A division of G. K. Hall & Co.
70 Lincoln Street
Boston, Massachusetts 02111

Copyediting supervised by Barbara Sutton.
Book production by Janet Z. Reynolds.
Typeset by Compset, Inc., Beverly, Massachusetts.

10 9 8 7 6 5 4 3 2 1 (hc)
10 9 8 7 6 5 4 3 2 1 (pb)

The paper used in this publication meets the minimum requirements
of American National Standard for Information Sciences—Permanence
of Paper for Printed Library Materials, ANSI Z39.48-1984. ∞™

Printed and bound in the United States of America.

Library of Congress Cataloging-in-Publication Data

Blumberg, Rhoda Lois.
    Civil rights : the 1960s freedom struggle / Rhoda Lois Blumberg.
—Rev. ed.
        p. cm.—(Social movements past and present)
    Includes bibliographical references (p.   ) and index.
    ISBN 0-8057-9733-5 (hc. : alk. paper).—ISBN 0-8057-9734-3 (pbk.
: alk. paper)
    1. Afro-Americans—Civil rights. 2. Afro-Americans—Legal status,
laws, etc. 3. United States—Race relations. 4. Civil rights
movement—United States—History—20th century. I. Title.
II. Series.
E185.615.B558   1991
323.1′96073—dc20   91-6425

for Sarah, Rachel, and Benjamin

Contents

Preface

The publication of a second edition of this book reflects the continuing interest of scholars, readers, and the author in this great American social movement. The first edition has been well received and used in many classes. Why, then, should there be a revised edition of a book about events that occurred some 30 years ago? There are at least two reasons for revising and adding. First, like any author, I had occasional second thoughts about aspects of my own work. There were times when I regretted not having said more about a particular event or adding another emphasis. Second, the literature on the civil rights movement has been enriched by a number of important new books, including vivid personal memoirs written by individuals who were actively involved in the movement on a day-to-day basis. Some of these were written by key women activists, who bring out the important role of women in behind-the-scenes organizing, educating, and risk-taking. Their work generally did not make headlines, nor were headlines sought. Too, it is now clear that mass mobilizations depended greatly on the participation of large numbers of females, old and young (see Morris 1984). Female high school and college students were prominent among those serving as test cases for desegregation and were not spared beatings, jailings, and attempted humiliation for their pioneering roles. I hope this second edition will be even more fully reflective of the significant part played by women in the civil rights movement. Some of the more recent books by men as well as women concur in this assessment.

In addition to the personal memoirs written by participants, scholars have painstakingly combed the compendious FBI files on movement organizations and individuals, and they have studied original records and communications. In the first edition, I referred to the FBI's surveillance of key leaders of the movement, especially Martin Luther King, Jr. Activists often joked about their telephones being tapped and their homes, hotel rooms, or offices being bugged. This was far from paranoia. The now-available record of highly intensive surveillance of civil rights and black power leaders and infiltration of their organizations shows that their concern was warranted. The FBI role becomes a powerful subplot in this whole narrative, one that some students might prefer not to believe. But the record is there, made available to us through the research of such scholars as Taylor Branch (1988), David Garrow (1986) and Kenneth O'Reilly (1989). At the famous 1963 March on Washington, speaker John Lewis was persuaded not to ask his question, "Which side is the federal government on?" O'Reilly provides an answer: "the FBI's conduct and the executive leadership that tolerated it constitutes as much a legacy of the 1960s as the Civil Rights Act of 1964 or the Voting Rights Act of 1965" (1989, 357). The reader will find more emphasis on the FBI role in this edition.

This edition has also tried to ferret out some discrepancies that appear in different accounts. Even eyewitnesses, however, vary in their recollections. My approach has been to interpret the civil rights movement sociologically, as a social movement. Many events occurred simultaneously and were interrelated; hence they cannot always be presented in sequential order. This book's brief chronology of major events may prove of help in placing them historically.

In the first edition I referred to the reaction of the 1980s that threatened to roll back black gains, making movement goals ever-relevant. There is little argument among civil rights proponents that the Reagan years were detrimental to civil rights—and that the legacy of that administration, in the form of judicial appointees, will be with us for some time to come. Unfortunately, the few black appointees made by President Reagan did little but mirror his views. This history reminds us that the need for a resurgence of movement activity occurs cyclically, as problems reemerge.

One successful movement goal—the reenfranchisement of African Americans—has continued to have visible results. In addition to increases in the numbers of black elected officials (some of them former civil rights leaders), Jesse Jackson's strong second-place showing in the 1988 Democratic party presidential primaries could only have occurred after the struggle described in these pages. Jackson himself was, of course, an important civil rights movement participant.

Two persons whom I somehow missed thanking in the first edition were my editor, John LaBine, who worked closely with me on that edition and contributed enormously, and Lynda M. Glennon, a former colleague, who was ever available for the sharing of ideas and problems. JoAnn Cunningham, of the Rutgers Africana Studies Department, provided valuable criticism of some of the material that is new in this edition. Responsibility for errors is, of course, my own. Thanks again to family members and friends who provided warmth and support, and to the Twayne social movement series editors, especially John Martin, for their graciousness and interest.

Preface to the First Edition

This book is about the black struggle for freedom that erupted in the mid-twentieth century and that was widely known at the time as the civil rights movement. The period from approximately 1955 to 1968 is viewed as the modern phase of a general social movement that began when the first Africans were brought to North America, soon to be permanently enslaved. The analysis utilizes but is not wedded to recent developments in social movement theory. It is guided by recognition of the interaction between active human agents that push a movement forward and societal forces that both facilitate and oppose it.

The 1955–56 bus boycott by the black citizens of Montgomery, Alabama, is taken as the key event that introduced nonviolent protest on a mass scale, mobilized and organized the aggrieved community with great effectiveness, and brought to the fore as a leader the Reverend Martin Luther King, Jr. The decline of this phase is marked by the death of King and the election of Richard Nixon.

The dialectical interaction between the movement and its environment effected change in the society and in the actors. Goals were achieved at a cost, both physical and psychological. Transformations in movement organizations and their leaders took place, as more diffuse economic and political goals replaced the earlier, specific objectives of desegregation and attainment of voting rights. A transition from allegiance to the ideology of nonviolence to one of black power and self-defense occurred within two of the major national civil rights groups and many local ones. The nation and the movement became embroiled in controversy over the undeclared war in Vietnam. Concomitantly, discontent with the powerlessness and poverty of ghetto life exploded in a series of urban rebellions.

The freedom struggle of African Americans was the major national issue during the presidencies of John F. Kennedy and Lyndon B. Johnson, until the Southeast Asian war supplanted it. Civil rights became a media event and a model for a decade of other social protest movements—those of youth, the women's movement, environmentalism, welfare rights, prison reform, and so on. Much was written about the movement while it was in process, both by scientific commentators and active participants. The literature of the 1960s reflects the spirit of the times, the hopes, doubts, criticisms, and predictions that were made.

Interest in civil rights remains strong for a number of reasons. The passage of years has brought forth hitherto concealed data about the interplay of forces as well as greater perspective on the movement's gains and disappointments. The Freedom of Information Act provided members of the public with previously classified information detailing the strategies projected toward the movement and its leaders by government agencies and officials. Strong suspicions of civil rights and black power leaders that their telephones were bugged and their movements electronically surveyed were proven correct. In addition, new research findings have been communicated that provide rich detail about specific organizations and specific movement events, as well as the lives and deaths of leaders. Finally, reaction in the 1980s threatens to turn back the clock on black gains, making movement goals more relevant than ever.

This book benefits from the new facts and retrospective insights, but also attempts to capture the spirit and drama of the movement as it occurred. The various elements are integrated into a comprehensive, nontechnical work, which, it is hoped, will bring the movement to life for the general reader and the college student. Apologies are offered in advance for any errors that have crept in, for it was not unusual to find sources disagreeing about factual details as well as interpretations. But all history is built upon a cumulation of such divergent sources. In addition to secondary data, the author's research on white women activists in the movement and her experience as a participant observer were utilized.

A book always reflects some personal involvement of the author, and in the present case the connection is clear. A white person, I nonetheless consider this "my" movement, the one in which I was daily and deeply involved for many years and which helped shape my life. After finishing a master's thesis that analyzed theories of race relations and their applications to the American South, I experienced the region firsthand—taking up a post as a research fellow at Fisk University in Nashville, Tennessee. Welcomed as two of the white junior faculty on campus, my husband and I had the great luck of being invited to share the home of the magnificent poet, the late Robert Hayden. A man of great principle and great kindness, Bob had not at that time received the recognition that would eventually be his.

My study of race relations continued at the University of Chicago with Louis Wirth before his untimely death. In that city, I met and had the privilege of working with another inspiring figure, Dr. Arthur G. Falls, cochairperson of the interracial Committee to End Discrimination in Chicago Medical Institutions. Later I continued my civil rights activities in a number of organizations in New Jersey communities. The demanding and stimulating juncture between intellectual and movement work created a high point in personal history.

There are insiders and outsiders in social movements: the insider is a member of the group directly affected by the changes sought; the outsider is a nonmember who is convinced of the rightness of the cause and for whom insiders are a reference group. Outsiders learn much from the insiders; nonetheless they are products of a different socialization. I write cognizant of my perspective as outsider and sociologist, but also as one who has shared the day-to-day emotional and intellectual problems of leadership in local civil rights organizations.

Originally, it has been planned to have an insider—sociologist Joyce Ladner—contribute a chapter assessing the gains of the movement. Professor Ladner, now of Howard University, was a movement activist in Mississippi and is one of the persons most qualified to review its impact. Unfortunately, however, serious health problems interfered with the completion of her chapter, and the plan had to be abandoned. I thank her for her willingness to again contribute to a book of mine and for her efforts to see the project through.

Rutgers University provided me with an academic leave to complete the work, and a Douglass Fellows opportunity grant subsidized the cost of illustrations. The Schomburg Center for Research in Black Culture was a rich source of varied materials. For pushing me into the computer age and thereby facilitating the act of writing, I am grateful to university colleagues Cathy Greenblat and Larry Baron. Irwin T. Sanders was a most gracious and helpful series editor. Miriam Goldberg, a longtime social activist, combined provocative challenge with constant support. My children were interested in my progress and encouraged me, as always. Most especially, I would like to thank my friend and colleague, William M. Phillips, Jr., for his critical reading of the manuscript, and his help in trying to save me from errors. Over the years, we have learned that, however painful at the time, the greater kindness is to spare not when criticizing the other's work. Responsibility for those errors or omissions that remain is, of course, that of the author. Thanks, too, to a dear aunt, Bess, and the other friends and relatives whose warmth and caring helped immeasurably.

A short book can provide only the highlights of complex and many-faceted events and point the interested person toward other specialized works. I hope readers will be stimulated to probe further into the rich literature available on this most important American movement.

Key activists lead the historic Selma-to-Montgomery march. *Left to right:* Bayard Rustin, A. Philip Randolph, John Lewis, Ralph Abernathy, Juanita Abernathy, Ralph Bunche, Martin Luther King, Jr., Coretta Scott King, Frederick Reese, Hosea Williams.

Chapter One

The Shaping of Black Resistance

But one thing I know, and that is that there is no middle ground for us. We must either have all the rights of American citizens, or we must be exterminated, for we can never again be slaves; nor can we cease to trouble the American people while any right enjoyed by others is denied or withheld from us. . . .

If there is no struggle there is no progress. Those who profess to favor freedom, and yet depreciate agitation, are men who want crops without plowing up the ground. . . . Power concedes nothing without a demand. It never did and it never will.

—Frederick Douglass

Black Americans have had to wage a continuing struggle for political, economic, and social rights in the United States—a battle not yet fully won. Periodically, they have managed to propel the issue of their civil rights from the periphery to the center of American political life. The decades of the 1950s and 1960s were that kind of time, when a nonviolent form of black protest arose with compelling force. Active refusal to accept enforced segregation and subordination was coupled with determination to avoid physical retaliation no matter how much protesters were abused, insulted, or harmed. Nonviolence was linked with direct, sometimes provocative action such as sit-ins, pray-ins, and wade-ins, as well as marches, boycotts, and rallies. The central tactic of the modern civil rights movement was also a principle intended to transform the two separate racial groups into a "beloved community" (King, M.L., 1958), but this hope was not to be realized.

Integration—the full and equal participation of black people in American institutions—was the objective. Ideological support was drawn from the U.S. Constitution and the Bill of Rights as well as from the precepts

1

of Christianity. The movement challenged the southern caste system—official segregation with its daily humiliations and white superiority justifications. The aim of desegregation or integration, however, was not to foster intermarriage or social "mixing," but to insure equal access to such basic rights as seats on buses, education, the vote, and fair trials when accused. Initially it was believed that this could be accomplished within the framework of American laws and the judicial system.

The modern nonviolent resistance phase was known as it was occurring as the civil rights movement.[1] Some analysts prefer to place the beginning of the movement somewhere in the early decades of the twentieth century, marked by the formation of the integration-oriented National Association for the Advancement of Colored People (NAACP) in 1909. But full civil rights had been the objective of earlier black activists, like abolitionist Frederick Douglass. Whatever we call it, the movement for black liberation has been ongoing, with significant peaks and ebbs.

The Periodicity of Black Protest

The modern civil rights movement represents one such peak in the struggle that began during slavery. Race relations in the United States have always been unstable, governed by underlying conflict. As Gurr has written, "Men and women of every social background . . . have resorted to violence against their rulers" (1970, 357). But protest does not and cannot always take the form of open rebellion. Those who challenge the system risk death or retaliation. For a corollary to the quotation by Gurr is that ruling groups tend to resist with every means at their command the efforts of subordinated groups to break their chains. The majority of white Americans have never supported in practice the idealized goals of full equality and social justice. Hence, the necessity for black protest has not died out but has been reshaped by changing opportunities.

The political, economic, cultural, and ideological posture of the nation toward its citizens of African ancestry[2] has provided an elusive and variable context for the emergence of black insurgency. Periods of extreme repression have fluctuated with times of comparative tolerance—not randomly, but in dialectical interaction with major economic and political changes. The predominant white mood has been affected by economic prosperity and decline, unemployment and labor shortage, war and peace, changing international climates, and competition from other issues. During repressive periods, martyrs may fight alone; at other times, substantial numbers of blacks and whites join in the struggle. An effective tactic under one set of circumstances may bring violent retribution under another. Those ahead of or behind "the times" risk disapproval and lack of support. It is no wonder, then, that black strategists have disagreed among themselves, as they continually reassessed the limits of what was possible in a given environment.

The Contrast of Different Historical Periods

The recurrent resistance of black people to the degradation and inconvenience of segregated public transportation illustrates a tactic that has sometimes worked and sometimes failed. This grievance set off the modern civil rights movement, yet it had been attacked before with varying success. During the Reconstruction period of the 1870s, black folk had successfully boycotted streetcars in Savannah, Georgia, and were able to desegregate them in four other southern cities. In sharp contrast, boycotts of segregated streetcars undertaken in 26 southern cities between 1900 and 1907 ended in failure. These latter efforts "occurred at a time when southern racism was reaching its crest and when the white South had gained a respectful hearing in the North" (Meier and Rudwick 1969). Nor could the protesters hope for support from the courts, for in the infamous 1896 *Plessy* v. *Ferguson* decision, the Supreme Court upheld "separate but equal" transportation laws.

Conditions were different in the middle of the twentieth century when a bus boycott created the dramatic take-off of the modern civil rights movement. In an organized protest, 50,000 black citizens of Montgomery, Alabama, rejected the daily humiliations of segregation and refused to ride the city buses. The boycott lasted for almost a year, until the Supreme Court upheld a district court judgment that segregated buses were illegal. The Montgomery action brought a young minister, Martin Luther King, Jr., to national attention and initiated the nonviolent direct action phase of black protest.

Issues in Black Protest

Most of the other issues tackled by the civil rights movement were also not new in the twentieth century, but rather were variations on earlier themes. What are the objectives that have prompted black people to organize and struggle? Quite simply, they have wanted the same rights as other Americans and an end to color discrimination and prejudice. Here are their most pressing demands:

1. Freedom from enslavement and destruction of family
2. The right to earn a living: land, jobs
3. Freedom from harassment, terror, and violence
4. Equal justice
5. The right to vote
6. Quality education
7. Integration, or alternatively, escape from oppression
8. Recognition of the African cultural heritage
9. The right to self-pride and end to stereotyping

Freedom from enslavement is such an obvious entitlement that it is hard to believe that an image of "happy slaves" was ever promulgated. Africans had arrived in the North American British colonies in 1619, along with white indentured laborers, but within a few decades they were singled out for "perpetual servitude." Their bondage was made legally permanent in Virginia in 1666 and shortly afterward in the other slave states.

African Americans suffered three deprivations that other minorities did not. First, Africans were the only people enslaved, treated not as human beings with feelings but as pieces of property who—in the land of free enterprise—were unable to profit from the fruits of their own labor. Second, tribes and family members were cruelly separated from one another, weakening the personal bonds that give sustenance and strength. Slave breeding and the selling of family members thwarted attempts to develop a stable family life, despite many permanent marital unions. Black womanhood and manhood were violated as slaves were treated as subhumans and reproductive animals. Black women were subject to sexual violation by white owners, sometimes in front of their husbands.[3] No wonder then that the earliest hopes of black slaves were for freedom— this regardless of whether masters were "good" or "bad" (Litwack 1980). As slavery ended, many set out to find their lost relatives and to reunite their families.

The third severe deprivation stemmed from the first two. In order to justify slavery, an elaborate theory of biological inferiority based on color was constructed. African people were dehumanized and their cultures denigrated. This ideological system and its underlying assumptions became institutionalized; it confronted black folk every day and continues to be revived and reinforced during periods of racial unrest. Such a psychological assault was intended to create feelings of inferiority and resignation, lessening the need for constant surveillance and physical force. No other color group was as stigmatized in the United States as were people of African descent.

The earliest forms of protest against slavery were the efforts—sometimes successful—of captured Africans to jump off slave ships or to resist physically while being transported. Soon numerous measures were contrived to keep slaves docile. Whites could use physical force, but their subjects had no right to resist it. Both men and women were subjected to such cruelties as being lashed with whips and branded by hot irons. They were forced to labor hard for bare sustenance. Somehow they found ways of resisting their masters—ranging from play-acting the fool or the "Uncle Tom" to quiet acts of subversion, slow-down, and sabotage. Their narratives show that they managed to maintain a group life even in their desperate condition. Against overwhelming odds, a number of slave revolts occurred—most notably those led by Gabriel in 1800, Denmark Vesey in 1822, and Nat Turner in 1831 (Meier and Rudwick 1976, 81). Fear of revolts and the growing controversy over slavery just prior to the Civil War led to tighter, more vicious control over the subjugated people. Some free black leaders, such as the noted physician-activist Martin R. Delaney, proposed colonization to another land as the only avenue for full freedom—a position that would resurface more than once in the twentieth century.

Repression could only create periods of seeming adjustment or racial accommodation until new opportunities for protest arose. As southern whites intensified their struggle to maintain the dying system of slavery, free black persons joined the abolitionist movement, bought freedom for family members, and risked transporting slaves through the underground railroad. The celebrated escaped slave Sojourner Truth made numerous forays into the South to lead others out. Both free and slave blacks volunteered for the Union Army and, once allowed into combat, proved themselves courageous soldiers—although they were paid less than their white counterparts (Litwack 1980, 81).

The power struggle between the North and the South continued after abolition; policies toward freedmen were widely debated in Congress. The intransigence of the South led to the period of Radical Reconstruction (1867–77), and northern troops occupied the South. It was a relatively hopeful time for the former slaves. Many voted, and a number held important offices. National politics, however, determined the mood of the next period. To insure his contested election as president, Rutherford B. Hayes agreed to withdraw northern troops from the South. Helping the newly freed people lost priority, despite the efforts of a few important friends in Congress, such as Charles Sumner. By the 1890s, the southern states had begun to pass Black Codes, laws to disenfranchise black people, segregate them in all areas of life, and relegate them to a permanently subservient status. The "golden age of racism" had begun. Economic serfdom, bolstered by outright violence, became the rule for the masses of landless, uneducated, and impoverished former slaves.

Economic goals, or more simply the wish to make a living, are a motivating force for any people. The freed slaves dearly hoped the government would give them land to own and farm. They suffered a sharp disappointment when Reconstruction ended and the federal government returned land to the former slaveowners. Blacks continued to seek jobs and economic security and later protested against job and union discrimination. Some had been able to learn skilled trades before the Civil War. Competition between them and white workers began, spurred on by employers who could profit from their rivalry. In 1890 a serious national depression caused great unrest; and the Populist party, supported by black and white farmers, promised interracial unity and briefly threatened the hegemony of the southern Democrats. Terror, fraud, and the played-upon fear of black domination defeated the Populists (Bloom 1987, 39–43). The American Federation of Labor (AFL), founded in 1881, came to exclude black workers, alienating many blacks from organized labor. Unemployment and job discrimination would continue to be major issues for the African American population.

Similarly, the quest for freedom from harassment, terror, and violence has been a central theme in black life. Free blacks, always fearing a return to bondage, fought for their own rights as well as the end of slavery. Black women had little protection against sexual violation, and the personal safety of their men was always tenuous and uncertain. The Ku Klux Klan, a hooded terrorist group, arose during Reconstruction to preserve white supremacy; it would have a number of later, equally vicious reincarnations. White violence, often overlooked and ignored, created such an atmosphere of terror that protest followed the predominant slave pattern of indirection, secrecy, and withdrawal into a separate black world. Knowing that even a rebellious glance or word might bring retaliation, southern black folk practiced nonviolence as a survival technique. The learning of controlled response to white aggression may help explain the self-discipline exhibited by a later generation of movement participants.

Lynching—group murder of a person untried and unconvicted for an alleged or rumored act—was a widely used terrorist tactic directed against African Americans from Reconstruction on. Recorded lynchings of blacks reached a high of 235 in 1892 and averaged 150 a year in the late 1880s and early 1890s (Wilson 1973, 102). Leading a public struggle against lynching in the 1890s, Ida Wells Barnett, a black journalist and newspaper owner, personally investigated the circumstances of 728 lynchings and publicly exposed the myths surrounding them. Barnett's newspaper office was burned to the ground, and she was unable to return to her home in Memphis (Giddings 1984, 26–30). Klan members, responsible for much of the lynching and violence, were never brought to justice. For 40 years (1909–1950) the NAACP attempted to push legislation against lynching through Congress (Zangrando 1980).[4] During the latter half of this period (1931–50), nine young men, all but one of them teenagers at the time of their arrest, fought for their lives and freedom after being falsely accused of rape by two white women in Alabama. An example of "legal lynching," the case of the Scottsboro Boys, as it was called, was based on flimsy and contradictory evidence and drew national and international attention.

Violence has tended to increase immediately after instances of black advance, which appears to threaten the racial privileges of some whites. Post–Civil War bombings of black churches and murders of assertive blacks would find a parallel during the civil rights movement, which would be severely tried many times by the hostile acts of whites. Martin Luther King, Jr., has written movingly of his successful effort to prevent violent reaction when his home was bombed and his family only miraculously escaped injury (King 1958).

Equal justice is a related issue that has strongly motivated black protest. The right to a fair trial, to a jury of one's peers, to restrained and courteous treatment by police, sheriffs, courts, and other agencies of law enforcement, to fair verdicts and sentences—all have been frequently denied to African Americans. The unequal justice system in the American South was documented in 1944 by Swedish social scientist Gunnar Myrdal. He found that black crimes against whites were routinely treated much more severely than white crimes against blacks; Caucasians were almost never found guilty of any crime against blacks (Myrdal 1944, ch. 26). This pattern continued during the civil rights movement, as unsolved bombings of black homes and churches and murders of activists proliferated.

The attainment of voting rights has been another major goal—sought by blacks and their white allies after the Civil War, won and again denied by the manipulations of state and local governments in the post-Reconstruction era, and once more a key issue of struggle in the 1960s. Voting rights have been seen as essential for the attainment and protection of other rights.

Satisfactory education has been another recurrent but elusive objective. The furtive acquisition of literacy by slaves who had been formally denied this right became a massive rush to school by ex-slaves after the war, which culminated in the 1950s and 1960s battle to end separate and unequal education. White resistance to court-ordered desegregation would continue into the 1970s and 1980s, given a new impetus by changing executive policy.

Proposed Solutions

A small educated leadership class had developed even as early as the 1830s when free blacks debated the problems faced by their people and tried to formulate solutions. One strand of thought held that African Americans, like other ethnic groups, had shared in the building of the country, belonged here, and should become assimilated into the general society. This belief underlay the goal of integration, usually an instrumental goal. That is, access to all institutions of the society is required to attain educational, economic and political progress. Alternately, as suggested earlier, a belief in the need for separation from whites has flourished during some historical periods—especially during times of disillusionment. This view holds that white Americans will never accept black people on an equal basis. Early black nationalist thought contained the seeds of a later flowering in its emphasis on the international bonds between people of African descent, their proud cultural heritage, and the need to direct their own fate.

Why should black people view separation from whites as necessary? First, reliance on one's own group may be the only secure response to threatened white hostility, rejection, and violence. Self-help minimizes contacts with whites. Second, withdrawal from whites can also encourage unity and create a stronger black consciousness. It reaffirms the value of the group and of African American and African cultures. Emphasis on pride in black culture, "soul," and group achievements provides an antidote to antiblack stereotypes. Self-pride and unity are necessary not only for psychological well-being but also for fueling the fires of black protest.

The struggle for basic rights has occurred within a fluctuating environment of national and international events. Some conditions would give black people increased leverage, such as defense and wartime needs for their labor. Others, such as postwar recessions, would reverse many of the advances. Open group protest could be mobilized when opportunity for change was combined with a belief in its possibility. As we examine the civil rights movement, we will take into account the factors in the environment conducive to protest and those that ultimately led to its decline.

The Rise of the Modern Civil Rights Movement

After scattered efforts to repeat the success that had been achieved by the Montgomery Improvement Association in 1955–56, a second major event occurred early in 1960 in Greensboro. Four first-year students from North Carolina Agricultural and Technical College took seats at a segregated lunch counter and refused to move until they were served. They adopted the nonviolent tactics and philosophy advocated by Martin King and practiced by the Congress of Racial Equality (CORE). Their return each day to the segregated lunch counter, despite increasingly hostile treatment, drew the support of other black and some white students throughout the South as well as adult leaders, and sparked sit-ins in hundreds of cities. Sympathetic demonstrations occurred throughout the nation. The movement was on, in full force.

The Deep South responded with massive resistance. Civil rights workers and black citizens were arrested, beaten, jailed, deprived of their jobs, intimidated, and killed. A reluctant federal government was ultimately forced to protect black Americans and to guarantee their rights. Important court decisions were handed down, major federal legislation was passed, public facilities such as transportation and waiting rooms were desegregated, and black citizens gained better access to the polling booths.

The Rise of the Black Power Movement

Toward the middle of the 1960s a fissure developed. The nonviolent direct action approach was overshadowed by an evolving black power philosophy among some of the activists. Both versions of black protest sought to improve the conditions of America's largest racial minority group, but they differed sharply on the means to that end. Analysis of the progress and disappointments of the civil rights movement—this book's major focus—helps us to understand how the black power movement came about. Young activists who had suffered beatings and jailings, who had been disappointed in their efforts to work within the official system, became increasingly disenchanted with integrationist aims and nonresistance. Nonviolent protest continued at a reduced rate, but significant leaders like Malcolm X arose to disagree with the nonviolent integrationist philosophy of Martin Luther King and his allies.

Black power was a nationalist, seemingly more revolutionary ideology that rejected white American culture and paralleled the nationalist movements of the formerly colonized abroad. It held that racism could not be eradicated from white hearts and minds, that blacks needed unity and self-pride rather than integration, and that self-defense was a proper response. The various black power groups of the late 1960s differed in the details of their analysis and their proposed programs (see Pinkney 1976). But once again the two responses to white racism—integration and separation—competed, now publicized through widespread and sometimes sensational media coverage. The themes were also reflected in the imagery of social scientists, from the race relations cycle of Park (1950), which envisioned ultimate assimilation, to the internal colonialism model of Blauner (1973), which portrayed blacks as a colonized people.

Riots and Rebellions

A third and related form of protest also surfaced in the 1960s. Urban rebellions or "riots" occurred in many American cities, beginning with a relatively brief one in Birmingham, Alabama, in 1963. Black citizens there responded to the vicious police treatment of nonviolent protesters and the bombing of homes of civil rights leaders, which seemed to occur with the acquiescence of the authorities. The next year, Harlem, Rochester, and Philadelphia experienced riots. Rampages of looting and burning were often targeted at stores owned by whites in black ghettos. Uprisings followed in a number of other cities between 1965 and 1968 (Waskow 1967; Pettigrew 1971). A wave of urban disorders was one of the pained and angry responses to the assassination of Martin Luther King, Jr., in 1968.

Scholars and activists who prefer to call them rebellions say that the riots were not random but expressed anger—anger at the conditions under which people were forced to live, at economic exploitation, and at official and unofficial white violence. Most frequently the disturbances were precipitated by police actions against black citizens. Riots earlier in the century had been directed against blacks; this new wave was called "property riots" because the main targets were ghetto property.

Class and Regional Differences in Black–White Relations

In many instances we have talked of blacks and whites without noting differences within each group. These shortcut references to racial groups are not intended to include *all* members of a given category but those who share their predominant thought and behavior patterns. Obviously, all black people do not think and behave and react alike, nor do all white people. Yet there has been a consistent and deep gulf between the two groups on *issues pertaining to race*. The Kerner Commission, investigating the urban rebellions of the 1960s, came to the conclusion that the country was severely divided racially. Periodic public opinion polls have revealed wide disagreements between blacks and whites regarding the pace of black progress (see, for example, Brink and Harris 1966, 120).

The overlapping of the major socio-economic divisions of the society with racial and ethnic divisions has long preoccupied social scientists. Speaking simplistically, some have argued for the primacy of class divisions over racial divisions or the reverse in determining life chances. The position taken here is less extreme. It postulates that racial divisions were first created to serve class interests and then developed into a powerful independent factor in American life. Class interests persist and continue to influence racial interaction.

Class analysis accepts as real that one's position as owner, worker, tenant, landless laborer, businessperson, or slave affects basic life conditions, motivations, and actions. These positions create different class interests. Class analysis notes the divisions *within* racial groups and that changes in overall group position affect each differently. Obviously, slave-owners served to lose if slavery were abolished; their slaves certainly stood to gain freedom from bondage and probably some of the other privileges and rights of freedom. Slaveowners failed to understand the extent to which slave behavior derived from accommodation and how much most slaves wanted freedom. Less obvious were the effects of Emancipation on poor nonslaveholding whites and blacks who were born free.

The different economic structures and class configurations of the North and South at the time of slavery helped shape consequent behavior. Prior to the Civil War, there were three main classes in the South: 2 million slaveholding whites, 5 million relatively powerless nonslaveholding whites, and almost 4 million black slaves. An oligarchy of 8,000 slaveholders really ruled the region (Du Bois 1969). According to Jack Bloom, "The racial patterns that developed in the South were shaped in an economic system that depended upon cheap, plentiful, and easily controlled black labor. . . . White supremacy . . . was the ideological foundation on which the Southern elite created a ruling coalition that it dominated" (Bloom 1987, 2).

The ruling elite established a belief system to support the notion that slavery was the true and proper state of the "inferior" race. All kinds of stereotypes (false and exaggerated images) were created as self-fulfilling prophecies. For example slaves were prohibited from learning to read; hence, most were in fact illiterate. Their use of such tactics as slowdowns or breaking tools led to their reputation as malingerers who needed the whip to motivate them. These images were not confined to the South but became part of the cultural baggage of many northern whites as well.

The nonslaveholding whites consisted of more than one group. There was a large bloc of yeoman farmers, artisans, and mechanics and a smaller number of the more familiar "poor whites" (Den Hollander 1953). Many of the latter were illiterate and degraded. Yet racial divisions distracted them from comparing their own position with that of the affluent white planters. From this class, whose only claim to status was their white skins, were drawn the overseers and vigilante groups who hunted escaped slaves. Poor whites could perform the more overt antiblack acts, while the upper class did not have to dirty its hands. Their later counterparts were the sheriffs, police, and hostile crowds of the modern civil rights era. This class continued to act out its hatred and compensate for its own problems, while richer and more powerful men in state legislatures and corporations made larger policies detrimental to black people.

A related issue is the question of the part played by different classes in social movements. Leaders often receive much attention, but the masses—the vast majority of everyday people—may, at certain periods of history, take crucial action as a collectivity. Du Bois's scholarly analysis of the role of slaves in the Civil War attributes enormous importance to the behavior of slaves in joining the Union Army en masse, first as workers and then as fighters. Du Bois explains "how the black worker won the war by a general strike which transferred his labor from the Confederate planter to the Northern invader, in whose army lines workers began to be organized as a new labor force" (1969).[5] The mass movement of African Americans out of the rural South northward to cities in the twentieth century would again show how significant the collective behavior of large numbers of people could be.

The issue of masses and elites surfaced in the modern civil rights movement, in a debate over whom its gains would benefit. The southern masses did mobilize for the movement even though its goals did not, at first, deal with their serious economic problems. Blacks were ready for a change when King appeared on the scene as minister of the Dexter Avenue Baptist Church in Atlanta. Clearly a member of the southern elite, King came from a line of ministers, held a Ph.D., and had received several offers of teaching jobs when he decided to assume a pastorate in his native region. His leadership and that of the southern ministry around him clicked with the mood of the African American masses at a particular moment in history.

North–South Differences

The old South's paternalistic pattern of race relations (van den Berghe 1967) represented extreme power differences between two major groups in an agrarian economy. Members of the so-called inferior group were stereotyped and treated like children; the ruling group assumed responsibility for those it had enslaved. A living contradiction to racial stereotypes were the free blacks, some of whom had acquired property and learned skilled trades. As the Civil War approached, they suffered much discrimination.

The paternalism of master-slave relations did not characterize northern racism. The northern slave population never numbered more than 70,000, and only a minority of upper-class northerners benefited directly from their labor. By 1804, all the northern states had either passed antislavery laws or provided for gradual emancipation. Still, many whites of this region had come to accept the theories of biological racism propounded by proslavery apologists.

The competitive form of race relations characteristic of the industrializing North focused on the relationships between laboring blacks and laboring whites. Free black persons competed with immigrants for jobs rather than forming alliances based on similar class interests. The brief attempt at labor unity by the Knights of Labor in the 1880s referred to earlier was overshadowed by the restrictive new AFL. For much of the twentieth century, A. Philip Randolph, head of the Brotherhood of Sleeping-Car Porters, would wage a relentless battle to break down the barriers of racial discrimination in white unions.

White labor, fighting for its own rights, took little interest in the abolition of slavery and was less aware of the effects of unpaid slave labor than it was of free blacks competing for jobs in the cities. (Interestingly, the reluctance of northern whites to take part in the Civil War hastened the acceptance of black troops and their ultimate emancipation.) Employers sometimes preferred black workers because they could pay them less; but frequently the only jobs available were as strikebreakers. This increased the hostility of white workers, even precipitating race riots. A white mob wounded and killed free blacks and fugitive slaves and destroyed property for three days in 1829 in Cincinnati, Ohio (Du Bois 1969).

The border states (Delaware, Kentucky, Maryland, Missouri, and Virginia) were also tied into the slavery system but wanted the southern cotton states to remain in the Union. Their economic interests lay in preserving the internal slave trade and the slave-breeding industry, which had flourished when the international slave trade was successfully limited.

The divisions between the North and South continued after Emancipation, when the South tried to reinstitute a slaverylike system. To gain better representation in Congress, the white South preferred to have blacks counted as part of the population—but without the vote, for if they were to vote, they might swing the balance of power to northern interests. On the eve of the civil rights movement, major differences existed between North and South with regard to black people's ability to register and vote without harassment and to the prevalence of legal segregation.

The North was not necessarily more moral than the South, but its interests were different. During the years of lynchings, the North never took the problem seriously enough to pass an antilynching bill in Congress. Yet the migrations of black people to the North in the twentieth century and their use of the ballot became crucial factors in the eventual passage of civil rights legislation. Moreover, the North could sympathize with blacks protesting against particularly southern discriminations. In subsequent years, when the fight against de facto school and housing segregation extended to the North, some northern communities proved to be as resistant and racist as the South had been.

Whites in the Movement

Sympathetic whites have been involved in the black struggle for freedom from the earliest times. John Brown, who led a slave revolt, was considered a fanatic by other whites and a martyr by the people whose cause he championed. It was easier, at first, for northerners to join in the civil rights struggle. Nevertheless, despite intimidation and abuse, a small number of courageous white southerners, and sometimes their families, participated—such as members of the clergy, college students, journalists, lawyers, medical workers, and a few outstanding judges who, unlike their peers, upheld the constitutional rights of black people and movement workers.

There are always some "outsiders" who, because of their own intellectual, political, or psychological development, come to understand the perspectives of disadvantaged groups in their midst. Particularly in the beginning stages of movements, these outsiders may provide important resources and support. But because of the different life experiences of insiders and outsiders and their previously segregated worlds, they frequently encounter difficulties in working together. The outsider, no matter how dedicated, may be seen as one who can escape if necessary. Thus, a person's degree of sensitivity and of commitment becomes an issue. No definitive analysis of the role of white people in the civil rights movement has emerged as yet. It is a topic to which we will return.

The movement was trying to create changes in a society dominated and run by white people. Some of them, the nation's leaders, would be forced to take positions in support of the black struggle, guided by such diverse factors as the need to preserve law and order, to prevent the disruption of business, and to garner the votes of blacks and liberal whites. Other forces within government, like the FBI, strongly opposed the movement and were covertly attempting to discredit the man whom most black people saw as their most important leader, Martin Luther King, Jr. (Garrow 1981, O'Reilly 1989). Like Lincoln before them, Presidents Roosevelt, Truman, Eisenhower, Kennedy, and Johnson were forced to take important public actions in response to the civil rights issues.

Conclusion

Some of the central themes outlined above will be fleshed out in succeeding chapters as we examine the civil rights movement—the first major movement of the 1960s, and one that clearly influenced movements of other ethnic groups as well as the peace, student, and women's movements of that turbulent decade. The question we will examine is not why the civil rights movement occurred but why it was able to grow, to mobilize tremendous support in the face of so much opposition, and to gain national media attention and significant financial resources at its peak. The dynamics of the movement, its organizational expressions and leaders, the opposition it faced, its problems and victories will all be explored. In order not to interrupt the narrative, the social movement theory that informs this analysis appears in an appendix.

I hope, finally, that the spirit of the movement, as well as its factual aspects, will be conveyed.

Paul Robeson, scholar, lawyer, actor, singer, and athlete, persecuted for his early struggles against colonialism and racism. *Laurance Henry Collection, Schomburg Center for Research in Black Culture.*

Chapter Two

From Accommodation to Protest

We wear the mask that grins and lies,
It hides our cheeks and shades our eyes,—
This debt we pay to human guile;
With torn and bleeding hearts we smile,
And mouth with myriad subtleties.

Why should the world be overwise,
In counting all our tears and sighs?
Nay, let them see us, while
    We wear the mask.

We smile, but O great Christ, our cries
To Thee from tortured souls arise.
We sing, but oh, the clay is vile
Beneath our feet, and long the mile;
But let the world dream otherwise,
    We wear the mask.
                —Paul Laurence Dunbar,
                    "We Wear the Mask"

Trends and events in the first half of the twentieth century significantly affected black people and provided the necessary conditions for the successful take-off of the civil rights movement. Militant free and ex-slave black leaders had come forward prior to the Civil War; whites as well as blacks had struggled in the abolitionist movement. Yet by the end of the nineteenth century, the main spokesperson for the race was the accommodationist leader Booker T. Washington, who espoused gradual change rather than political action.

Poverty, segregation, and violence were rampant when Washington came to prominence. Most former slaves had been deprived of their newly won right to vote and were still members of a rural peasantry in the South. Washington advised adjustment to the biracial situation and to disenfranchisement. He stressed self-help, racial solidarity, economic accumulation, and industrial education. His polite, conciliatory stance toward whites was coupled with the premise that black folk should take responsibility for their own advancement—to prove themselves worthy of the rights many thought they had already won.[1]

Washington's 1895 speech at the Cotton States and International Exposition in Atlanta was hailed by whites. He gained the financial backing of foundations and controlled, through the "Tuskegee machine," important governmental appointments of b¹ack individuals during the Theodore Roosevelt and Taft administrations.

Protest had not entirely died out. The Afro-American Council, in existence from 1890 to 1908, had a militant outlook. Ida Wells Barnet took her campaign against lynching to the British Isles, gaining international attention. Through her efforts the incidence of lynching began to decrease in 1893. "The decline in the murders can be directly attributed to the efforts of Ida B. Wells," according to Giddings (1984, 92). Black women formed the National Association of Colored Women, a confederation of nationwide clubs oriented to the progress of the race and its women. Wells Barnet and William Monroe Trotter, editor of the outspoken *Boston Guardian,* lashed out against Booker T. Washington. W. E. B. Du Bois gradually made public his growing disagreements with Washington. Through his role as editor of *Crisis* magazine, Du Bois would renew the move toward integration and equal rights. But until his death in 1915, Booker T. Washington remained the most influential political figure of the race.

What happened to move a people from accommodation to protest? The most important interacting events that made the transition possible included:

1. A mass migration of black peasantry out of the South, eventuating in their transformation to a predominantly urban group

2. White violence against the black urban newcomers, which demanded response

3. Two world wars and an economic depression

4. Years of litigation culminating in important legal victories
5. The development of community institutions and organizations in the cities
6. The rise of leaders who utilized opportunities for protest and were able to mobilize potential participants
7. A changed international climate confronting American racism

These interrelated developments and the efforts of particular leaders and organizations will be presented chronologically.

The Migration of Black Peasantry Out of the Rural South

The unorganized movement of a large mass of people is not a social movement, but it may create the necessary preconditions for one. Migrations had occurred immediately following the Civil War, but most were over relatively short distances, from county to county or rural to urban areas within the South. As of 1910, 90 percent of black people were still living in the rural South. Isolated and dependent on whites, they were preoccupied with economic survival and physical safety.

Emancipation and the brief Reconstruction period provided legal freedom but left former slaves destitute in the rural South. The Freedmen's Bureau, a federal agency, had attempted to distribute abandoned lands to them but was thwarted by Andrew Johnson's decision to return these properties to the former Confederates (Meier and Rudwick 1976). A labor contract system instituted during the Civil War and early Reconstruction years so strictly and legally bound the farm workers to the plantation owners that it seemed like another form of slavery. The sharecropping system that succeeded it differed in that the freedman rented land and paid the owner a proportion of his cotton crop.

Although sharecropping was preferred to the labor contract, many abuses arose—such as a credit system that kept the tenants in debt to landlords and store owners. Economic bondage was supported by intimidation and an unequal justice system, in which a black person could never successfully challenge a white person's word. Frequent lynchings made the point that black folk should not protest the white man's economics. White riots against blacks were the South's response to those who tried to vote or hold office.

Movement to urban areas and the North would be a necessary precondition to open group protest, and such movement occurred. Almost half a million rural black people did indeed leave their homelands in the

Members of a tenant farming family near Greensboro, Alabama, 1941. *Delano, Farm Security Administration photograph, Schomburg Center for Research in Black Culture.*

crucial decade of 1910–20. The proportion making interstate moves was larger than in any previous 10-year span (Kennedy 1930, 23). Two important developments pushed them out of the South and into northern cities.

Natural events combined to make agriculture disastrous in the important 1910–20 decade: the ravages of the boll weevil, an insect pest that destroyed acres and acres of crops, and the terrible 1915 floods in Alabama and Mississippi, two states heavily populated by blacks. Kennedy (1930) maintains that hope for greater freedom and justice in the North was an additional motivating force.

A second development that pulled blacks away from the South was the need for black workers in northern factories. The coming of World War I had cut off the heavy flow of European immigrants. Defense industries needed replacements for this source of labor and for men entering the armed forces. Northern recruiters traveled southward, offering black workers free transportation and the promise of better conditions. The federal government and northern newspapers joined in the plea, and they were supported by personal accounts of friends and relatives (Ottley 1968, 34).

Similarly, the onset of World War II led to another major migration to the North. (Both wars had other important effects—as shall be seen later in this chapter.) For the first part of the century, the energies of black people would be devoted primarily to defensive measures against white violence. The two wars, a major depression, and decades of litigation would intervene before the nonviolent offensive against southern segregation and disenfranchisement could take off.

Unfortunately, the movement of black people to cities did not go unresisted. Major riots occurred in the early 1900s—pogroms of violence directed against African Americans. The Atlanta riot of September 1906 was precipitated by a local political campaign in which disenfranchisement was the issue. The white press helped to stir up white mobs who were then aided and abetted by the police. Many were killed and injured, more blacks than whites—a pattern true of most race riots.

The year before, the debate between the accommodationist Washington and the militant Trotter had come to a head at a disruptive public meeting in Boston. Trotter's arrest and imprisonment for interrupting the meeting so angered Du Bois that he called black leaders together to form the Niagara Movement, an important precursor of the NAACP. Note the basic ideals of democracy enumerated in the principles of the Niagara Movement:

1. Freedom of speech and criticism
2. An unfettered and unsubsidized press
3. Manhood suffrage
4. The abolition of all caste distinctions based simply on race and color
5. The recognition of the principle of human brotherhood as a practical present creed
6. The recognition of the highest and best human training as the monopoly of no class or race
7. A belief in the dignity of labor
8. United effort to realize these ideals under wise and courageous leadership (Du Bois 1968, 249)

In 1909, the Niagara Movement merged with the new interracial organization, the NAACP. According to Du Bois, "The NAACP started with a lynching 100 years after the birth of Abraham Lincoln, and in the city, Springfield, Illinois which was his long time residence" (1968, 254). An August 1908 riot in Springfield had reached major proportions. Whites lynched two black persons and forced two hundred others to flee (Zangrando 1980). Property damage was high, and business activity was paralyzed for ten days. It took 4,000 militia to restore order.

Shocked by this violence, white liberals and reformers, led by Mary White Ovington and Oswald Garrison Villard, called for an organizing meeting. Many scientists and social workers attended, and most of those in the Niagara Movement joined. Others were wary of an interracial organization. Du Bois agreed to leave Atlanta University to become director of publications and research for the NAACP. From then on, he played a major role in black life, serving as editor of its magazine, the *Crisis,* from 1910 to 1934.

Another still-extant black organization with branches in major cities, the National Urban League, was created in 1911. Basically a social welfare agency, the League would concentrate on employment issues but use a conciliatory approach for most of its national history. (Occasionally, individual branches departed from official conservatism.) The NAACP, in contrast, would use investigation, education, litigation, lobbying, and publicity to seek federal action against lynching and other abuses. Seen as radical by southern whites, the NAACP would be a frequent target of more militant black organizations.

The alliance of blacks and white liberals continued in the NAACP, but not without problems. White liberals and reformers could be stirred by outright violence against unarmed blacks, but many carried the heritage of conscious or unconscious feelings of white superiority. Du Bois writes the following about Villard, one of the founders of the NAACP:

To a white philanthropist like Villard, a Negro was quite naturally expected to be humble and thankful or certainly not assertive and aggressive; . . . . There was much that I liked in Villard himself, but one thing despite all my effort kept us far apart. He had married a wife from Georgia, a former slave state, and consequently I could never step foot in his house as a guest, nor could any of his colored associates. Indeed I doubt if any of his Jewish co-workers were ever invited. I knew the reasons for this discrimination, but I could hardly be expected to be happy over them or to be his close friend. (Du Bois 1968, 256–57)

The Impact of World War I

In spite of its horrors, war nevertheless provides new opportunities and the hope for greater equality. A nation at war urgently requires internal unity and the full cooperation of its citizens. Out of necessity, exclusionary practices are modified, providing members of minority groups with a chance to demonstrate their loyalty and ability. Labor needs increase as men go off to battle, industries gear up for military production, and the armed forces seek new sources of recruitment. However, gains made during wartime frequently occur under a cloud of discrimination and segregation. When the war ends, segments of the population must compete for the decreased pool of jobs and the neglected, deteriorated housing supply.

Paralleling these developments are changes in the consciousness of both blacks and whites. The former seek to retain the small gains they have earned. The latter feel entitled to their former advantages in jobs and housing, and many are alarmed by the increased presence of black people in cities. This is what occurred after World War I.

Black Americans have volunteered for every U.S. war despite the government's reluctance to utilize them in combat or provide equal treatment.[2] During the Civil War, the North began to experiment with the use of black troops under white commanders only when it encountered resistance from white draftees and appeared to be losing the war. When slaves were finally permitted to fight, rather than being confined to the hard labor of supporting other troops, they could expect no mercy from the southern white enemy. Black prisoners were rarely taken alive. Nonetheless, they continued to enlist, proving their bravery and valor.

During World War I, black soldiers had to struggle to be allowed into combat once again. They trained and fought in segregated units and often were allowed to perform only the most menial of tasks. Their housing and recreational facilities were inferior and segregated. The much-decorated 369th Infantry Regiment fought alongside the French army because they were not allowed to fight with white Americans.[3] Blacks who found civilian employment in the North were often confronted with continuing racism by both employers and unions. President Wilson maintained segregation in all governmental agencies during World War I.

The end of the war saw the return of the armed forces from abroad, the resumption of a normal labor pool, and economic cutbacks. The nation no longer needed the labor of its "last hired, first fired" black population. Moreover, the returning white servicemen could use their traditional scapegoat, black people, to explain their own problems, encouraged by their employers and the unions. Management used black workers as part of a dual labor force, relegating them to lower-level jobs or paying them less than white workers. During the war, a committee of nationally known black leaders had met with the AFL Executive Council to oppose union discrimination, but were rebuffed.[4] That powerful union continued to permit the exclusion of blacks from its locals. The media also helped foster the anti-Negro mood. The 1915 motion picture *Birth of a Nation* glorified the Ku Klux Klan and ridiculed newly enfranchised Negroes. Its influence was strong because of both its racist sentiments and its technical excellence. Antiblack violence was growing, and activist William Monroe Trotter journeyed to Paris in February 1919 to register an international protest against it.

White hostility toward black people burst out in a series of major confrontations—urban riots—in 27 widely dispersed cities, including Chicago, Longview and Houston, Texas, Washington, D.C., and Elaine, Arkansas. The summer of 1919 became known as the "Red Summer." In many cases, returning servicemen of both races were involved. For the first time, African Americans openly fought back when attacked. In each of these riots, according to Meier and Rudwick, "the typical pattern was black retaliation to white acts of persecution and violence, and white perception of this resistance as an organized, premeditated conspiracy to 'take over,' which unleashed the armed power of white mobs and police" (1976, 240). Lack of government support or protection coupled with economic depression and joblessness inhibited further widespread black protest.

Disillusioned, black people were ready for a new leader. The riots provided fuel for a separatist movement—a rejection of the rejecters—and the Jamaican Marcus Garvey appeared at the right time. In the harsh period just preceding the Civil War, physician-activist Martin Delaney had similarly concluded that justice was unattainable in the United States, and he had sought a country to which ex-slaves and free blacks could emigrate. For blacks, emigration constituted an abandonment of the hope for integration and acceptance. For some whites, it was a way to get rid of an unwanted, unassimilable group. Nevertheless, a separatist movement also threatens the dominant group, for by demonstrating a great split between the races, it makes clear the failure of American democracy.

Secessionist Marcus Garvey's Universal Negro Improvement Association, founded in 1914, grew during the heightened white racism of the 1920s. Garvey directly opposed its tenets by stressing the beauty of blackness, black pride, and self-esteem. He developed doctrines and methods that had great appeal for the urban masses; his organization claimed a peak membership of 6 million at a time when the NAACP membership, predominantly middle class, numbered in the thousands. Cheered by his huge parades and problack rhetoric, many poor blacks invested in Garvey's projects. One of these, the Black Star steamship line, was intended to take them back to Africa. Garvey's recognition of the primacy of economic factors in the deprivation of black people would find renewed expression in the programs and actions of the Nation of Islam, or Black Muslims.

Du Bois and Randolph had been so angered by the 1919 violence that they supported the idea of retaliation in kind, but they thought Garvey's approach was wrong. They and the NAACP opposed not only his separatism but his racism against light-skinned blacks. Garvey was convicted on a charge of mail fraud in 1923 and was jailed and eventually exiled. Given the state of legal justice for black people and the mood of the times, one is led to wonder about the adequacy of the grounds for Garvey's prosecution (persecution?) and exile (see Pinkney 1976, ch. 3). Garvey died in London in 1940, but his influence, frequently underestimated, was to reemerge. Another outlet and response to poverty, racism, and life in the urban slums was the growth of religious sects, such as those of Father Divine and Daddy Grace, and storefront churches. Father Divine attracted many. Religion was often used as a substitute for political action.

Between the Wars

During the interval between the two world wars—from 1919 to the beginning of defense preparations in the early 1940s—the nation continued to be troubled by severe economic problems. The wartime boom ceased, unemployment grew, and conditions worsened until the crash of 1929.

In the South, violence against blacks continued, with numerous lynchings reported every year.

During this period, labor unions actively organized workers, the Communist Party USA recruited among the disillusioned, and Franklin Delano Roosevelt was swept into office, promising a New Deal. The Depression hit black Americans even more severely than others since they were already at the bottom economically. Roosevelt's main thrust was to regain national confidence in the country's financial structure, to aid agriculture, and to provide work and relief to the unemployed. Though not specifically aimed at them, many of the programs helped blacks survive. Others proved damaging, such as the restriction of cultivated farm acreage. Some policies were administered more unfairly in the South, so that black migration to the North continued, though at a slower rate. Federal housing agencies supported and extended racial segregation in housing, even while making more housing available.

Black organizations attempted to influence government and to sponsor demonstrations, which, while not as massive as some of the later ones, presaged what was to come. These groups established a Joint Committee on National Recovery in 1933 to monitor and fight discrimination in federal agencies. In some ways, the federal government appeared to be ideologically committed to greater equality. FDR appointed race relations advisors in major federal departments, a "kitchen cabinet"; the Democratic party sought and gained the votes of urban blacks. But the president's record was much spottier than one might think, given the general esteem accorded him by black people. His wife, Eleanor, was more committed to racial equality. Symbolic acts, like her resignation from the Daughters of the American Revolution because of its discriminatory behavior toward Marian Anderson, gave moral backing to black aspirations. At meetings and conferences that took place in the South, Eleanor Roosevelt openly violated state statutes by refusing to accept segregated seating arrangements.

The birth of the Congress of Industrial Organizations (CIO) in 1935 coincided with the New Deal period. Because it was an industrial union, it included all workers, not just skilled craftsmen. It actively aimed at incorporating and upgrading black workers, an objective made easier by the labor shortages of World War II. In 1939, the median income of non-white wage and salary earners was only 41 percent of that of whites; by 1950, it had risen to 60 percent (Rosen 1968). But by 1955, the CIO had merged with the stronger, less liberal AFL after major battles within its ranks over the issue of communism.

The economic catastrophe of the 1930s had brought economic and class issues to the forefront for everyone. The Abyssinian Baptist Church of Adam Clayton Powell was drawn into social activism on the issue of black jobs. The 22-year-old Powell believed it right to take action on the firing of five black doctors. He organized picketing and other demonstrations, which led to significant successes at Harlem Hospital (Haskins 1974, 29–32). Powell questioned the hiring policies of the stores in New York's black ghetto, organizing a "don't buy where you can't work" campaign. Thousands joined him in demonstrations that would be a prototype for later protests. Meanwhile, the NAACP was criticized for its lack of attention to economic problems, and Du Bois left his editorship of the *Crisis*. Ralph Bunche and A. Philip Randolph helped to form a new organization, the interracial Negro National Congress, in 1936.

The radicalized American thinking at that time made the American Communist Party (CP-USA) a more significant force than it is today— for blacks especially, because it was the only political party that professed a deep concern with racial issues. The party believed the CIO to be an important vehicle for the organization of black labor. Prior to World War II, the CIO enrolled hundreds of thousands of blacks into unions through both Communist and non-Communist organizers. At the height of its popularity, the Communist party was able to attract a percentage of the black population roughly comparable to its percentage of the white population, but some fatal errors cost it its black support. Several reversals in official policy led to disagreements with black leaders. Randolph was attacked at the 1940 convention of the National Negro Congress, and a number of pro-Communist union leaders walked out. Consequently, Randolph and other prominent black people withdrew from the organization; many were unwilling ever to work with Communists again. At the onset of World War II, Hitler's attack on the Soviet Union ended the CP's opposition to American involvement in the war, but this reduced its commitment to fighting discrimination. The party put wartime unity above its concern with race. Randolph was denounced for organizing a march on Washington, and other black leaders were criticized.

The NAACP, which would take a strong anti-Communist stance, spent much time challenging the CP when both groups were involved in the same racial issues. The Scottsboro case provides a fascinating example of this rivalry. The immediate response of the International Labor Defense, a CP front organization, to the railroading of the black youths pushed the NAACP into a more active role in the case. Both groups vied to be the men's legal representatives. And it appears that the CP was effective in bringing international pressure to bear on this travesty of justice (see Carter 1969).

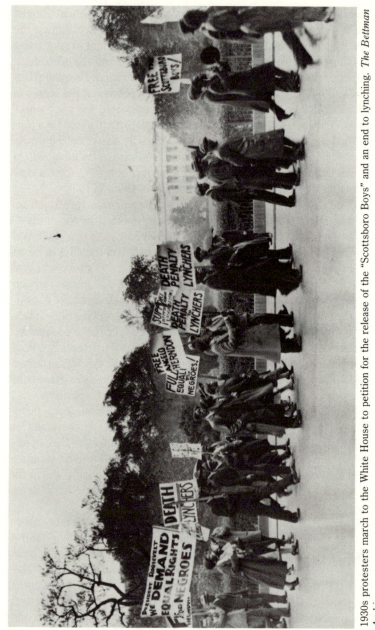

1930s protesters march to the White House to petition for the release of the "Scottsboro Boys" and an end to lynching. *The Bettman Archive.*

Although communism has never achieved a major foothold in American life, anticommunism has been a strong and effective theme. During the cold war period of the late 1940s and 1950s, the label "Communist" was applied indiscriminately to individuals and organizations interested in social change. One man who suffered severe persecution because of his openly proclaimed views was the black artist, intellectual, and humanist Paul Robeson. The most illustrious graduate of Rutgers University, Robeson had excelled in both scholarship and athletics. The man's talents were immense and varied. Unable to utilize adequately his training as a lawyer, he moved into the arts. Finding less racial discrimination abroad, especially in the Soviet Union, he spent a number of years concertizing and acting outside of the United States. His criticism of colonialism in Africa and Asia and of discrimination in his own country earned him the enmity of the U.S. government. In 1950, his passport was revoked, and the many appeals he subsequently made to regain it were turned down.

Robeson maintained that his support of anticolonial and antidiscrimination efforts was behind the revocation, citing the following statement from a State Department legal brief that opposed his claim to the right to travel: "Furthermore, even if the complaint had alleged, which it does not, that the passport was cancelled solely because of the applicant's recognized status as spokesman for large sections of Negro Americans, we submit that this would not amount to an abuse of discretion in view of the appellant's frank admission that he has been for years extremely active politically on behalf of the independence of the colonial people of Africa" (Robeson 1958).

Black equality is seen as a radical goal by many whites, and the red label has conveniently and indiscriminately been used to discredit black organizations—even the religiously oriented Southern Christian Leadership Conference (SCLC). The Southern Conference Education Fund (SCEF), one of the few predominantly white pro–civil rights groups, was labeled subversive, its officers arrested, and its files confiscated (Kinoy 1983, 209–55).[5] Martin Luther King's enemies, including most notoriously the FBI, would continuously seek to link him with persons suspected of Communist ties (Garrow 1981; O'Reilly 1989). Mobilizing support against Communists is more acceptable than openly fighting against struggles for minority rights.

The Development of the Black Metropolis

World War II stimulated another major migration to the North, so that by 1950 almost one-third of all black people lived outside the South

(Downes and Burkes 1969, 330). Over 20 million people, more than 4 million of them black, were forced to leave the land after 1940 (Piven and Cloward 1972, 201).

Although the federal government subsidized farmers to take land out of production in order to reduce agricultural surpluses at the end of the war, few sharecroppers received their share of the subsidies. Vastly increased mechanization made much human labor power obsolete. The result was the loss of 1 million farms between 1950 and 1969, with only the larger ones remaining. By 1960, 73 percent of black people were urban, and by 1965, the figure had risen to 80 percent (Piven and Cloward 1972, 214). Another important fact was that by 1960, about half the black population lived outside of the most repressive areas—the old slave states.

The movement to the cities resulted in conditions favorable to protest: the amassing of large numbers of people with similar grievances, a slight economic improvement over rural poverty so that folks could be less concerned about their daily bread, a nucleus of organizations through which communication and mobilization could occur, and a cultural support system for black pride and militancy. The segregated black world contained contradictions, from which both problems and strengths derived. Among the latter was the possibility of high population concentrations creating a rich, varied, all-black group life. On the other hand, urban conditions were crowded, dangerous, and unhealthy, and the black population was subject to exploitation. There also came to be vested interests in preserving segregation.

Even during slavery, free African Americans had gravitated to cities, finding relatively more freedom there to seek their rights. They acquired property, created schools and churches, met in conventions, petitioned state legislatures, and protested segregation. As abolitionists, they were largely responsible for the escape route to the North and Canada—the underground railroad. Denmark Vesey, the leader of a major slave revolt in Charleston, South Carolina, in 1822 was a freeman and a successful carpenter. These urban-dwelling free blacks and former slaves became the nucleus of a more educated class. Within the black communities, a vast network of organizations grew—churches, fraternal orders, lodges, and protest groups. These provided forums for working out survival and protest strategies.

Mass migration to northern cities in the twentieth century provided an even stronger base for dealing with racism. Unlike the white immigrants who preceded them, ghetto blacks found no escape route to "better," more healthful neighborhoods. Housing segregation became increasingly rigid; neighborhood businesses continued to be controlled by whites. The separate black world came to share a sense of oppression and a sense of community. The black press became a vital source of communication, supplementing white newspapers with race news—full coverage of black problems, issues, personalities, and cultural life. Through their own publications, leaders publicly and heatedly debated the correct course of action. Fiery critics, such as Marcus Garvey and Malcolm X after him, seemed best able to capture the imaginations of urban blacks and to verbalize their smoldering resentment.

These large concentrations of people had ready access to one another and to the mass communication media. By the early 1940s, New York's Harlemites were able to elect one of their own, the young minister and race leader Adam Clayton Powell, Jr., to the city council. In 1945, black urbanites of the new Eighteenth Congressional District started sending him to Congress. Although most African Americans were concentrated in unskilled or semiskilled jobs, some found additional avenues of employment and status. The city became the center of intellectual thought and cultural development. It placed black protest leaders in contact with white liberals and radicals and created the possibility of a northern support system for the southern-based civil rights movement of the 1960s.

Harlem, the mecca of African American culture, began to take shape and character as a black community around 1910 (Ottley 1968). The Harlem Renaissance, a creative outburst of talent and nationalism, was led by black poets like Langston Hughes, Countee Cullen, and Claude McKay. Black theater and black music became popular.

Many of the writings of the 1930s projected themes of protest. Richard Wright's works, such as *Native Son,* gained him recognition as a major American writer. This literary movement accelerated as such giants as Ralph Ellison and James Baldwin incisively examined the effects of white racism on black life. The growth of this literature provided ideological and emotional impetus for the protest movement and gave sympathetic whites a greater understanding of black life.

White liberals had supported the Harlem Renaissance. Their later critics, such as Harold Cruse (1967), say that white patrons and sponsors influenced the directions of black artistic expression, preventing it from fully achieving its promise. Others view this cultural era as significantly fostering black pride and black consciousness. Always there would be this debate about the influence of white liberals. They brought black interests to the attention of the public, but, it was argued, they did so in a patronizing fashion that would have to lead eventually to rejection. A somewhat different criticism would be made intermittently of white Communists. They were frequently accused of using racial issues for their own purposes. The question of whether to work with white leftists would plague black organizations; paradoxically, some of the most anti-Communist black organizations were accused of being reds by their white enemies.

World War II and the First March on Washington

As World War II approached, black leaders remembered the bitter experiences of World War I, and the Red Summer of 1919. Two issues loomed large—continued segregation in the armed forces and the inability of blacks to work in defense industries. As whites began to profit from these burgeoning industries, African Americans were blocked from entering training for some of the newly available jobs. The 1940 statistics on the employment of blacks in war industries showed that only a tiny proportion had been hired. The armed forces were strongly racist: the Selective Service System operated under discriminatory quotas; the navy restricted blacks to messmen and other menial positions; the army segregated them. As national rhetoric proclaimed the contrast between the free and totalitarian worlds, black leadership initiated a "double V" campaign—victory abroad and victory over racism at home.

Black anger was growing. In September 1940, the executive secretary of the NAACP, Walter White, along with Randolph and other prominent blacks, met with President Roosevelt to protest segregation in the armed forces. This effort proved futile, despite the fact that the black vote had helped FDR gain a second term. Not only did the president reaffirm the segregation policy, but he seemed to imply that the black leaders had gone along with it. This they immediately denied. The NAACP held a national protest day, 26 January 1941, calling it "National Defense Day." African American newspapers, firmly supported by the black public (as shown in polls), unanimously called for an end to racial discrimination during the national emergency. In contrast, the white press ignored the grievances of blacks, confining itself to the usual reporting of black crimes.

It was in this context that Randolph, who had tried so hard to move organized labor from within, took bolder action. He created the March on Washington Movement (MOWM), threatening a mass protest demonstration of 100,000 black people in Washington on 1 July 1941. The black press fully supported the proposed march, the aims of which were to secure the admission of blacks into defense industries on a nondiscriminatory basis and to end segregation in the armed forces. FDR finally became convinced that he could not deter the leaders. At the last moment, on 25 June 1941, he created the first national Fair Employment Practices Commission through Executive Order 8802. It took this combination of circumstances to move the federal government into the area of employment discrimination.

A student of the first March on Washington action ranks it as a high point in black protest and sees it as the best example of pressure unanimously and militantly applied against a president up to that point (Garfinkel 1969). A short-lived but extremely significant event, the MOWM incorporated several elements that would reappear in the civil rights movement of the 1960s. Randolph tried to build mass participation and recognized the importance of black consciousness in the development of racial protest. Randolph had become distrustful of white allies and planned an all-black march. The CP opposed the planned march until close to its deadline, when an event abroad led it to reverse its position—the Nazi attack on the Soviet Union in June 1941. Integrationist in orientation, the NAACP was lukewarm about it, providing little coverage in its official publications. But much successful grass-roots recruiting took place.

The NAACP and the Urban League had become the main bastions of black leadership following the demise of Garvey. Yet for a year and a half, from the inception of the MOWM until its decline, A. Philip Randolph was the major black leader in American (Garfinkel 1969). A member of the board of directors of the NAACP, Randolph was never averse to starting a new organization when he thought one was needed. This strong leader met tremendous opposition from white unionists and received little acknowledgment from other white Americans.

Shortly after the first FEPC hearing, the Japanese bombed Pearl Harbor, and the United States became formally involved in the shooting war. Black leaders persisted in seeking equality during the war but were unable to achieve desegregation in the armed forces. That would not occur until President Truman signed an executive order in 1948. Nevertheless, the mood of black people during the war is probably accurately reflected in this statement by Ottley in a book published in 1943:

Tradition must be overturned, and democracy extended to the Negro. . . . The color problem has become a world-wide issue to be settled here and now. Should tomorrow the Axis surrender unconditionally, Negroes say, the capitulation would provide only a brief interlude of peace. . . . There is nothing mystical about the Negro's aggressive attitude. The noisy espousal of democracy in the last war gave stimulus to the Negro's cause, and set the race implacably in motion. By advancing it in this war, democracy has become an immediate goal to the Negro. His rumblings for equality in every phase of American life will reverberate into a mighty roar in the days to come. (344)

Ottley's dramatic projection into the future was based not only on internal developments within the United States but also on a changing international environment. During the war, black soldiers went abroad again in the name of democracy, experienced segregation in the armed forces and their recreational facilities, and met Europeans who were far less prejudiced than white Americans. Racial clashes between white and black servicemen occurred. But the aftermath of World War II would differ from that of the first war. White supremacy in Africa and Asia was in decline: between 1945 and 1960, 40 new independent nation-states were formed. The impact on the United States was considerable. Says Isaacs, "The downfall of the white-supremacy system in the rest of the world made its survival in the United States suddenly and painfully conspicuous. It became our most exposed feature and in the swift unfolding of the world's affairs, our most vulnerable weakness" (1963, 6–7).

The United States competed for the friendship of the newly independent nations, but reports of American segregation and discrimination interfered. In the world of sports, for example, blacks had been almost totally excluded. In the fight ring, where they could compete, Joe Louis reigned as world heavyweight champion. The color barrier in baseball was finally breached when Jackie Robinson was hired by the Brooklyn Dodgers in 1945, which some saw as a hopeful sign.

The Soviet Union, engaged in a cold war with the United States, could point to this country's hypocrisy. The CP-USA publicized cases of racial injustice and championed the victims. The foreign press gave full coverage to America's racial disgraces, such as the 1955 murder of the teenager Emmett Till in Mississippi. Though there were other killings of blacks by whites in the state that year, the vicious beating, mutilation, and killing of Till brought special pain and anger to black people throughout the United States.

Emmett Till had been a 14-year-old Chicago youngster, unused to the ways of the South, when he went with his cousin Curtis Jones to visit relatives near Money, Mississippi. One evening in August 1955, Emmett and Curtis stopped at a country store. Some versions have it that Emmett whistled at a white woman, Carol Bryant, who was in the store; other versions, that he made some remark to her. In Mississippi, that was enough to get him killed. Bryant's husband, Roy, and his brother-in-law J. W. Milam came to the modest home of Mose Wright, Curtis's grandfather, and dragged Emmett Till away. He was never seen again alive. Wright had protested, citing the boy's age and lack of knowledge about the South, but the men's retort had been a threat on his own life. Three days later, Till's bruised and mutilated body was found, a bullet through his head. Milam and Bryant had been charged with kidnapping; now the charge was murder. Local authorities wanted to bury Till's body immediately, but his mother, Mamie Bradley, insisted that the corpse be sent back to Chicago. Defying instructions not to open the casket, Emmett's mother did so and was horrified. She insisted on an open casket funeral so that everyone could see what had been done to her only child. Pictures of the body were published by black newspapers and magazines throughout the country, and the funeral was attended by thousands. Meanwhile, a trial was to be held. A trial requires witnesses, but "in 1955, for a black man to accuse a white man of murder in Mississippi was to sign his own death warrant" (Williams 1987, 45). In an act of sheer courage, the elderly Mose Wright took the witness stand to point out Till's abductors. Other black witnesses, who had seen the defendants with Till, also testified, then were hurried out of town. Despite the evidence, the all-white jury took a little over one hour to return a not guilty verdict. While national leaders fretted over America's tarnished image abroad, incensed black groups rallied in large numbers to protest the lynching and the verdict. Many of the future civil rights workers were deeply affected by this case; it is probably no accident that the Montgomery bus boycott was initiated less than six months after Till's death.

Battles over school desegregation after the 1954 Supreme Court decision (*Brown* v. *Board of Education*) also made headlines. In particular, a famous confrontation at Little Rock, Arkansas, gained national and international attention (see chapter 4). A reluctant President Eisenhower was forced to send in airborne troops to enforce a federal desegregation order and escort nine black students into high school. The incident so embarrassed the president that he went on television and radio to criticize the actions of the governor of the state and to justify his own.

Incidents involving ambassadors or citizens of new African or Asian states were also causing the country acute chagrin. A number of them were refused service or segregated in restaurants and motels along U.S. Route 40, which leads into Washington, D.C. Sometimes official apologies were necessary. The capital city itself discriminated against dark-skinned peoples. Route 40 would become the target of demonstrations by CORE, intended to test desegregation laws. But meanwhile, the NAACP was continuing its pursuit of desegregation through the courts.

The end of World War II did not see a resurgence of race riots for several reasons. Labor shortages provided some employment gains for blacks, and the country did not experience a severe recession. Larger numbers of black people now lived in the North, where they could vote and did. The 1948 Democratic party convention adopted a strong civil rights plank, but it was challenged by a separate Dixiecrat candidate. Against this rival and Progressive and Republican party candidates, Harry S. Truman pulled off his surprising victory. In the same year, black citizens received their reward for support—Truman's executive order ending segregation in the armed forces. Black voters were beginning to play a pivotal role in national elections.

The Litigation Phase

A final but major precondition to the modern civil rights movement was the continuing battle in the nation's courts. The NAACP had fought and finally won a number of cases against segregation in graduate and professional education, successfully demonstrating the inferiority of schools for blacks.

As early as the 1930s, the Supreme Court had begun to reverse its post–Civil War negativity to the black cause. A 1938 Missouri case was decided favorably when the Court insisted that equal educational opportunities had to be made available to black students. Two important cases followed. In *Sweatt* v. *Painter,* the Court ruled that the state law school set up in Texas for blacks was not comparable to the white school. The following year, the Court went even further in *McLaurin* v. *Oklahoma.* By maintaining segregation in the classroom, cafeteria, and library, the University of Oklahoma was judged to have deprived a black student of the equality guaranteed by the Fourth Amendment (Woodward 1974). By the fall of 1953, blacks had been integrated, in a token manner, into 23 publicly supported colleges in southern or border states at the graduate level. There was even a small amount of integration at the undergraduate level. But in the five states in the lower South, the public schools were totally segregated, and black schools were vastly unequal in resources and in the education they offered. As many of the southern states made a last-ditch effort to improve black schools, the NAACP decided to attack the principle of segregation itself. Five cases challenging the constitutionality of school segregation were moving up to the Supreme Court from South Carolina, Virginia, Kansas, Delaware, and the District of Columbia. In December 1952, the Supreme Court ordered the litigants to submit briefs on a list of questions for a new hearing in the case of *Oliver Brown et al.* v. *Board of Education of Topeka, Kansas.*

The unanimous ruling of the Court under Chief Justice Earl Warren favored the black plaintiffs. In often-quoted words, the Court declared that segregation has a detrimental effect upon colored children because it "generates a feeling of inferiority as to their status in the community that may affect their hearts and minds in a way unlikely ever to be undone" (Woodward 1974, 147). These victories of the litigation phase were crucial developments. Willie (1981) considers the years 1930–54 the first stage of the movement; Blackwell would start with 1920, labeling 1920–54 the period of "Accommodation and Agitation" (1982). Their mutual cut-off dates affirm that 1954, the year of the Supreme Court's famous *Brown* decision, was a turning point.

The Supreme Court decision was greeted with hope by black Americans, who did not realize at the time how long and hard a struggle lay ahead. Soon they would turn to nonviolent action to protest the much-hated, humiliating segregation in public transportation. More and more, it was felt that mass action was necessary to supplement the legal process. This impulse was abetted by the South's open attack on the NAACP, the organization that depended upon the legal approach. In the years 1956–59, the southern white power structure would attempt to destroy the NAACP. States passed measures that would force the organization to turn over its membership lists, imperiling the lives and jobs of those on the lists. Throughout the South, NAACP leaders were called before investigating committees and labeled Communists; Alabama succeeded in outlawing the NAACP completely for nine years (Morris 1984, 30–35). Paradoxically, the void left by the beleaguered or outlawed NAACP chapters fostered the creation of new action-oriented, often church-related organizations. Instead of the historic protest group, "civic leagues," "improvement associations," and other innocuously named local groups arose to pursue black rights.

Beginning in 1955, nonviolent protest spread significantly, backed by a clearly enunciated ideology. The proliferation of leaders and the escalation of involvement lasted over most of the 1960s and was popularly called—at the time—the civil rights movement. So we move to the first major battle in the modern civil rights movement—a struggle that had never died of black people for their rights as Americans.

Rosa Parks, whose action sparked the Montgomery boycott, is fingerprinted after her indictment for violating a seldom-invoked antiboycott law. *Wide World Photos, Inc.*

Chapter Three

Montgomery's Nonviolent Revolution

It is an axiom of social change that no revolution can take place without a methodology suited to the circumstances of the period.
—Martin Luther King, Jr.

Montgomery and Martin Luther King, Jr., created a revolutionary point of departure which the sit-in students carried to a new stage of development.
—LeRone Bennett

Nonviolent protest was the method and "revolutionary point of departure" that took a nation by surprise in Montgomery. The philosophy had been enunciated before and practiced most effectively in India's independence movement, but never before had the black population of an entire American city used it so determinedly in a sustained and eventually successful struggle.

Riding a bus to work was accompanied by daily indignities for the ordinary black folk of Montgomery, Alabama, and every other southern city. In Montgomery in 1955, "there were no Negro drivers, and although some of the white men who drove the buses were courteous, all too many were abusive and vituperative. It was not uncommon to hear them referring to Negro passengers as 'niggers,' 'black cows,' and 'black apes.' Frequently Negroes paid their fares at the front door, and then were forced to get off and reboard the bus at the rear" (King 1958, 40–41).

Another humiliation was the practice of forcing black people to stand while seats reserved for whites remained empty. If these seats were occupied and other whites boarded the bus, blacks sitting immediately behind the white section were supposed to give up their seats. If they refused to stand and move back, they were subject to arrest. And refuse to stand is precisely what Rosa Parks did on that fateful first day of

December 1955 when she was arrested. She was returning home from her day's work as a seamstress. Shortly after she took a seat directly behind the section reserved for whites, she was ordered to stand and move back. Think of the double affront of a middle-aged woman being expected to rise for a male passenger, when the customary norm is the reverse. This incident followed very closely upon the arrest of a 15-year-old high school student, Claudette Colvin, who had been pulled off a bus, handcuffed, and taken to jail for not giving her seat to a white passenger. She was given a suspended sentence, but members of the angry black community had protested to authorities. When Rosa Parks, a respected figure, was arrested, the news circulated widely.

Public transportation was still guided by the Jim Crow legislation that had been officially instituted by the southern states when racial attitudes hardened in the 1890s. Later critics would say that the eventual desegregation that occurred was a shallow victory, doing nothing to help the economic position of African Americans. The viewpoint here is that the victory was significant for working people and highly symbolic. It is probably difficult to imagine in the South of today (and especially in its more progressive cities) how pervasive and degrading segregation was and why this issue could galvanize thousands into action. But anyone aware of South Africa's apartheid should know that America had its own version. State laws mandated racial separation in schools, parks, playgrounds, restaurants, hotels, public transportation, theaters, restrooms, and so on. Water fountains were labeled with signs for "white" and "colored."[1] The allocation of funds for every segregated facility demonstrated unmistakably who was entitled to the best and the worst. Everywhere segregation was a symbol of black inferiority. The segregation creed included many related assumptions, such as that the Bible and Christianity sanction inequality and that blacks are fit only for menial labor (Silver 1963, 22).

Montgomery was the place where southern segregated transportation was challenged over a sustained period for the first time in many years, in a successful action that resounded throughout the region and the nation. A bus boycott began on the Monday after Rosa Parks's arrest, and it drew the steady support of almost 100 percent of the city's black residents. Group protest tends to erupt in many localities, and segregated public transportation had drawn sporadic resistance efforts from its beginnings. Morris (1984, 17–25) reminds us that a less publicized but successful bus boycott took place in Baton Rouge, Louisiana, in June 1953, just prior to the Montgomery action. It lasted only 10 days and succeeded in its demand for the modification of certain insulting segregation practices. Segregation as such was not challenged, and the Baton Rouge event did not gain widespread media attention. Importantly, it was known to black leaders and provided a partial model for the Montgomery boycott.

Now, in Montgomery, the right combination of factors made the city a landmark. For when a local action like this one mobilizes extensive support and opposition, gains national media attention, and stimulates repetition in many other places, it becomes a turning point in history. If the momentum continues, a new phase in a general social movement is ushered in. Montgomery signaled the end of reliance on litigation as the major strategy of civil rights activists and accelerated the use of nonviolent direct action to test and supplement laws. It demonstrated the ability of black leaders to mobilize all segments of the community—the elite and the masses—through their churches, organizations, and communication structures, and to gain moral and financial support from sympathizers throughout the country.

The boycott also engendered organized resistance as white officials of the city used every possible legal tool to defeat it. Segregationist whites resorted to violence, bombing, or burning the homes of the major participants and the few local white supporters. The nonviolent response to these acts set a tone and reflected the strength of a philosophy that would direct the movement for years to come. The boycott of nearly one year's duration brought to prominence the young Martin Luther King, Jr. King was an improbable leader—fresh out of theological school, intellectually oriented, newly married, and the father of a baby.[2] His career in the ministry had just started, and he had been selected to head a prestigious black church. Offered the presidency of the local NAACP, he had declined. But when leadership of the Montgomery boycott was thrust upon him, he accepted and became its guiding spirit. Out of the Montgomery Improvement Association grew the Southern Christian Leadership Conference, which would play a major role in the movement until the assassination of its founder in 1968. *Stride Toward Freedom,* a graphic account of the origins and day-by-day developments in Montgomery, was written by the person whose leadership and philosophy took shape in the process (see King 1958).

Acts of rebellion that occur out of their time tend to go relatively unnoticed. But one act at the right moment, like a match setting off a fire, may become the precipitating incident that sharpens awareness of dissatisfaction. Such was the case in Montgomery. The black community was already angry about the humiliations and discourtesies experienced on buses. Yet until there was belief in the possibility of change, expressions of ignorance or agreement with whites were a necessary charade played out by blacks. Says King, "White people in the South may never fully know the extent to which Negroes defended themselves and protected their jobs—and in many cases, their lives—by perfecting an air of ignorance and agreement" (1958, 28). Many whites were caught off guard by the unanimity with which the other race responded to Mrs. Parks's arrest and the events that followed. Though some feel that 1960 and the beginning of the student sit-in movement was the "year of massive awakening for the Negroes of the South" (Woodward 1974, 169), there is little doubt that Montgomery ushered in the nonviolent era. The students who initiated the sit-ins were familiar with King's account of the boycott, had heard him speak, and adopted his methods.

The Significance of the *Brown* Decision

We shall see how the dynamically interacting forces of the movement and its environment combined to produce the Montgomery movement. The previous chapter discussed the many developments in the twentieth century that led to the renewal of protest. Very important was the changing pattern of Supreme Court decisions, from the 1896 low point of *Plessy* v. *Ferguson*, through the outlawing of the white primary in 1944, to the high point of the 1954 *Brown* decision.

The Supreme Court had ruled that deliberately created segregation placed a stigma of psychological inferiority on the black child and was morally wrong. From then on, the black struggle for desegregation was even more clearly a "norm-oriented movement," in the language of Smelser (1962). Black people were not opposing the American system but were trying to make it work for them. Yet the South had made segregation and its accompanying ideology a central value, writing it into hundreds of state laws. The day of the Court decision was called Black Monday by Mississippi Judge Tom Brady, but it was a day of hope for black Americans. The federal government would be forced to take action against state laws that violated its principles.

The *Brown* decision had placed the federal government on the side of those who saw segregation as evil. It encouraged attack on other forms of segregation and hence had a broader significance:

Much of *Brown*'s meaning lay outside schools, in the groundwork it laid for a massive attack upon Jim Crow itself. Before *Brown*, "enforced separation of Negroes and whites, the American precursor of South African apartheid, was common." After *Brown*, public beaches and buses, golf courses and parks, courtrooms and prison cell-blocks began to open to black and white alike. *Brown* was the catalyst that shook up Congress and culminated in the two major Civil Rights acts of the century, one opening restaurants, hotels, and job opportunities to blacks and the other making black voters a new southern and national political force. (Wilkinson 1979, 48–49)

Mobilization and Tactics

Immediately following the precipitating incident in Montgomery, the community began to mobilize—first informally, then formally. On Monday morning, 5 December, the public buses would roll bereft of black passengers—their main source of business. A young woman and a middle-aged woman had acted on their own in individual protest. Though a somewhat retiring person, Parks had challenged segregation before, and was well known and admired by the community. She had long been active in the NAACP and had recently attended a workshop at Highlander Folk School, an interracial adult education center. Despite the risks and her family's fears, she agreed to have her action become a test case.[3]

Rosa Parks used her one phone call to inform her mother that she had been arrested. Word of the arrest was transmitted to E. D. Nixon through the mother's frantic call. Nixon had headed the NAACP and hence worked with Rosa Parks for many years. Unable to find out what the charges were, nor to reach black attorney Fred Gray, Nixon called upon white lawyer Clifford Durr to make inquiries. Durr was told that Parks had been charged with violating Alabama bus segregation laws. Along with Durr and Durr's wife, Virginia (who had introduced Parks to the Highlander workshops), Nixon went to the jail to post a bond.

Back at the Parks's home, Nixon gained Rosa Parks's approval to proceed with a test case. Fred Gray was now in contact and agreed to represent her. He also called his friends on the Women's Political Council, who had been bringing bus segregation grievances to the city commissioners for a period of years and had even threatened a boycott. According to JoAnn Robinson, president of the Council at that time, her group made a decision to proceed with a one-day boycott that very night (Robinson 1987, 43–54). As she tells it, Robinson, with the aid of two trusted students, spent the night of 1 December 1955 running off leaflets that announced the boycott. On the morning of 2 December these leaflets were distributed by the thousands throughout the entire African American community. Meanwhile, a meeting of Montgomery's black civic leaders had been initiated by Nixon and was scheduled to be held at King's church that very night. Networking among the minority community's top people was so effective that more than 40 leaders assembled there.

Some accounts of these fast-moving events leave out Robinson's part altogether and credit Nixon with initiating the boycott and the leaflet distribution (Raines 1977, 37–39, 43–46; Durr 1985, 279–81). But the influential role of women in prodding male leaders and starting the boycott is made clear in King's descriptions (1958).[4] Both Nixon and Robinson were part of Montgomery's protest leadership and were probably in contact, directly or indirectly, on the issue. King cites Robinson as one of the most active participants in planning and executing the boycott.

The clergy represented the largest leadership group among black people, joined together in a ministerial alliance. Other independent professionals, such as doctors and dentists, often played important civic roles. In the past, many black clergymen had been accused of being too compliant in their relations with the white community. This time, the ministers were galvanized into action in support of the boycott, and their constituents received moral justification from their own long-accepted leaders. Help was also needed from businesspeople. Segregation had spawned separate taxi companies, since white Birmingham drivers would take only customers of their own race. There were 18 black taxi companies in the city; initial plans were to use the more than 200 cabs available with reduced group fares. However, white officials soon outlawed the use of the taxis.

King viewed the Montgomery protest as the withdrawal of cooperation from an evil system, as massive noncooperation rather than as a boycott. But under any name, this had been a tactic used or threatened by black people many times before, from the Atlanta streetcar boycott of 1894 to the economic boycotts of the 1930s. This time, the effort would be thorough, prolonged, and ultimately successful. The courts would rule, after one year, that the Alabama segregation statutes were illegal. Initially, though, the boycott was set for only one day—Monday, 5 December 1955.

The previous weekend, the white press published critical articles intended to expose the planned action—an attack that backfired because it provided needed publicity. A 60 percent participation rate would have been deemed a success by the leadership; instead, the boycott proved almost totally effective. As young Martin and Coretta King watched the first early bus pass by their window—a bus that ordinarily took domestics to their places of employment—they noted with awe that it was empty. The spirit of the movement was already evident that day as an army of black walkers cheered the empty buses rolling by. Rosa Parks was found guilty and fined $10, one of the first clear-cut instances of conviction for disobeying a segregation law. She appealed the verdict to test the law's validity. Meanwhile, a new organization was formed to guide the protesters, the Montgomery Improvement Association. King was elected president.

Another tactic utilized in Montgomery was the evening mass meeting. One of these was scheduled to take place after the first day's boycott. An overflow crowd of thousands massed outside the meeting place proved the community's readiness for action. In his first movement speech, King expounded on his belief that protest was necessary but that it should be guided by Christian love. The huge turnout convinced him that the boycott should be continued. The response to King's speech and to Rosa Parks, who was present, was tremendous. A list of demands was read to the audience. Initial demands are frequently more moderate than later ones: The black community did not demand an immediate end to segregated buses, but voted unanimously for the following resolution:

It was resolved not to resume riding the buses until:

1. courteous treatment by the bus operators was guaranteed;

2. passengers were seated on a first-come, first-served basis—Negroes seating from the back of the bus toward the front while whites seated from the front towards the back;

3. Negro bus operators were employed on predominantly Negro routes. (King 1958, 63)

The Developing Boycott

Mass meetings continued to be held in the city's black churches throughout the boycott. They served to promote morale, unity, and an esprit de corps, regardless of the day's difficulties. It is no wonder that so many churches would be bombed and burned; they were a source of power for the black community. But not everyone was a churchgoer, and King personally visited bars and nightclubs to keep the people informed.

In this first major action the black people of Montgomery showed amazing unity and strength. The white opposition—first the bus companies and then the city fathers—tried in varied ways to defeat it, by spreading false rumors and harassing and arresting people who volunteered as drivers in car pools. Many times the African Americans were underestimated, as they set up committees and met crisis after crisis innovatively and nonviolently. The NAACP was called upon for legal help in the case of arrest; meanwhile, Parks's appeal was proceeding through the courts. Negotiating meetings with white officials proved fruitless and soon ended, but the boycott went on. Mass meetings and fund raising continued as the determined community gained national support. There were some sympathetic whites in Montgomery, including a couple of ministers and a few drivers in car pools, but the boycott was basically a black effort with both men and women participating in car pools. A supportive advisory group formed around King, who had become the spokesperson for the movement.

As challenges occurred, King met them with renewed dedication to nonviolence, calling upon the Gandhian principles that he had studied earlier. CORE, the pioneering interracial civil rights organization, had also practiced nonviolent civil disobedience, but it was in Montgomery that the technique met its most significant test to that date. A brief digression here will describe CORE, an organization that determinedly entered the southern struggle and remained one of its major nationwide groups.

CORE: The Forerunner

Formed in 1942, CORE was an outgrowth of the Fellowship of Reconciliation (FOR), a Christian pacifist group that followed the ideas of the Indian leader Mahatma Gandhi. A number of race relations committees, or "cells," were formed in cities of the North and Midwest. The Chicago group was influenced by the prominent activist black physician, Arthur G. Falls.[5] Its members were also students of the labor movement and borrowed techniques from the sit-down strikes of the industrial unions. Even before the formation of a national organization, the Chicago cell engaged in direct action. In March 1942, it chose the White City Roller Rink as a site for a test of state civil rights laws. That April a mixed group of 24 persons sought admission. When blacks were turned away, the group negotiated with the rink manager. Like King, they believed in appealing to the conscience of the discriminator. Later in the same year, the Chicago group would attack discrimination in housing at the University of Chicago Hospital and Medical School and at the university barbershop.

In April 1942, the same month as the first action, 22 women and 28 men met to form a permanent interracial group.[6] CORE was a forerunner in many respects: its concern with interracialism, internal democracy, and nonviolence; its practice and development of direct action techniques; and its method of negotiation with the oppressor. It was one of the first organized groups to use these principles in confronting discriminatory restaurants and recreational facilities outside the South. In 1947, sponsored by CORE and FOR, 16 individuals engaged in a project called the Journey of Reconciliation to test compliance with a 1946 Supreme Court decision outlawing segregation in interstate travel. This early action served as a model for the first 1961 Freedom Ride, which would, because of the extreme violence encountered from racists, propel CORE to the front pages of the nation's newspapers. Internal dissension and the effects of the McCarthy period had weakened CORE in the interim. But in the winter of the Montgomery bus boycott, Bayard Rustin—who had served 22 days at hard labor because of his part in the 1947 ride—rushed to the city to offer his organizing skills and knowledge of nonviolent techniques. Rustin also brought in other experienced civil rights advocates.

King's Concept of Nonviolent Resistance

Martin King elaborated upon his concept of civil disobedience and nonviolent resistance in *Stride Toward Freedom*. This approach tries to awaken a sense of moral shame in the opponent to achieve redemption and reconciliation. Nonviolence involves the willingness to love others, to attack forces of evil rather than individuals, and to forgive—merging Christian and Gandhian precepts. Suffering is to be accepted without retaliation, and indeed it was, as civil rights demonstrators by the thousands maintained this posture in the face of insults, beatings, and jailings.

King's faith in nonviolence was tested several times during the Montgomery boycott; each time he felt stronger and more committed to his principles and was able to convince others of their correctness. When actions by city officials appeared to be failing, the Klan put out leaflets and made harrowing phone calls at all hours of the day and night. King was informed of a plot against his life and had to confront the possibility of his own death. On 30 January 1956 his house was bombed and his wife and baby were lucky to escape injury. An angry crowd gathered outside, some with guns, ready to defend the young minister. This event proved to be a major test of nonviolence and of King's charismatic abilities. He asked the crowd not to resort to retaliatory violence and successfully prevented a possible riot. The home of boycott leader E. D. Nixon was bombed two days later; the bombings and burnings of homes and churches would continue even after the boycott was won.

For the first of what would be many times, King was arrested and jailed. The pretext was that he had been speeding, a charge frequently used against members of the movement. News of his arrest spread, and large crowds gathered around the jail. This time King was released. He experienced jail as what Gerlach and Hines call "a bridge-burning act," a dramatic movement experience that intensifies commitment to a cause. Attempts at intimidation had backfired, strengthening rather than destroying the movement.

Some black participants were so exhilarated by the boycott that they chose to walk many miles daily to their jobs rather than accept rides. A favorite, oft-repeated movement story relates the words of an elderly woman, familiarly known as Mother Pollard, who steadfastly walked to her destination. When asked if she wasn't tired, she replied, "My feets is tired, but my soul is rested" (Branch 1988, 149).

As time went on, arrest became a badge of honor. A transformation occurred in people. Those who had once feared arrest were now proud of it. Thousands of other civil rights activists would willingly subject themselves to the same fate in the ensuing decade. When King was arrested again, he used his March trial to throw a floodlight on the degradation imposed by segregated buses. His dignity and strength garnered increased support. The opposition's tactics provided momentum for the movement, drawing its participants closer together. The discipline of the protesters, their adaptability in gaining access to resources, and the rise of national pressure against segregation laws all contributed to making Montgomery a momentous event. The environment had become conducive to protest.

The Legal Battle

Supplementing direct action, a legal battle was being played out. With the help of the NAACP, a suit was filed in the U.S. Federal District Court asking for the end of bus segregation on the grounds that it was contrary to the Fourteenth Amendment. The city commissioner was charged with violating the civil rights of black motorists and pedestrians. The original demands of the Montgomery Improvement Association had been made stronger and less equivocal. A three-judge federal court panel held a hearing on 11 May 1956, and on 4 June they decided that the city bus segregation laws of Alabama were unconstitutional. City attorneys filed an appeal to the Supreme Court and the boycott continued.

Meanwhile, the city tried additional legal strategies. On 30 October, Montgomery asked the court to grant it compensation for damages growing out of the car pool operation. The pool was termed a public nuisance and was accused of being a private enterprise operating without a franchise. A hearing was set for 13 November, almost a year after the start of the boycott. During a dramatic recess, King received word that the Supreme Court had affirmed the favorable decision of the district court. But the high Court's decision would take some time to reach Alabama officially, and the city was granted a temporary injunction halting the motor pool. The protesters responded by developing a share-the-ride plan for every area and street, to operate until the Supreme Court decision came into effect. Black citizens also received lessons in nonviolent behavior to prepare them for the soon-to-be-integrated buses. On 20 December the bus integration order reached the city. King rode the first integrated bus with a white minister, Glenn Smiley, in the seat beside him. A representative of FOR, Smiley had trained Montgomery people in nonviolence and had argued the fine points of the doctrine with King. Although Rosa Parks was photographed on the first day of bus integration, her picture was not the one the newspapers chose to flash around the world. Parks is now widely acknowledged as "the mother of the civil rights movement," but newspapers showed King and Smiley on the bus.

The successful conclusion of the protest brought forth a violent response from whites, a pattern that would recur. The White Citizens' Councils, organizations formed to combat implementation of the *Brown* decision, were spreading throughout the South. In Montgomery the Citizens' Council had used economic pressure against the boycott and its supporters, complementing the city's tactic of legal harassment. With the desegregation of public transportation, the terrorist Ku Klux Klan took over. City buses were fired upon, injuring some black passengers, and service had to be suspended after five o'clock in the afternoons. In early January 1956, a wave of bombings hit four black churches and the homes of King's closest associate, Ralph Abernathy, and a white supporter, Lutheran minister Bob Graetz. These terrorist actions had an unintended effect, again one that would be repeated in ensuing years. They mobilized the support of influential white persons who had heretofore been quiet. Up to this point, the black people of Montgomery had been joined only by a few courageous white ministers and some persons from a nearby army base who had volunteered as drivers. Now the forces concerned with law and order began to speak up. The editor of the *Montgomery Advertiser* wrote a strong editorial condemning the bombings. The Men of Montgomery, an influential business group, also publicly opposed this terrorist action. Although seven white men were charged with the bombings and five were indicted, the all-white jury found them not guilty. This was a verdict that would recur with painful regularity. The buses, however, were finally able to run.

The Citizens' Councils were a specific response of the so-called respectable segregationists to the prospect of school desegregation. They had open access to officials and legislators and claimed to be above the tactics of the Klan. But the actions and inflammatory oratory of acknowledged white leaders encouraged the more violent groups in their dirty work. The Ku Klux Klan had first arisen in the post–Civil War period to intimidate and terrorize the freed slaves and prevent them from voting.[7] In the period of active racism around 1919, it experienced a resurgence. Reacting not only to black cityward migration, it also turned against foreign immigrant groups, Jews, and Catholics. The Klan spread to the Midwest and the North, gaining considerable political clout in the 1920s. It influenced the outcome of elections and put known Klan members into office. In August 1925, at the peak of its power, 40,000 Klansmen marched openly in Washington, D.C. The organization had become quiescent in the early fifties, but with the 1954 school decision, it was reborn. Klans would stretch throughout the South from that time on and were clearly responsible for bombings, bloody confrontations, and murders of civil rights workers. (See the special report of the Southern Poverty Law Center 1981.)

The Origin of the Southern Christian Leadership Conference

Montgomery had an impact on other cities of the South, and similar protests began in places like Tallahassee and Birmingham. Both cities were the sites of what Morris has called local movement centers. That is, they had strong networks of activist individuals and organizations that were determined to fight racial injustice. In fact, one of their problems was the multiplicity of protest groups and the factionalism and disunity that sometimes resulted. If these separate but overlapping groups could be brought together under an umbrella organization, their various constituencies would constitute a major resource.

Obviously, the transportation issue could not only move black communities to take to their feet in protest, but could also provide a sufficient stimulus to unite its factions. Too, public buses represented an economically vulnerable target, since so many passengers were black. King and his aides met in Atlanta with 60 black leaders from 22 southern communities in early January 1957, focusing on transportation desegregation. The group reconvened in New Orleans on 13 February, with 97 members from 35 communities in 10 states (Ashmore 1982). This time it broadened its aims to include all forms of segregation and added voter registration as a major objective. The name of the group, which originally reflected its single goal, was changed to the Southern Christian Leadership Conference.

The SCLC would draw its official leaders mainly from the male ministers who headed its affiliates in various cities. Morris calls the SCLC "the decentralized political arm of the black church" (1984, ch. 4). (It was not until 1966 that a white person was added to its board of directors.) Many of these ministers had also been local NAACP officers—evidence of a strong action orientation not shared by some clergy. SCLC's leaders recognized the need for new organizational structures and tactics to supplement the NAACP's legal approach. Indeed, the NAACP's successful legal battles had subjected it to attack in the South even as its centralized bureaucratic structure inhibited rapid response to developments. In contrast, the SCLC would sometimes seem like organized chaos, with constantly changing schedules and delayed meetings. Tactically, such practices made it harder for its enemies to track.

As one of its first actions, the SCLC sent a telegram to President Eisenhower asking him to convene a White House Conference on Civil Rights comparable to those he had sponsored in other areas. Failing that, the organization said its members would engage in a prayer pilgrimage to Washington on 17 May 1957, the third anniversary of the *Brown* decision. This demonstration did take place and was attended by important black leaders, many celebrities, and about 25,000 people. Six years later—years of organizing, mass action, jailings, beatings, murders, and international publicity—the better-known 1963 March on Washington would take place.

By 1957, King was already being acclaimed as the movement leader, his gift of oratory electrifying audiences. A number of those who first rallied to the SCLC would become familiar names: Abernathy, King's closest confidant who would eventually officiate at his friend's funeral and become head of the SCLC; Rustin, who had joined others in the Journey of Reconciliation's early testing of southern interstate transportation, was one of the first to choose jail, and would masterfully organize the 1963 March on Washington; Andrew Young, who would become a controversial ambassador to the United Nations under Jimmy Carter and hold major public office in Georgia; Fred Shuttlesworth, the Birmingham leader who would invite King to his city for a crucial confrontation with segregationists; Ella Baker, a former NAACP field official, who would encourage the student movement to form its own organization and remain its trusted adviser; and many others. Among them was white lawyer and businessman Stanley Levison, who along with Rustin and Baker formed a New York–based organization, In Friendship, to support the Montgomery bus boycott. These activists recognized the boycott as a major breakthrough and offered their services. Baker was asked to set up the first SCLC office as "associate director" and, when the black minister chosen to replace her didn't work out, served a second tour of duty as "acting" executive director. Rustin, an adviser and organizer for many years, was often asked to take a low-profile role because of his known homosexuality. Levison became King's closest white friend, one who assisted him in many ways, from fund raising to ghost-writing. Because of alleged Communist connections, which were never substantiated, this friendship was used by the FBI to discredit King and the movement.[8] Allegations that King was unduly influenced by Levison and others were easily belied by those who knew Martin. King did consult many people officially and unofficially, and he was known to be a patient listener. But the principals involved agree that King acted independently and exercised the final word in the SCLC's decisions.

Many black youth would be influenced by the new breed of activist ministers and would enter into nonviolent demonstrations by the thousands. Long dissatisfied with the NAACP's approach, they were soon to eschew formal ties with the SCLC to create their own organization, the Student Non-Violent Coordinating Committee (SNCC, pronounced "snick" by insiders). SNCC would play a major role in sustaining the movement and in developing local grass-roots leadership.

Nonviolence as a Tactic

King was not the originator of nonviolence in America, but he was the one who made the most extensive use of the tactic. Labor people and pacifists had employed nonviolent techniques in the labor organizing drives of the 1930s and during World War II. A number of the pacifists had helped to form CORE. But the combination, in Montgomery, of nonviolent direct action with successful legal pressure "provided a model for subsequent agitation in the areas of public accommodation and the right to vote" (Lynd 1966, xi).

The practice of nonviolence was not easy, nor was it totally accepted by all black folk. There would be times during the movement years when ordinary citizens could no longer contain their rage over church bombings, beatings of unarmed demonstrators, and assassination of their leaders. There were dangerous times when the need for self-defense against what appeared to be certain death brought out the show of weapons.

Nevertheless, whether or not one agreed with Martin Luther King about the philosophical basis for nonviolence, there was little doubt about its effectiveness as a tactic at that time and place. As has been pointed out repeatedly, black people were the victims of white violence for many years. Slave revolts were quickly put down. The rate of lynchings declined only slowly after massive efforts for federal legislation failed. Sharecroppers who tried to organize were viciously attacked. The government, the sheriffs, and the police were all white at the time of the Montgomery bus boycott. Any aggressive act on the part of protesting blacks would have given the authorities the needed justification for overwhelming retaliation. Nonviolence provoked white terrorism, but not the sort of openly condoned killing ("in self defense") that would have occurred had blacks taken the offensive. Nor would the sympathy of the North and liberal whites have been so aroused had black folk fulfilled the stereotyped image of "the aggressive Negro." The oppressor was forced to commit his brutality openly.

If self-defense was more natural than nonviolence, the latter nevertheless was a hard-learned technique that African Americans had applied in daily life. They knew that acts of rebellion would be met harshly. Hence, the smiling face and seeming acquiescence were developed as survival techniques. Seeing nonviolence transformed into a movement technique gave it honor and dignity for the first time, a tremendous psychological boost. Moreover, the Montgomery movement was justified on moral and religious grounds by the black leaders most familiar as spokespersons for the race in the South—the ministry. These men had long placated the white power structure in the fashion of Booker T. Washington, tolerating their reputations as Uncle Toms in exchange for minor gains. In more recent years, many had accepted official roles in NAACPs and had begun to organize their local communities. Some, such as Birmingham's Fred Shuttlesworth, were recognized protest leaders. Now the ministers, headed by one who was ready to die and who had the sense of mission and the oratorical ability necessary for a holy crusade, were telling their congregations to engage in massive noncooperation with an evil system, the system of segregation. When the people took this advice and proudly withdrew their patronage from a business economically dependent on them, their protest worked.

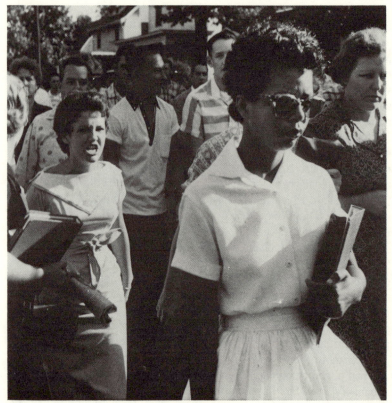

White students and adults jeer Elizabeth Eckford, one of the nine black students admitted to Little Rock High School. *Wide World Photos, Inc.*

Chapter Four

The Counter-Movement

Nowhere in the region did black rights make good white politics. Seldom in the Upper South and almost nowhere in the Deep South did the black man have an open white friend. . . . Political courage in the late 1950s meant standing for open schools, refusing to sign the Southern Manifesto or admitting that Brown, *however hateful, still was the law.*

—J. Harvie Wilkinson III

The success of the Montgomery boycott buoyed the hopes of black southerners; their leaders tried to maintain the momentum. Similar actions gained temporary media attention, and news of them was spread further by informal communication networks. But it was not until 1960 that the movement would gain full force, recharged by the action of the four freshmen from the Agricultural and Technical College in Greensboro, North Carolina. The Woolworth lunch counter sit-in would spread over North Carolina within two weeks and to the other southern states almost as rapidly (Chafe 1981). (Chapter 5 chronicles the events at Greensboro.)

The Montgomery movement had given rise to a new organization, the SCLC, and the Greensboro sit-ins would lead to the creation of another movement spearhead, SNCC. Dedicated and self-sacrificing youth would have their own vehicle for action in SNCC, unhampered by the conservatism of some of their elders.[1] SNCC would play a key role in future voting rights campaigns and in the later transition to the black power philosophy.

The years from 1956 to 1960—from Montgomery to Greensboro—were not quiet, as many local groups prepared to combat southern inequality. Struggles occurred in such places as Tuskegee, Alabama, and

Fayette and Haywood counties, Tennessee (discussed later in this chapter). "Citizenship Schools" for adults who wanted to vote were being organized by Septima Clark, director of workshops at Highlander Folk School in Monteagle, Tennessee. But none of the scattered demonstrations took on the national significance of the Montgomery bus boycott. What was happening in the interim years?

As the NAACP quietly pressed desegregation suits in numerous southern localities, the white South became engaged in a counter-movement to the Supreme Court's 1954 decision. The South Carolina state legislature passed a law specifying that no state or city employee could belong to the NAACP. When Septima Clark refused to deny her membership in that organization, she was fired from a teaching job she had held many years. South Carolina's loss was the civil rights movement's gain, for at Highlander, where she moved in June 1956, Clark developed methods for teaching adults that would be widely applied by movement organizations (Clark and Brown 1986).

As long as the resources of government were either neutral or on the side of segregation, there was no need for an antidesegregation movement. The 1954 decision had postponed discussion of implementation for another year. In 1955, the *Brown II* decision came out, specifying that black plaintiffs would have to be admitted to public schools on a racially nondiscriminatory basis "with all deliberate speed." The Court then left it to lower courts to interpret its ruling. Immediately following the *Brown* decision, some voluntary and peaceful desegregation had occurred in border states such as Missouri, Oklahoma, and West Virginia and in cities such as Baltimore, Washington, D.C., and Louisville. Some moderate southerners counseled a degree of compliance, and segregationists hoped that the district judges, many of whom were Southerners, would not support the Supreme Court.

The NAACP filed petitions for desegregation signed by local blacks with 170 school boards in 17 states in the summer of 1955 (Woodward 1974, 154). It sought parents who were brave and committed enough to become litigants. But even earlier, in July 1954, the first Citizens' Council had been formed in Indianola, Mississippi—the state historically known for its extreme racism. Organized to oppose desegregation, Citizens' Councils were linked in a loose federation that became a powerful political and social force, intimidating black and white citizens, public officials, newspaper editors, and almost any moderate person.

To the South's consternation, lower courts had begun to rule that enforced segregation was a denial of equal protection of the law. By January 1956, 19 school court decisions had been rendered, all of which supported the Supreme Court's position. In a major case, Louisiana-born Federal District Judge J. Skelly Wright invalidated his own state's plan to preserve school segregation. Such southern judges would become infamous in their own region by their decisions.

The Counter-Movement to School Desegregation

By the beginning of 1956, the segregationists began to panic. Citizens' Councils spread from Mississippi into Louisiana, Alabama, Texas, Arkansas, Florida, and Georgia. State legislatures attempted to nullify and void the *Brown* decision. Die-hard segregationism became the issue on which politicians won and held office in the South. Worldwide media attention was directed to scenes of ugly confrontation between southern governors and neatly dressed black schoolchildren trying to enter white schools. The scenario was supplemented by white mobs, encouraged by their state leaders' predictions of violence.

The antidesegregation movement was a counter-movement. Participants in a counter-movement share a consensus that a change-oriented social movement constitutes a threat and that something can be done to stop it. Movement and counter-movement then mutually influence each other, competing for legal and governmental backing, money, and the support of the uncommitted public. Like the movement itself, the opposition develops strategies and tactics and takes many organizational forms. In this case, the anti–school desegregation forces became extremely creative in their efforts to impede implementation of *Brown*. They became a dangerous part of the civil rights environment.

The counter-movement drew attention away from black nonviolent protest efforts in the years under discussion, even as the NAACP continued to pursue its legal cases. It became obvious that mass action would be needed to enforce favorable court decisions. Southern branches of the NAACP came under highly organized attack, creating an even greater need for new protest organizations.[2] A vital question remained—would the courts be supported by other branches of the federal government? Most important, on whose side would the president come down? Dwight Eisenhower was unwilling to take a position in favor of the Supreme Court decision. His statements (when he made any) were ambiguous. Many felt that had he supported the *Brown* decision with the moral weight of his office and his personal popularity, the whole course of school desegregation would have been different.

Harry S. Truman had won the post–World War II 1948 election with a strong civil rights platform and the support of black voters, but the nation's mood had changed since that time. The country had been through the red-baiting McCarthy period of the 1950s and was only now beginning to recover. As we have seen, the major civil rights organizations had experienced their own internal strife over the communism issue.[3] The McCarthy hearings were over, but many in the national government, especially the chief of the Federal Bureau of Investigation, J. Edgar Hoover, still tended to see racial protest as Communist-inspired. Thus, in 1956, neither political party would take a firm stand against segregation in its national platform. That same year, a young black woman, Autherine Lucy, tried to enter the University of Alabama for graduate study. She was met with violent mobs, but the Supreme Court ordered that she be admitted. When the university trustees used the device of expelling her, the federal government failed to intervene, and the University of Alabama remained segregated for seven more years. But only one year after the Lucy case, in 1957, a major confrontation would take place between the federal government and the state of Arkansas over a similar issue.

A counter-movement develops its own ideology and rationale, reconceptualizing the impending change as negative and destructive of long-cherished values. Here words play an important part in convincing neutral or less-committed individuals. Note the rhetoric of Senator James Eastland of Mississippi, the principal spokesperson for southern resistance, who called for "'all patriotic organizations . . . to cooperate in a united movement for the preservation of America under a constitutional form of government'—which he claimed had been abandoned when the [Supreme] Court bowed to 'pressure groups bent upon the destruction of the white race. . . . The Court has responded to a radical, pro-Communist movement in this country. . . . We in the South cannot stay longer on the defensive. This is the road to destruction and death. We must take the offensive'" (Ashmore 1982, 225).[4]

State governments were in the forefront of the antidesegregation forces. The Alabama State Legislature was the first to call the Supreme Court decision "null, void and of no effect." In Virginia, conservative leaders claimed the right of "interposition" of state authority against the alleged violation of the Constitution by the Supreme Court. Pupil placement statutes were a successful delaying and time-consuming device enacted in 10 southern states shortly after *Brown*. They required a case-by-case procedure for gaining entry to schools. In the first three months of 1956, the legislatures of five states—Alabama, Georgia, Mississippi, South Carolina, and Virginia—adopted at least 42 prosegregation measures. States such as Virginia went as far as closing down public schools and creating subsidized white private schools. When various ploys were ruled out, the school systems still had the option of choosing tokenism, admitting one or two black students to prove compliance.

Southern politicians had seen the vote-getting possibilities in the school desegregation issue, and some former moderates began to adopt hard-line postures. Since most southern blacks were excluded from voting, politicians could appeal to a white electorate. In spring 1956, the school issue figured prominently in seven state primary elections. Two North Carolina representatives who refused to sign the Southern Manifesto were defeated.[5] Governors in Florida, Arkansas, North Carolina, and Texas took strong segregationist stands.

Economic reprisals were taken against whites who seemed sympathetic to black people and against blacks who took part in desegregation suits. Liberal ministers were forced out of the South. The Citizens' Councils maintained important links with state politicians and legislatures. Seemingly less blood-thirsty than the Klan, the Councils provoked violence through their antiblack rhetoric.

Little Rock, Arkansas

Against this background, an event of major importance took place in 1957—the confrontation between Arkansas governor Orval E. Faubus and the United States government over the desegregation of Little Rock's Central High School. Other major role players in the drama were nine black high school students (six young women and three young men) and their adult adviser, Daisy Bates, president of the state conference of NAACP branches. The crisis forced President Eisenhower to finally support the Supreme Court, temporarily hastened the pace of desegregation, and encouraged hopes for continued federal support. It also showed how racism could be manipulated by state politicians and that legal victories would be challenged and rechallenged by the opposition.

The issue amounted to whether or not a governor could use the National Guard to enforce segregation, defying court-ordered integration. Elected as a moderate, Faubus was seeking an unprecedented third term. Ironically, black students had already been admitted to the University of Arkansas and to other formerly all-white colleges in the state without incident. The superintendent of schools, Virgil T. Blossom, and the school board in Little Rock had prepared the community for orderly desegregation, which was expected. But by August 1957, Faubus believed that he could gain political mileage out of the race issue. What is more, he was challenged to take an antidesegregation stand by Governor Marvin Griffin of Georgia and Roy Harris, the president of the Citizens' Councils of America, who came to Arkansas that month to rally supporters.

The Little Rock school board had scheduled the first phase of its school desegregation plan to begin in September 1957. Meanwhile, Mrs. Clyde A. Thomason, a member of a newly organized segregationist group called the Mothers League of Little Rock Central High School, filed suit in Chancery Court seeking a temporary injunction against school integration. The suit was heard on 29 August 1957, and Thomason had none other than the governor of the state as her surprise witness (Bates 1962, 57). Both the governor and Thomason predicted violence if integration were to take place. Judge Murray O. Reed granted the injunction. The next day, NAACP lawyers took the case to Federal Judge Ronald N. Davies, who overruled the decision and ordered the school board to go ahead with its integration plan.

The night before the nine selected students were to start their first day of integrated education, National Guardsmen appeared, surrounding Central High. On television, the governor asserted that "blood would run in the streets of Little Rock" if the black students tried to attend the school (Bates 1962, 62). He declared the school off limits to them.

Attorneys Wiley Branton and Thurgood Marshall of the NAACP asked Federal Judge Davies for an interpretation. Taking the governor literally as intending to protect life and property against mob violence, the judge ordered the school board to proceed with its integration plan. Superintendent Blossom met with the parents of the nine students and Daisy Bates to discuss how this would be achieved. Bates was serving both as adviser to the students and as nerve center of the Little Rock integration struggle. She had been in touch with the children and their parents throughout these events, and they looked to her for guidance. Her role, as the undisputed strategist and liaison with authorities for the desegregation effort would continue through the next tumultuous school year, despite threats to her personal safety, rocks thrown through her living-room window, the need for armed guards to protect her house, and even an arrest. Eventually, because of their activism, she and her husband, L. C. Bates, lost the *State Press,* a newspaper they had successfully published for 18 years (Bates 1962).

Blossom asked the parents not to accompany their children to school the first day, claiming it would be safer. Meanwhile, segregationists from all over the state were rallying to join white mobs at the high school. To provide some assurance of the children's safety, Bates was able to recruit a few ministers to accompany them. She also asked the local police to be on hand the next morning. The officer in charge promised to do so, but he pointed out that city police could not approach the school while it was being "protected" by the National Guard. The various changes in plans about where the students were to assemble had kept Bates busy until three o'clock in the morning of the fateful day they were to enter, 4 September.

Overly fatigued, Bates failed to inform 15-year-old Elizabeth Eckford of the last change in plans. This human error resulted in one of the now-famous scenes of the civil rights struggle—Elizabeth, alone, trying to make her way past jeering mobs to the entrance of Central High School on 4 September. The National Guardsmen did nothing as hate-filled whites threatened and vilified her. Although some of the reporters and photographers at Little Rock became victims of the violence themselves, they managed to capture the scene; it was flashed around the world. Turned back by the raised bayonets of the Guardsmen, Elizabeth walked a gauntlet past the frenzied mobs again, maintaining dignity and control amid cries of "Lynch her!" She headed for a nearby bus stop. Two white people are remembered as coming to her aid that dangerous day. Benjamin Fine, education editor of the *New York Times,* sat down beside her and tried to comfort her. Grace Lorch, the wife of a professor, helped get her away, boarding a bus with her. Meanwhile, the other eight African American students, accompanied by four ministers, approached the school and were told by a National Guard captain that the governor had forbidden their entry.

The NAACP attorneys went back to federal district court, and Judge Davies granted them an injunction barring the governor from interfering with integration by use of National Guard troops. The troops withdrew, and city police prepared to protect the students the day they were to try again, 23 September.

Now large mobs assembled that belligerently defied the police. The students slipped through a side entrance to the school, but they did not stay there long. By 11:30 that morning, police chief Gene Smith (believed by the group to be sincerely doing his duty) decided it was too dangerous for the nine to remain in school, and they were spirited out. Numerous newspapermen had converged on Little Rock to record the events and many—including the entire *Life* magazine staff—were beaten (Bates 1962, 93). Later that day, random white violence occurred throughout the city.

Pictures of the confrontation between orderly schoolchildren and Little Rock's snarling white adults were flashed around the world. Eisenhower, the former wartime general, finally acted. He ordered 1,000 paratroopers to Little Rock and placed 10,000 National Guardsmen on federal service. He appeared on radio and television to explain his response. Eisenhower had never put his moral weight behind the 1954 Supreme Court desegregation decision. His statement that "you cannot change people's hearts merely by laws" had been repeated publicly several times (A. Lewis and the *New York Times* 1964, 48). Now his hand was forced by the widespread national and international publicity and the blatant challenge to federal authority.

Thus, in 1957, Little Rock (along with Montgomery and, in 1963, Birmingham) became a name that conjured up images of rioting and interracial strife. This was so even though, according to an on-the-scene newspaper editor, the confrontation had been contrived by the governor and, miraculously, there were no serious injuries (see Ashmore 1982). Bates's description of the level of violence differs from that account: she experienced many sleepless nights while cars filled with hostile whites circled her home. Threatening phone calls were a constant, and she and her supporters were prepared—as had been many beleaguered blacks before them—to defend themselves with arms. The nine integrating students experienced injury and continuing insult. After observing some initial gestures of friendliness, they found the school taken over by hardline segregationists. These racist students harassed, kicked, and pushed the black students and otherwise tried to force them to withdraw. Finally, after many requests for protection, two guards were assigned to accompany each student. Every afternoon, the students would gather at the home of Daisy Bates to share their day's experiences and encourage each other. Perhaps this is what helped all but one survive the year at Central High. (Minnijean Brown was suspended after responding to repeated provocations by white students, and had to finish her education elsewhere.)

Movement events such as the Little Rock showdown are experienced vividly in personal lives, but they also have broader significance. The Arkansas example showed both the importance of elected leadership in affecting social change and the role of national media coverage. But the confrontation also had important implications for resource mobilization.

Eisenhower's action taught the leaders of the developing civil rights movement that open, highly publicized incitement to violence by local authorities had to be understood as inimical to the nation's interest. Mob action or vicious behavior by whites was likely to bring the prestige and resources of the federal government to the side of black people and, what is more, could sway public opinion. People who believe in the rule of law would sympathize with victims of mob brutality and might be influenced to support a position they had previously rejected. Southern moderates were strengthened temporarily, and the North found it easy to moralize about southern resistance. According to Ashmore, editor of the only white Arkansas newspaper willing to take a position against the governor, "Orval Faubus was a hero to the mob; the nine courageous black children he failed to keep out of Central High were heroes to the world" (1982, 267). To many black people, Daisy Bates was also a heroine. Her courage and militancy proved a source of strength to the pioneering children and their families. Many times in the future, high school and college students would play important and dangerous roles in the movement, often stimulating adult participation. Many other women, too, were extremely important in local battles, although their leadership was frequently not as openly acknowledged as that of Daisy Bates.

In a way, Faubus had been a valuable enemy, as Roy Wilkins, head of the NAACP maintained, because he had forced a reluctant Eisenhower to finally back the Supreme Court. But the Arkansas governor was not yet defeated. When an effort to postpone integration was denied by the Court, Faubus closed the high school for the 1958–59 school year. Although he was reelected to a third and subsequent terms, the school closing nevertheless brought out those forces in the white population who opted for public education. Such was the situation of mixed progress and resistance that faced civil rights advocates as they tried to calculate their next lines of attack.

The strength of the antidesegregation movement had proven greater than expected. The year 1958 saw three Virginia cities close their public schools rather than comply with court orders. As various tactics spread, desegregation slowed down, then came to a halt. Many analysts believe that this resistance after a brief period of rising expectations was a key factor fueling the continuation of the civil rights movement.

The 1957 Civil Rights Act

On the national scene, the politics of race was also having a significant effect. The first civil rights act in 82 years was passed by Congress in 1957 through the efforts of presidential hopeful Lyndon Johnson. Although it was a weak act by later standards, it created an independent bipartisan Civil Rights Commission with investigative and advisory functions and the power of subpoena. Passage of the bill is credited to the amazing political astuteness of the then Senator Johnson of Texas, who was able to gain support for his version of the civil rights bill from fellow senators with widely differing points of view. Another role was being played by Johnson's supporter, the publisher Philip Graham, who convinced some major civil rights leaders to accept the compromise bill. Despite a 14-hour filibuster, the act passed the Senate by a substantial majority.

The Civil Rights Commission was given the important power to investigate complaints that the right to vote was being denied by reason of race. The campaign for voting rights would take activists into the heart of Klan territory. Hence, the commission, made up of six members appointed by President Eisenhower, could be crucial. Most of the appointees to the first commission did not seem promising, but one of them, Father Theodore Hesburgh, the president of Notre Dame University, proved a strong advocate of the purposes of the new commission and moved it to positive action.

No complaints were entered by the still-skeptical blacks for the first eight months of the commission's existence. But when the first case (from Gadsen County, Florida) received a careful field investigation, civil rights leaders began to encourage use of the commission. The year after its formation, it received complaints from 29 counties in eight states, citing denial of the right to vote.

The agency encountered resistance in areas of high Citizens' Council activity. A showdown occurred when officials at Lowndes County, Alabama, refused to present voting records. Black people comprised over 80 percent of the county's population, but not one of them had ever been able to register. The commission used its power of subpoena and held a hearing in Montgomery. Based on the facts acquired by the commission, the Department of Justice filed suit, and local officials were ordered to make their records available. But black would-be voters and civil rights workers were subjected to harassment, physical abuse, imprisonment, and death over the elementary American right to vote, and many felt that the Justice Department could be moved to act only in the most extreme cases (see chapter 6).

Meanwhile, two local actions showed that the movement was beginning to affect widely separated types of people. A highly educated black constituency in Alabama and poor sharecroppers in Tennessee were the principals involved; in both cases, the issue was voting rights.

Tuskegee

Tuskegee is located in Macon County, Alabama, and was the home base of Booker T. Washington from 1881 until he died in 1915. An all-black-staffed Veterans' Hospital was established there in 1924. The combined staff of Tuskegee Institute and the VA Hospital gave the county the distinction of having a higher proportion of highly educated African Americans than any other in the state. However, Alabama had set up a maze of difficulties for potential black voters. In its literacy test, the applicant had to read, write, and interpret a section of the U.S. or state constitution. It was up to the white local boards of registration to determine the results of each applicant's literacy test. In addition, each black person had to have two whites vouch for him or her in order to register.

Tuskegee blacks had created a local organization, the Tuskegee Civic Association (TCA), a somewhat conservative body whose main focus was education. This group would take the lead in the fight for voting rights. For despite the devious voting regulations and the traditional racial peace that prevailed in the county, white leaders feared the potential voting power of the educated blacks. They persuaded the state legislature to pass a law gerrymandering the city of Tuskegee, which it did on 13 July 1957. Tuskegee's boundaries were changed to make a four-sided municipality into a 28-sided city. Only 10 black voters out of 400 were left in the city, and no white voters were eliminated. This was more than the black community could accept. The TCA called for a selective buying campaign against the white merchants in town, inasmuch as the state had outlawed boycotts. The campaign (actually a boycott) lasted for about four years at a high level of effectiveness and caused a significant number of white businesses to close down. It was not until 1961, however, that a federal court ruled that the gerrymandering had been racially motivated in violation of the Fifteenth Amendment, the former boundaries of the city were restored, and the vote returned to black citizens.

During the period of the gerrymandering dispute, the new U.S. Commission on Civil Rights conducted investigations in Macon County and revealed a longtime denial of voting rights. The TCA produced a record of every black person who had applied for a voter certificate since 1951 as well as other corroborating data. Thus, in this case, mass action was combined with fact-finding, an appeal to a federal agency, and use of the courts. In 1959, Macon County had become one of the first targeted by a Justice Department suit charging voting denials.

Tent City, in Fayette County, Tennessee: home to sharecroppers evicted because they registered to vote. *Ernest C. Withers.*

The human face of eviction: sharecropper family members looking out of their living quarters in Tent City. *Ernest C. Withers.*

Fayette and Haywood Counties

As in Tuskegee and Montgomery, local black civic leagues were springing up throughout the South. The Fayette and Haywood County Civic
and Welfare Leagues, in southwestern Tennessee, held a highly successful voter registration drive in 1958. The counterattack by whites
took the form of extreme economic retaliation. Three hundred sharecroppers were evicted from the plantations where they had been working. In 1960, a "tent city" was set up for the refugees, and national civil
rights organizations, especially CORE, sought donations of food and
clothing. Had their plight not drawn national attention and the help of a
major organization, the ousted farmers could not have held out. But
northern liberals were beginning to provide the southern movement with
financial and moral support. Representatives of the Fayette County and
Haywood County sharecroppers were sent north to address sympathetic
interracial audiences.[6] As the North was being mobilized to help, southern resistance to desegregation and the black vote continued to mount.
At this time, the North and the South had differing reputations for
racism.

Movement Halfway Houses

There were still some voices of moderation in the South, although it was
increasingly difficult for whites to take an open stand against segregation.
Among those sympathetic to black rights were several white or interracial groups that engaged in educational, informational, and/or leadership-
training efforts. Morris calls the major ones *movement halfway houses*
because, although they did not have a mass base, they facilitated the
movement wherever possible. Among those he discusses are Highlander
Folk School, the Fellowship of Reconciliation, and the Southern Conference Educational Fund (Morris 1984, ch. 7).

The Southern Conference Educational Fund produced valuable research and disseminated information about southern inequities. The Fellowship of Reconciliation provided training in nonviolence and initiated the
test of interstate transportation that would be reincarnated as "Freedom
Rides." The interracial Highlander Folk School in Tennessee, an innovative grass-roots educational experiment, was targeted many times.
Miles Horton, who founded it, was an extraordinary figure who brought
blacks and whites together in one of the only integrated settings in the
South. Highlander recognized and encouraged Septima Clark's special

talents. Clark knew how hard it was for illiterate or semiliterate blacks to attempt to register to vote and she pioneered literacy training. Starting with respect for the intelligence and adult status of the students, she developed appropriate and meaningful teaching materials and trained lay teachers. Clark reports that "by the spring of 1961 eighty-two teachers who had received training at Highlander were holding classes in Alabama, Georgia, South Carolina and Tennessee" (Clark and Brown 1986, 60). During the summer of 1961 the citizenship education program was moved away from Highlander, which was under threat of being shut down. Its funding from the Marshall Field foundation was transferred to the SCLC, and Martin Luther King invited Septima Clark to join its staff.

Southern white liberals tended to condemn violence but to avoid taking a public stand against segregation. Their voice was a weak one, in contrast to that of the rabid racists, and their position was compromised in the eyes of many black people. A few courageous lawyers, judges, newspaper editors, and professors took positions in opposition to those of the majority in the region. Some, such as Judge J. Waties Waring, were forced to leave their home states (Clark and Brown 1986, 29). In contrast, white liberals and radicals in the North were more able and willing to speak out on racial issues. Interracial CORE chapters were operating in a number of northern and western cities; when the organization went South it would have to modify its constitutional provision requiring a racially mixed membership. Attracting white members would probably have been very difficult in the region.

Another difference between North and South was that of de facto and de jure segregation. The latter, segregation by law, was typical of the South. The North resorted to informal practices and manipulation, such as the drawing of gerrymandered school districts or the selection of school sites centrally located in predominantly white or predominantly black neighborhoods. That these neighborhoods existed testified to the reality of widespread housing segregation. The North's informal discriminatory practices created dilemmas for black people. Some even said they preferred the clarity of the southern patterns to the indefiniteness, hypocrisy, and unpredictability of the North.

The posture of leading political figures also differed in the two regions. Segregation was spoken of as a lofty principle in the South, but not publicly so in the North. There black voters usually were not intimidated or prevented from registering, although some politicians might try to buy their votes. These politicians moderated their official positions to reflect their new racial constituency. A number of northern and western states had passed fair employment laws and had set up antidiscrimination agencies. Local human relations committees were springing up, and some nonsouthern NAACP branches became more active at the very time that the South was trying to outlaw the organization.

The student sit-in movement further galvanized northern and western support. Interracial groups would become involved in sympathetic picketing and boycotting of chain stores that had segregated southern branches, and some white volunteers would go south. As the battle escalated, regional differences appeared sharp. The voting rights campaign would take black and white civil rights workers into the most feared counties in Mississippi, Alabama, and Louisiana. With little legal justification now for the withholding of voting rights, terrorist intimidation would be increasingly used to supplement the evasive and discriminatory behavior of white voting registrars. But a major assault on segregated eating facilities set the pace for the accelerating civil rights movement—the student sit-ins.

Freedom Riders rest on the ground beside their bombed and charred bus. *Schomburg Center for Research in Black Culture.*

Chapter Five

Sit-ins and Freedom Rides

"Which one should I get first?" a big husky boy said.

"That white nigger," the old man said.

The boy lifted Joan from the counter by her waist and carried her outside the store. Simultaneously I was snatched from my stool by two high school students. I was dragged about thirty feet toward the door by my hair when someone made them turn me loose. As I was getting up off the floor, I saw Joan coming back inside. We started back to the center of the counter to join Pearlina. Lois Chaffee, a white Tougaloo faculty member, was now sitting next to her. So Joan and I just climbed across the rope at the front end of the counter and sat down. There were now four of us, two whites and two Negroes, all women. The mob started smearing us with ketchup, mustard, sugar, pies, and everything on the counter. Soon Joan and I were joined by John Salter, but the moment he sat down he was hit on the jaw with what appeared to be brass knuckles. Blood gushed from his face and someone threw salt into the open wound. Ed King, Tougaloo's chaplain, rushed to him.

—Ann Moody

The scene: The F.W. Woolworth store in Greensboro, North Carolina.

The time: about 4:30 in the afternoon.

The date: Monday, 1 February 1960.

An historic event is about to unfold, the telling of which cannot fully recapture the drama of the moment. Four black college students are among the shoppers: Ezell Blair, Jr., Joseph McNeil, David Richmond, and Franklin McClain. The money of black shoppers is welcome at all the departments but one—the lunch counter. That is for whites only in Woolworth's, as well as in every other variety store in the South. Black people are not to be seated with white people at even the most modest of eating facilities.

The four students sit quietly at the lunch counter, ask for service, but are refused. They read their books, and after an hour the store closes. That night their campus is alive with word of the sit-in, and 20 more students are recruited to return with them the next day. Today's events have been a milestone in a movement that will change the entire South and affect the whole nation. Some have chosen to call this, rather than Montgomery, the real turning point because, "Montgomery was a reaction; Greensboro was an act. . . . The students knew what they were about: they did not stumble into it" (Bennett 1966, 217).

Despite some accounts to the contrary, the action of the first-year students from North Carolina Agricultural and Technical College was neither spontaneous nor hasty. They had spent hours discussing the integration movement and their wish to take action. They had seen the promise of the Supreme Court decision of 1954 compromised by massive white resistance and violent confrontations like that in Little Rock. They were familiar with the Montgomery boycott. Indeed, the Reverend King had brought his message to Greensboro in 1958 and had been provided with a chapel facility by President Willa Player of Bennett College in what was for that time a courageous act. She would be a tower of strength for the youths in days to come. Students from Little Rock had also come to Greensboro to talk about their experiences.

Two of the younger men who initiated the sit-in had lived in Greensboro all their lives; the others were from Washington, D.C., and Wilmington, North Carolina. They were not northerners come down to make trouble but had grown up under segregation. Within that context, they had come into contact with adults, black and white, who took a stand against the southern system, including the father of one, Ezell Blair, Sr. All the students had been members of NAACP college or youth groups and were impatient with the pace of change and the ability of local boards to circumvent the *Brown* decision (Chafe 1981).

In Greensboro itself, the school desegregation issue had revealed the transparency of its "good" race relations. At first, some token desegregation had occurred. Josephine Boyd, a black honor student at segregated Dudley High, had applied for and been admitted to the white senior high school, which she attended despite harassment. Gradually, local white resistance had hardened, encouraged by the efforts of the state of North Carolina to disempower the Supreme Court. This was one of the states that had, in 1955, passed a Pupil Assignment Act. The act prevented any action on behalf of a group. Every application by a black student for reassignment was treated as a separate case with tremendous discretionary power vested in local school boards. School desegregation had been brought to a standstill in North Carolina by 1959. The effects of the countermovement were vivid facts of life for the young people in Greensboro.

It was against this background that the four young men decided upon a tactic and a target. The tactic was meant to point up a contradiction— that black people were served at all other counters but not at the lunch counter. The sit-in was simple: a student would take a seat or try to place an order at a "white" facility and remain seated if refused service. If struck or pushed, the individual would not retaliate. The students dressed neatly and acted politely. They chose Woolworth's, a chain store with many branches, because it was vulnerable to pressure in the North as well as the South. And that indeed proved to be the case because sympathetic picketing would occur all over the country. Other variety stores were targeted as well. The quotation at the beginning of the chapter is from the autobiography of a young Mississippi woman and illustrates the vicious treatment that many of the students faced.

Actually a NAACP youth council in Oklahoma had organized a sit-in by predominantly black students on 9 August 1958. Another lunch counter sit-in occurred in Wichita, Kansas, that same month, and several sporadic and unpublicized sit-ins followed in other border states. They did not ignite the movement, however. The Greensboro students, Matthews and Prothro assert, "managed to create a region-wide 'movement' from what had been scattered and sporadic protests. And they managed to commit this movement to the use of direct highly provocative tactics in its struggle for freedom and equality" (1966, 412).

The Sit-ins Escalate

The Tuesday sit-in was followed by larger ones. In the first week, students from Bennett, a black women's college, and a few white students from the Women's College of the University of North Carolina (located in Greensboro) joined the demonstrations. Saturday morning was the high point. Hundreds of black students, including the AT&T football team, went to the downtown area to participate. Hostile young whites, waving Confederate flags, were there to greet them. In midafternoon, amid an atmosphere of tension, the store manager said he had received a bomb threat and closed the store. The students felt they had won and that evening held a huge mass meeting. They voted to cease demonstrations temporarily to provide time for negotiation. When Woolworth's opened the next Monday, the lunch counter did not.

Despite much evidence of community willingness to accept equality of service for black people, the white leadership and store managers would not act without further pressure. On 1 April, the students resumed their demonstrations, picketing the variety stores and testing lunch counter segregation. National leaders such as King and Thurgood Marshall, national counsel for the NAACP, supported their actions. The accomodationists among Greensboro's black citizens seemed to disappear, and a more unified, militant spirit was evident. Woolworth's sales went down 20 percent in the city in 1960, and its profits were off by 50 percent. But it was not until 25 July that the first black person was able to eat at the Woolworth lunch counter. The pressure had finally worked. Greensboro would continue to experience protest action as targets shifted and the pace of change slowed.

Meanwhile, the sit-ins had struck a responsive chord in the hearts of both black students and a number of white students. As television, newspapers, radio, and word of mouth carried news about the sit-ins, youths started their own demonstrations wherever they were. Bob Moses, a former Harvard graduate student who was to become a legendary hero in the South, left New York to join the struggle. Julian Bond, then a Morehouse College student, immediately set about launching the Atlanta student movement. Six weeks later it "erupted into one of the largest and best-organized sit-in demonstrations of all" (Zinn 1965, 17). Within a year and a half after the first Greensboro sit-in, demonstrations had occurred in over a hundred cities and towns in every southern and border state as well as Illinois, Nevada, and Ohio. Sympathetic boycotts of Woolworth stores were being conducted in every major city of the North.

Nashville, Tennessee, the site of the famous Fisk University and a number of other black and white institutions of higher education, became a focal point of massive sit-ins and violent retaliation. There, college and theological school students had been preparing themselves for nonviolent confrontation with the system. Nashville became the source of dynamic movement leaders such as Diane Nash, John Lewis (who would head SNCC), James Lawson, and James Bevel, to name just a few. Many of them turned from secure middle-class futures to the unknown dangers of defying the South. The Nashville students drew up a code of conduct that was used by the whole movement:

Don't strike back or curse if abused.

Don't laugh out.

Don't hold conversations with floor walkers.

Don't block entrances to the store and aisles.

Show yourself courteous and friendly at all times.

Sit straight and always face the counter.

Remember love and nonviolence.

May God bless each of you. (Bennett 1966, 216)

The Nashville movement had begun only 12 days after the first Greensboro action and involved 40 students, some white, sitting in at Woolworth's. On the fourth day of the Nashville sit-in, violence erupted. Lighted cigarettes were pushed against the backs of young women sitting at the counter. When a white sit-inner regained her composure in the face of racist jeers, she was pulled off her stool, thrown to the floor, and kicked. At another store, a white man kept blowing cigar smoke into the face of a Fisk University student. He then repeatedly pulled the student, Paul LePrad, off the stool, hitting him. At this, the police arrested the student and the 17 other sit-inners (Zinn 1965, 20–21). Such incidents would be repeated elsewhere as thousands of students rallied to the cause. Some would be subjected to tear gas and billy clubs, to sentences on chain gangs, and to overcrowded and putrid jails. By April, 2,000 had been arrested and thousands had marched on state capitols and downtown areas in Alabama, South Carolina, Georgia, and Louisiana. Students had inaugurated their massive involvement in the movement.

Diane Nash, whose own leadership is unquestioned by those who were there, emphasizes the continuing impact students would have: "The media and history seem to record it as Martin Luther King's movement, but young people should realize that it was people just like them, their age, that formulated goals and strategies, and actually developed the movement" (Williams 1987, 131). Indeed, many times the students' resolve and daring pushed the other civil rights organizations to greater militancy.

CORE, the NAACP, and the SCLC Join the Students

All the major civil rights organizations seemed to understand that a new phase had begun. Through George Simkins, Jr., head of the city NAACP chapter, the four originators of the sit-in made contact with CORE's national office. CORE leaders rushed to North Carolina to offer their aid.

By the end of the first week of sit-ins, the NAACP and SCLC representatives were on the scene. The interaction of these three major civil rights organizations, and the independent one that the students would soon form, continued throughout the sixties and proved to be complex and even controversial at times. Each sought a major role in the struggle and competed for personnel, resources, and publicity. Their rivalry was complemented, however, by patterns of mutual aid and the practice of sending in reinforcements or a charismatic leader to aid other organizations at crucial times. A division of labor and of territories evolved that was sometimes shaky. All banded together in uneasy union at major events. The NAACP, frequently discounted for its gradualism, and the NAACP Legal Defense and Educational Fund, in addition to other lawyers' groups, remained an important backup for legal aid.

The paths of the major national organizations would increasingly diverge after the resumed Meredith march of 1965 (see chapter 8). Together, they and the many state and local pro–civil rights groups formed what Zald and McCarthy have called a "social movement industry" (1979). While industries usually are part of the established order and have connotations that set them apart from social movements, the term does suggest the complex network of interrelated organizational ties that bound together individuals and groups engaged in a similar enterprise.

From the time of the first Greensboro sit-in, simultaneous actions were taken in many communities, some achieving national attention and a degree of success, others not. Often they would extend over months, even years.[1] Some were spearheaded by local groups, not necessarily affiliated with the big-name organizations, in the South as well as in other regions. Each of the major groups, in carving out a national role and seeking funds, selected targets for concentration. James Farmer of CORE and John Lewis and Stokely Carmichael of SNCC, in addition to King and Abernathy, made frequent headlines. Hundreds of others were less well-known, and many background advisers saw themselves as intellectuals rather than popular figures. Perhaps the most controversial of the major organizations was SNCC, which underwent a metamorphosis in the course of the movement.

The Birth of the Student
Non-Violent Coordinating Committee

SNCC was born out of the generation gap between more mature leaders and the college and high school students. The difference, perhaps, lay in the fact that among the former were accommodationists, whose voices of moderation combined with their positions of influence could hold the more daring in check. The NAACP and SCLC were willing to consult community influentials; SNCC preferred a free hand. The mood was such that peer pressure urged youth on to more dangerous confrontations. But there was also a continuity of generations, which is sometimes overlooked. Many of the activist youth had been inspired by the courage of parents, teachers, and university presidents.

The survival of black colleges in the South had often been at the cost of at least outward subservience to the power structure. Some college presidents, such as Stephen Wright of Fisk, Benjamin Mays of Morehouse, and Willa Player of Bennett College, openly supported the students. But hundreds of students were dismissed and many teachers fired by other black college presidents. James Lawson, a black divinity student at predominantly white Vanderbilt University and a leading activist in the Nashville movement, was expelled a few months before his graduation. A number of the white faculty members subsequently resigned over the refusal of the school to readmit Lawson.

Perhaps because of the inconsistency in adult behavior, the students decided to form their own organization. It would strive for internal democracy rather than hierarchy and emulate in its Spartan living conditions the bulk of the people it was trying to serve. Nonetheless, the initial conference leading to the formation of SNCC was financed by the SCLC. King and his aides, principally Ella Baker, took the lead in calling student leaders together on the campus of Shaw University in Raleigh, North Carolina. The 15–17 April 1960 conference drew more than 200 delegates, representing over 50 colleges and high schools in 37 communities of 13 states (Lynd 1966, xli). The group met again at Atlanta University and created a structure and identity for their organization. Ella Baker remained an inspirational adviser, encouraging the youthful activists to remain independent of the SCLC.

Many of the original members of SNCC were students and ex-students who had participated in the sit-ins. Predominantly black but initially interracial, the new group drew some of the most dedicated and well-accepted of white activists: Jane Stembridge, a white Virginian, was entrusted with setting up the first SNCC office. The students tended to be middle class and intellectually oriented, but they would take the movement into the poor Black Belt counties of Georgia and Mississippi, living on subsistence wages and facing great danger as they tried to organize local folk.

The courage and dedication of the early SNCC workers is legendary, although only a few of their names are well known. Just as it is challenging

Ella Baker, longtime civil rights organizer who helped students from SNCC, in photo taken from the documentary film about her life, Fundi. *The Southern Patriot.*

to try to recapture the drama of the 1960s on paper, so it is hard to appreciate the extent of the bravery of the SNCC field staff. Howard Zinn, who was close to many of the students as their teacher and adviser, has movingly described their willingness to "drop everything—school and family and approved ambition—and move into the Deep South to become the first guerilla fighters of the Student Nonviolent Coordinating Committee" (1965, 3).

By early 1964 the number of field workers was up to 150. The cause of voter rights and voter education would take the young volunteers into the heart of the Deep South and would bring jail, beatings, and death to some. The violent response of white authorities would then bring the movement back to the centers of national power, confront the Democratic party with difficult choices, and eventually lead to a new direction—black power.

Meanwhile, the sit-ins continued. A year and a half after their origin, at least 70,000 blacks and their white sympathizers had taken part in demonstrations, according to the Southern Regional Council (Matthews and Prothro 1966, 408).[2] And by spring 1961, about 140 cities had reported changes in their segregation practices. At year's end, several hundred lunch counters had been desegregated in scores of cities in Texas, Oklahoma, the border states of the South, and even Atlanta, Georgia. Resistance still was strong in the rest of Georgia, South Carolina, Alabama, Mississippi, and Louisiana.

CORE leaders joined the scene of many student sit-ins and also inaugurated some of their own. One of its major efforts occurred in Rock Hill, South Carolina. On 31 January 1961, Tom Gaither of CORE and nine students took seats at a McCrory's lunch counter and were arrested and taken to jail. They were convicted of trespassing and sentenced to 30 days hard labor on a road gang or $100 fines. Nine out of the 10 chose jail instead of bail. This was the beginning of a "jail, no bail" tactic that made national headlines and was repeated many times elsewhere. Students continued to demonstrate in Rock Hill and to volunteer for jail. SNCC leaders arrived, demonstrated, were arrested, and began serving 30-day jail terms. Rock Hill was of considerable significance as a model for the jail-ins of the Freedom Rides that were soon to occur (Meier and Rudwick 1973). Massive jail-ins would stretch local facilities, gain national attention, and solidify the commitment of those involved. The students sang freedom songs, went on hunger strikes, and drew strength and support from each other. Wrote one observer, "There has never been a singing movement like this one. . . . Every battle station in the Deep South now has its Freedom Chorus, and the mass meetings there end with everyone standing, led by the youngsters of SNCC, linking arms and singing 'We Shall Overcome'" (Zinn 1965, 4).

Inspired by the uprising, concerned black and white people in the North grasped the opportunity to provide moral and financial support for the southern movement, as well as to initiate projects in their own communities through branches of CORE, the NAACP, and local human rights groups. CORE brought the North into the movement through sympathetic picketing of variety stores almost immediately, sponsoring a demonstration in Harlem in February 1960. There were dozens of such demonstrations each Saturday at variety store outlets throughout New York and other states.

Northern support of southern desegregation efforts mushrooms; a picketing scene in New Brunswick, New Jersey, 1960. *Personal collection of the author.*

The Freedom Rides

CORE had proven itself a responsive ally when it came to the aid of the students. Its tactics were being widely practiced, even when its philosophy was not fully accepted. Two decades of nonviolent action in scattered northern and western cities had given CORE organizational skills, but it still lacked a strong national presence. In contrast, King and the SCLC had rapidly gained widespread fame. What CORE needed to gain attention and increased financial resources was a charismatic black leader and a major original initiative. This it got by appointing James Farmer national director and creating the Freedom Rides.

Farmer took office on 1 February 1961. As early as 1942, he and Bayard Rustin had organized race relations conferences in a number of cities and formed nonviolent direct action groups. The Freedom Rides, modeled after the 1947 Journey of Reconciliation that CORE and FOR had sponsored, began on 4 May 1961 and established CORE as one of the central organizations active in the South. This status was achieved because of bloody beatings, bus burnings, and unbelievable bravery, all of it captured in the country's media.

The Freedom Rides were precipitated by a 1960 Supreme Court decision—*Boynton* v. *Virginia*—which extended the prohibition against segregation in interstate travel to terminal accommodations. The Freedom Rides, to be undertaken by trained interracial groups, intended to expose illegal segregation practices at terminals all the way to the Deep South. CORE decided on this action while the other organizations were considering their next targets. The Freedom Riders's bloody reception soon brought them reinforcements.

Many accounts of the Freedom Rides have appeared, some differing slightly.[3] It is worth describing them in detail to illustrate not only the concrete events but the interplay of civil rights organizations, the press, and government officials. The NAACP, SNCC, CORE, and the SCLC both assisted and upstaged each other at times. In doing so they brought more power, more ideas, and more collective bravery to the movement—while experiencing a conflict in outlook that would eventually break their alliance. The organizations developed different styles, the SCLC tending to select a series of major projects and to act with careful deliberation and planning. SNCC workers lived quietly in local communities, subject to the greatest hazards, returning to previous scenes of beatings and jailings without retreat. Initially the most interracial, CORE created innovative nonviolent techniques but also engaged in community organizing and voter registration in the Deep South. Major white repression often brought members of the competing groups to demonstrations others had initiated, in a show of defiance and unity.

This time it was the turn of CORE and James Farmer to have their moment in history. Tom Gaither, of Rock Hill fame, made a preparatory trip around the proposed route of the Freedom Rides, arranging rallies and overnight housing. He notified and sought the cooperation of local NAACPs. The facilities of two bus companies, Trailways and Greyhound, were going to be tested. Thirteen people, seven blacks and six whites, trained for the journey in Washington, D.C., and on 4 May 1961 they departed on one Greyhound and one Trailways bus. The four CORE staff members who took part included Farmer, James Peck (who had been on the original Journey of Reconciliation), and John Lewis, a 21-year-old member of the Nashville Christian Leadership Conference, who would eventually head SNCC. Lewis had already been arrested five times and had sacrificed his June graduation from a theological seminary. The white volunteers were somewhat older than the black ones, and most had been associated with peace organizations. The two causes were seen as closely allied by many white activists.[4]

The buses traveled through Virginia and North Carolina, with riders insisting on their right to use terminal waiting rooms and lunch counters. A CORE field secretary, Joe Perkins, was arrested and acquitted two days later. The Rock Hill Greyhound station became the first scene of violence for the Freedom Riders. A waiting mob at the entrance of a white waiting room beat John Lewis and Albert Bigelow, a 58-year-old white architect and pacifist. The next day, two men were arrested after attempting to eat at a white luncheonette in Winnsboro, South Carolina, and were released seven hours later. Continuing the journey to Atlanta, the riders found the restaurant at the Greyhound terminal closed but were able to eat at the Trailways terminal. Increasing publicity helped in some ways, but it also alerted the Ku Klux Klan. The white mobs would grow in size and violence until only luck or last-minute federal intervention prevented actual deaths. Many riders would be hospitalized or jailed. A cautious Robert Kennedy would have long, cajoling conversations with segregationist governor of Alabama John Patterson and be the recipient of alarmed phone calls from Martin Luther King and other embattled civil rights workers.

The Reverend Fred Shuttlesworth, president of the Alabama Christian Movement for Human Rights (ACMHR), an affiliate of the SCLC, had warned of the possibility of attack in that city, but the riders continued. Unfortunately, he was correct. Violence broke out even before the riders reached Birmingham. When the first of the two buses crossed into Alabama, the Klan was waiting. At the Anniston station, an angry mob wielding chains, sticks, and iron rods began breaking the bus windows and slashing tires. The vehicle took off, followed by the attackers. Several miles out of town, the bus driver realized that his tires were going flat and he pulled off the highway. The mob used bricks and an ax to smash the windows one by one, used pipes to batter the exterior, and tried to force open the door. An incendiary bomb was tossed into the bus, bursting into flames.

Fortunately, two Alabama state investigators were traveling on the vehicle under cover, along with some regular passengers. As the bus started to fill with acrid smoke, investigator E. L. Cowling forced the door open so that all could exit. The mob attacked the passengers as they stumbled out through smoke and heat, stopping only when state troopers arrived. As a photographer captured the scene that would be distributed around the world, the troopers took the passengers to Anniston Hospital. The police finally arrived but refused to guarantee protection from a mob waiting outside the hospital. Meanwhile, hospital officials were telling the battered riders to leave. It is generally agreed that there was a daring and successful rescue, with carloads of armed black churchmen getting the riders away to relative safety. Says Ashmore, "A flying squadron of blacks led by the Reverend Fred Shuttlesworth" came from Birmingham to the rescue (1982, 326). Shuttlesworth's fearlessness was legendary; he had risked his life many times to develop Birmingham as a protest movement center.[5]

The pictures of the flaming bus had hit the front pages, making the Freedom Rides a major media event. The second group of bus riders encountered white mobs both at Anniston and Birmingham (Meier and Rudwick 1973). At Anniston a group of white men boarded the bus, knocking riders down, stomping on them, and beating them. Then this second bus was allowed to proceed to Birmingham. There the Klan was ready in numbers with pipes, chains, and baseball bats. There is undeniable evidence of collusion between the notorious police commissioner of Birmingham and the Klan, and of the indifference if not hostility of the national FBI. "A detailed battle plan for this operation had been forwarded to Washington by the FBI, whose paid informant within the Klan reported that Police Commissioner Bull Connor had agreed to give the bullyboys twenty minutes before he sent in his police, saying that he wanted the Freedom Riders beaten 'until it looks like a bulldog got ahold of them'" (Ashmore 1982, 326).[6] He got his wish; they were bloodied. James Peck was knocked unconscious, and Walter Bergman, a retired white schoolteacher, suffered permanent brain damage from a blow on the head (Sitkoff 1981, 102). At this point, no bus driver would take the Freedom Riders farther. CORE decided to abandon the rides; the battered group boarded a flight to New Orleans that had been arranged by the Department of Justice. Despite prewarnings, the federal government had entered the scene only after the beatings and injuries had taken place—a pattern that would be followed with disheartening monotony in the difficult years ahead. Yet when Martin Luther King made a remark somewhat critical of the response of the FBI to violence against blacks, he was targeted as a dangerous enemy by its top officials (Garrow 1981; Lane and Gregory 1977; O'Reilly 1989). Over the years, evidence has increased that J. Edgar Hoover not only despised King but held the Kennedys in contempt—despite their efforts not to offend him.

The repeated scenes of vicious attack highlighted by the international press embarrassed President John F. Kennedy as he prepared for an upcoming summit meeting with Soviet premier Nikita Khrushchev. Some presidential advisers and Justice Department members were sympathetic to the demonstrators—notably, Harris Wofford, Burke Marshall, John Doar, and John Seigenthaler. Yet they were also sensitive to President Kennedy's fragile relations with southern governors. They hesitated to bring federal power to bear unless requested by the states or unless an obvious state of extreme crisis compelled intervention. Not surprisingly, the Kennedys sought to establish a cooling-off period, a cessation of the Freedom Rides.

Nashville student leaders decided otherwise. Diane Nash, John Lewis, and other SNCC activists determined that violence should not be allowed to stop the movement; students would continue the Freedom Rides into Alabama and Mississippi. A selected group of SNCC veterans were chosen and given tickets for a bus, headed for Birmingham on 17 May. Her peers insisted that Diane Nash was too valuable as the central strategic contact for her to leave Nashville, but John Lewis, who had been on the first Freedom Ride, was on the bus. In a new tactic, Bull Conner intercepted the group as it reached Birmingham and arrested the students. Then, in the middle of the night, he removed them from jail and drove them to the Alabama-Tennessee border. Finding refuge with a black farm family, they called Nash, who dispatched cars to get them. They decided to return to Birmingham and start their journey anew, aware that they were facing possible death. Indeed, the Freedom Rides proved to be one of the most dangerous undertakings of the movement.

Now the Kennedys worked harder behind the scenes to assure state protection for the Riders, but Governor John Patterson ignored even the president's calls. Finally, he agreed to meet with John Seigenthaler, the Justice Department aide who was monitoring the situation for the administration. Patterson, whose language dripped with the word "nigger" and other racial epithets, told Seigenthaler in front of various officials that he would protect all persons in the state. Among those present was Floyd Mann, head of the State Highway Patrol. Mann was one of the few law enforcement officials in Alabama who was intent on protecting those under his authority.

Mann protected the bus as it headed toward Montgomery, but he could not continue within the city limits, where his jurisdiction ended. Despite official and unofficial warnings about mobs gathering, city police commissioner L. B. Sullivan removed his forces from the bus terminal just before the Freedom Riders got there. Suddenly, the riders were alone and the governor's promised protection proven a lie. The waiting mob at Montgomery was even more vicious than previous ones. The Justice Department's John Doar observed the scene from a window of the Federal Building and described it over the phone to his superior, Burke Marshall, in horrified tones. He noted the absence of police anywhere and the raucous crowd. "Less than five minutes after the bus door opened in Montgomery, official Washington knew that pipes and bare knuckles nullified all the painstaking federal-state agreements" (Branch 1988, 447). President Kennedy sent 600 federal marshals to Maxwell Air Base outside of Montgomery, while Governor Patterson continued to insist that a federal presence was not necessary.

Seigenthaler, arriving at the bus terminal by car, decided to attempt to rescue Susan Wilbur, a white female Freedom Rider, who was being pummeled from the front and behind. When she hesitated to enter his car, Seigenthaler became one more victim. As he called out that he was a federal agent, he was hit on the head with a pipe and fell to the ground unconscious. The crowd kicked his body halfway under the car, where he lay for about a half an hour, bleeding and unattended. Meanwhile, John Lewis had also been knocked unconscious, Zwerg was lying facedown on a patch of warm tar on the pavement, and Lewis's schoolmate, William Barbee, was being stomped and kicked. Floyd Mann appeared on the scene, and acting without authority, he brandished his revolver to free Barbee. He moved on to aid others, some of whom were newsmen under attack. The injured faced delays in getting ambulances or taxis that would take them to a hospital willing to accept them. After about 10 minutes of the violence, Police Commissioner Sullivan arrived on the scene, but he did nothing to help in the evacuation.

Those Freedom Riders who could had found refuge in hiding places around the city. In contact with Diane Nash by phone, they were directed to the home of the Reverend S. S. Seay. There they were all welcomed and given news about others. The world had been informed about the day's events, and notables of the civil rights movement were on their way to Montgomery.

Now Martin Luther King and the SCLC came to show their presence and support. King was protected on his way from the airport to Ralph Abernathy's First Baptist Church, where 1,500 people were assembled. At least twice that many hostile whites surrounded the church, in which young and old were singing freedom songs and honoring the Riders. CORE leaders from New York reentered the scene, not without difficulty. Against all advice, Fred Shuttlesworth left the church to meet James Farmer at the airport. As they approached the church, their car was blocked and they continued the journey by foot. In the kind of unbelievable action for which he was famous, Shuttlesworth waved the hostile crowds aside with huge gestures, bellowing "let him through, let him through." They made it into the church.

In Washington, Robert Kennedy and his aides were monitoring the situation, trying to determine when and what kind of federal help was needed. On the phone with him, King described the conditions in the church and the mood of the mob, where a token number of federal marshals sent out earlier were trying to keep things under control. The need to reinforce them grew urgent, as no local police were to be seen. Finally, additional marshals were ordered in from Maxwell Field.

The new marshals fired tear gas into the mob, temporarily unsettling them. But the gas also wafted into the church, almost creating panic. Eventually, Governor Patterson declared a state of martial law. Montgomery police finally got into the action, just as soldiers from the Alabama National Guard appeared. While those in the church welcomed the National Guard, they were surprised to find themselves contained within the church long after the danger had seemed to subside. The Guard was under the control of Governor Patterson, and the federal government had to again intervene to convince the commanding officer, General Henry V. Graham, that people should be allowed to leave the church. They had been there most of that terrible night. King sought the attorney general's assistance to obtain safe passage into Mississippi for the next Riders. He also stated that arrestees would serve their sentences rather than accept bail. Kennedy tried to arrange a cooling-off period as well as safe passage, but he was rebuffed by James Farmer.

The Riders proceeded on the route to Jackson, Mississippi. Jail-ins were frequent as Farmer and many other prominent persons were arrested and refused bail. The participants included college students, blacks and whites, northerners and southerners, members of the clergy, and a disproportionate number of Quakers and Jews. Many remained in jail for 39 days, the limit of the time they could serve and still make an appeal. The NAACP Legal Defense and Educational Fund appealed the convictions of the Mississippi courts all the way up to the Supreme Court—achieving success only in April 1965 when the Court reversed the convictions. The Interstate Commerce Commission ordered the abolition of Jim Crow facilities in interstate transportation much earlier, in September 1961.

The Freedom Rides had been a high point that drew the involvement of every major civil rights organization. Word of mouth and the media kept the leadership in touch with the volatile, rapidly changing scene. Skills, funds, man- and womanpower were derived from varied sources. The creative competition as well as cooperation of the organizations made all of this possible. Starting in relative obscurity on 26 May, the Freedom Rides had "changed many lives and come to the attention of millions." CORE was now "allied formally with the heirs of the Montgomery bus boycott and the student sit-ins, maneuvering along a collision course with the federal government as well as the Southern states" (Branch 1988, 47). Here is an assessment of long-term experts on the movement about the effects of interorganizational rivalries in the early sixties:

Disagreements over strategy and tactics inevitably became intertwined with rivalries between personalities and organizations. Each civil-rights agency felt the need for proper credit if it was to obtain the prestige and financial contributions necessary to maintain and expand its own program. The clashes between individuals and organizations, both nationally and locally, were often severe, and the lack of unity was often deplored. Actually, down to 1964, the overall effect of the competition was to stimulate more and more activity as organizations attempted to outdo each other, and thus to accelerate the pace of social change in city after city. (Meier and Rudwick 1976, 280–81).

President Kennedy had been elected with the support of blacks, based upon his more positive posture toward desegregation than that of his predecessors. Nevertheless, he was very cautious. Planning a tour of Europe, he preferred to have his brother take the more visible role. In doing so, Robert Kennedy came to be seen as a reluctant ally by those risking their lives but as a conspirator with the movement by segregationists and state officials. Critics claimed that the president's concern with maintaining a congressional majority in support of his international programs led him to sacrifice seemingly controversial measures. Ironically, his successor Lyndon B. Johnson would achieve much more for black Americans but would eventually lose the support of King over the Vietnam war issue. And during both presidencies, J. Edgar Hoover, whose antiblack feelings were well known, would attempt to convince his superiors of Communist influence in the civil rights movement (Garrow 1981).

Robert Kennedy and Burke Marshall, civil rights chief in the Justice Department, maintained that the federal government could move in only after severe violence and the failure of local authorities. And indeed, the early 1960s saw the terrorism of the Freedom Rides repeated many times. It would produce many martyrs, some known and others still anonymous. The sequence of responses to the Freedom Rides was: first, there would be violence by whites against nonviolent demonstrators or jail sentences for violations of state laws that the federal courts would eventually hold unconstitutional; second, the federal government would intervene when mob rule took over; and finally, federal agencies would have to act to remove the original cause of the demonstrations. By the end of 1962, the civil rights organizations had achieved their objectives in interstate travel, but only because the process described had been pursued. As it took place, newspaper and TV accounts swung public sympathy to the side of the protesters, and international pressures mounted to force the federal government's hand. There seemed to be no shortcut that could eliminate the sacrifices of the activists.

The Meaning of the Sit-ins and Freedom Rides

Since the end of the 1960s, questions have been raised about the importance of the sit-in targets. As attention became directed to the conditions in the ghettos and to basic economic issues, earlier civil rights goals were sometimes labeled middle class, symbolic, or inconsequential. The position here is that these early goals were prerequisite to later phases of the movement, that they were important psychologically and ideologically, and that they affected the daily lives of working people.

The masses would not have responded to the sit-ins and freedom rides if they were inconsequential or meaningless. Leaders have to be guided by the issues that the majority of their people consider relevant at that time and place. And for southern blacks, the remnants of slavery were increasingly hard to live with. The middle-class students who joined the sit-ins were not part of a wealthy middle class, but of a black middle class striving for education as the road to upward mobility. They were widely supported by other students and eventually by the adults of their region, who had spent their lives subservient to whites. Bennett maintains that the demonstrations finally made clear that black people were not satisfied and wanted their citizenship rights (1966). The split personality they had so painfully maintained was shattered when they finally showed the white South their true feelings. The polite, deferential posture of blacks and the paternalistic attitudes of whites toward "their nigras" were replaced by a more honest, if more tense communication. Conscientious whites were forced to examine their values, stimulated by the courageous few who brought the issues into their own white churches and communities. The accommodationist stage was clearly a thing of the past, and the United States would have to face continued racial turmoil until black rights were won.

A distinction must be made between gains that can be measured in dollars and cents and the other gains of the movement. The poor were the ones who rode the segregated buses to work; these segregated buses were thereby part of their working conditions. It is true that middle-class black shoppers, spending money in white stores, were demeaned by the refusal to serve them at lunch counters. But poor people of the race also patronized the variety stores, and they, too, may have wished to stop off for a cool drink. The more educated intellectuals may have started the southern movement, but its success confirms its general appeal. A whole people made enormous psychological gains as they were finally able to openly reject segregation, the demeaning symbol of inferiority. Also being rejected were the inadequate facilities such as restrooms and waiting rooms that were their usual lot. Like the Montgomery bus boycott, sitting-in gave black citizens a sense of pride in self and group. For thousands of people, taking part in the assault on the most public symbols of their inferior position in American life was an important starting point for further efforts. As for the Freedom Rides, the federal government had been provoked by the sacrifices of the riders and world public opinion to intercede in the most blatant cases of white aggression against nonviolent freedom fighters.

Black citizens of Clinton, Louisiana, a site of CORE voter registration efforts, wait in line as they attempt to register. *Bob Adelman.*

Chapter Six

Voting Rights and the Mississippi Challenge

Slavery is not abolished until the black man has the ballot.
—Frederick Douglass, 9 May 1865

The pursuit of voting rights was an ongoing process for black people, but the years between 1961 and 1964 were especially momentous. During these years all the civil rights organizations and many local ones were actively engaged on many fronts. Rather than trying to deal with all the events that were taking place simultaneously, this chapter focuses on the voting rights campaigns that brought the black struggle to the center of national politics. In the next chapter we shall go back to some of the other major campaigns that occurred during this time.

Segregated interstate transportation facilities had been challenged head-on and a dangerous battle won. There were many more to be fought. Now, in the summer of 1961, the committed students and other activists who came out of jail as Freedom Riders had to consider their next move. While the issue was debated, forces were at work that would make voter registration and related community organizing the main thrust of the movement from 1961 to 1964. All the major organizations, but especially SNCC and CORE, would participate. During these years, the mass involvement of grass-roots people, strengthened and supported by outside volunteers, would be largely responsible for two major pieces of legislation, the Civil Rights Act of 1964—pushed through Congress in the name of the assassinated John Kennedy—and the 1965 Voting Rights

Act. In 1964, Congress would also pass the Twenty-fourth Amendment to the U.S. Constitution, outlawing the poll tax in federal elections.

The movement was represented in Congress by Harlem's fiery Adam Clayton Powell, Jr. It was not until 1961 that he successfully countered opposition to gain significant power in the House. His seniority entitled him to the chair of the important Education and Labor Committee, where he vigorously promoted civil rights and labor legislation.[1]

Despite the eventual legislative victories, there would be disappointment, disillusionment, and burn-out along the way—not to mention the deaths of a number of civil rights activists. The brutality of local government and law enforcement officials buttressed white supremacist violence, and weak support from the attorney general's office made victories costly. Large numbers of black people remained unable to register.

The events of these tumultuous years were transforming for both the civil rights workers and the African American communities involved, as movement experience so often is. Intense, firsthand involvement in the lives of local people in the Deep South brought SNCC and CORE field-workers face to face with the reality of black folks' poverty and fear. The early SNCC workers carefully encouraged the development of indigenous leadership. Constantly reassessing their strategies and tactics, the key young activists debated among themselves while pushing the other organizations toward greater militancy. Eventually some of the most seasoned of the former students turned toward black power and separatist philosophies. Being beaten and jailed for helping others secure their rights tends to be a radicalizing experience. Later recruits, too, were drawn from a broader base in the black class system, were often less religiously oriented, and tended to consider self-defense more appropriate than nonviolence.

The transformation process also affected many black southerners who were finally able to stand up to openly white supremacist forces, as they literally risked their lives, livelihoods, and health for the right to vote. The presence of the volunteers provided support for those who had taken courageous positions in the past and now welcomed their help. "The situation that SNCC usually encountered in the Delta was that while most people were initially afraid, some were interested right away and, given the tightly-knit social bonds of rural communities, they were able to pull others in." (Payne 1990, 163). The two community struggles of local origin described in chapter 4, in Tuskegee and in Fayette and Haywood counties, Tennessee, attest that black southerners truly cared about their right to vote and that voter registration was a meaningful goal.

The History of Black Disenfranchisement

Black people had been gradually disenfranchised since the 1877 compromise ending Reconstruction. The short-lived Populist movement of the next decade had shown how the southern black vote could become pivotal under a two-party system. Soon one party dominated the South, and the Democratic primary was the only scene of contest. The white primary became the most common way of preventing black people from registering or voting as the Democratic party became a private association.

However, a Texas law of 1923 requiring white primaries was legally vulnerable, and it was challenged in lawsuits. The winning of such cases resulted in new manipulations by the southern legislatures to create technical compliance by changing legal and party rules. Finally, the important 1944 Supreme Court decision in *Smith* v. *Allwright* declared the white primary unconstitutional under almost any condition. After this, the proportion of black people registered to vote, especially in the border states, increased. By 1952, about 20 percent of black adults compared with over 60 or 70 percent of whites were registered (Matthews and Prothro 1966, 17). But black registration had begun to slow down in response to the Citizens' Councils, the Klan, and other manifestations of the countermovement.

Congress provided some encouragement by passing a number of civil rights acts. The 1957 act gave the U.S. attorney general power to seek injunctions when people were deprived of or about to be deprived of their right to vote. In 1960, this was slightly strengthened by providing for the appointment of federal voter referees to register potential voters once the courts determined that a pattern of depriving black people of their vote had been demonstrated. The zeal with which a given attorney general would choose to enforce this provision was still an open question.

The Significance of Voting Rights

The sit-ins, boycotts, and Freedom Rides had been successful in the Upper South but had met with massive resistance in the Deep South; and it was there that black voters were most severely disenfranchised.

Mississippi was the most dangerous challenge—one that thousands of SNCC workers would nonetheless take on. Fifty percent of voting-age whites but only 5 percent of blacks were registered in the state. The latter constituted over 40 percent of the population but held no political offices. To confront the exclusionary practices of the most racially backward state and to attack the most difficult target first contradicts conventional wisdom. It was the boldest ploy possible, and one that could either be definitive or end in disaster. In Mississippi the white primary would meet its ultimate challenge—the creation by local Mississippians of a parallel Democratic party that challenged the legitimacy of the lily-white regular Democrats.

Multiple forces determine the course of a movement. Among the factors operating most powerfully to make voter registration a major goal were:

> The significance of the vote, historically, symbolically, and psychologically
>
> The lack of leverage and hence powerlessness of the black nonvoters
>
> The varied resources that could be mobilized to support the goal: the local black citizenry, southern liberals, the executive branch of the federal government, private foundations, and northern whites and blacks

Winning the right to vote would not, in itself, improve the basic conditions of life faced by the masses of black people, particularly those in urban ghettos. But many important leaders, from Frederick Douglass on, considered attainment of this right to be essential. Martin Luther King, Jr. proclaimed that "the biggest step Negroes can take is in the direction of the voting booths."

Symbolically, the inability to vote made many black people feel they were less than citizens, that they were not adults. Politically, their power and influence were minuscule. White elected officials had no black constituencies to please, and with no black elected officials, blacks had no voice in the inner councils of government. The same is true of the disenfranchised black South Africans, still fighting for the right to vote at the time of this writing.

Finally and crucially, the denial of voting rights was so flagrant an injustice that it could mobilize many types of support. As pointed out earlier, help could be expected from the North in matters that did not touch on northern-style discrimination. Outside the South, a number of black entertainers and writers had attained prominence and access to wealthy circles. Harry Belafonte, the actor and singer, comedian Dick Gregory, and writer James Baldwin were notable among those who would use their contacts and lend their presence to the southern campaigns. Belafonte, generous himself, became a major fund-raiser when the costs of bail and trials reached extreme proportions. A useful ally and friend to King, he could be called upon at any hour. Singers Mahalia Jackson and Joan Baez performed on many occasions, raising spirits and morale. They and other artists and celebrities were willing to risk reputations as well as donate time and money to a not-always-popular cause.

Of pivotal importance was the fact that the White House itself was eager to back the voter registration target. Presidents Eisenhower, Kennedy, and Johnson all professed that blacks having the vote would be the most effective means of their achieving equality. Kennedy believed that strong civil rights legislation could not be passed until black people could affect Congress. He undoubtedly hoped to benefit from an increased number of southern black voters in his expected 1964 presidential campaign. Voting rights was seen as a defensible area for federal concern. Further, focus on this goal would divert people, so the administration thought, from disruptive mass demonstrations that might further alienate white Democrats. Presidential efforts to "channel the black movement" are explained this way:

The Kennedy Administration's posture on these matters is not difficult to understand. Tactics of confrontation, together with the police and mob violence which they provoked, were polarizing national sentiments. The excesses of southern police and of white mob violence generated one excruciating political dilemma after another for the Kennedy Administration. . . . Each [federal] intervention, or the lack of it, angered one or the other major constituency in the civil rights struggle, thus worsening the electoral lesion in the Democratic Party. (Piven and Cloward 1979, 231)

The administration was to find that "voter registration was every bit as threatening to the white community as direct action," and that all civil rights work "melded together in the field" (Rothschild 1982, 15).

Financial resources are almost always a pressing concern of movements once they get under way. Harris Wofford, special assistant to Kennedy, whose civil rights sympathies were deemed too extreme to give him a more important title, believed that voter registration was a worthy target. Hence, he used his contacts to encourage private foundation grants and served as a catalyst between Kennedy, King, and the foundations (Branch 1988, 382–83). In this case, the offer of funds was probably a key factor in convincing the civil rights organizations to move ahead with an extensive voting rights campaign. One faction in SNCC wanted to continue direct action, whereas another wanted to pursue voting rights. The direct actionists knew the Kennedy administration was acting politically, in hopes of ending what it considered disruptive actions. Yet other members of the group felt strongly that voting rights were crucial. After long discussion, a compromise, in which both goals would have equal priority was worked out by Ella Baker. Diane Nash would head up direct action efforts, while Charles Jones would be in charge of voter education for SNCC. John and Robert Kennedy and their aides encouraged foundations to donate funds. The Taconic, Field, and Edgar Stern Foundations agreed to channel funds to the civil rights organizations through the interracial Southern Regional Council. The Voter Education Project, which was expected to last two and a half years, received $870,000, most of it from these foundations (Meier and Rudwick 1975, 175).

The Voter Education Project Gets under Way

With the encouragement of the Kennedys, a residential training school for fieldworkers was set up in Georgia under Andrew Young and Wyatt T. Walker. Although the SCLC was in agreement, CORE and especially SNCC played the major role in voting rights organizing activities. While others in SNCC were still arguing for direct action programs, Bob Moses, one of the most selfless of the black leaders, went to McComb, Mississippi, in August 1961 to begin voter registration work. Maintaining an unassuming posture, he engendered loyalty and love on the part of local black citizens and other staff members. Moses's pioneer effort occurred in Pike County, where the first voter registration school was opened. By early 1962, all the major organizations—CORE, SNCC, the SCLC, and the NAACP—were loosely bound together in the foundation-funded Council of Federated Organizations (COFO), which coordinated the Mississippi voter registration campaigns. Moses became its director and a legend in spite of himself. He was probably the one important leader who struggled against his own charisma, eventually stepping down from the highly respected role he had achieved in Mississippi and changing his name to his mother's maiden name, Parris.

Despite warnings from their elders in the more established groups, SNCC field secretaries spread out into dangerous southern localities, including some of the known Klan-infested areas, to live with and organize local people. Voter education schools were needed to teach disenfranchised blacks how to thread through the labyrinth of contrived registration procedures. The SNCC volunteers hoped to bring voter education to Mississippi on a large scale.

Most of the field secretaries and early volunteers were black but some were white, such as Jane Stembridge, Casey Hayden, and Mary King. They tended to be southerners who had sought out the movement, unlike the 1964 and 1965 summer volunteers who were actively recruited. The earlier white activists were often more knowledgeable about racism and were better accepted than were the later summer recruits. Although living on subsistence wages, the workers were not vulnerable to the severe economic reprisals faced by local people who dared to defy tradition. And this they did by opening their homes and churches to the SNCC workers. Charles Sherrod, project director in southwest Georgia, noted that there was usually an elderly black woman in every community who was willing to put herself on the line by taking in the activists.[2]

McComb, Mississippi

McComb, one of the first sites of action, illustrates patterns that occurred elsewhere in Mississippi and the South. In order to be certified to register, a Mississippi citizen had to be ready to interpret any section of the state constitution—the correctness of which would be decided by the same voting registrar who presented the passage. Moses started the practice of accompanying local people to the designated place to share with them the long wait in line to register, which most often ended in disappointment. He, as other SNCC workers would, returned to the scene time after time after being harassed, hit, or arrested.

It soon became apparent that local high school and college youths in the area were yearning for freedom and would defy their elders to join the movement. Attempts to desegregate public facilities continued. Brenda Travis, a high school student, was expelled from school for sitting-in and was eventually sentenced to a year in a school for delinquents. Herbert Lee, a farmer who had helped Bob Moses, was killed in Amite County, Mississippi, and the accused white man was acquitted. The slaying of Lee and expulsion of Brenda Travis from high school led to a demonstration by more than 100 high school students in McComb. In Birmingham, as in McComb, youthful heroism would force older people into action and provide increased impetus for the movement. But some older people were also models for youth. Fannie Lou Hamer, then a Mississippi sharecropper, was fired from her job for trying to register to vote and was arrested and brutally beaten in jail. Out of that experience, she joined SNCC to become a field director and influential political activist and eventually played a significant role on the national level. Works that record the movement in specific localities are replete with the names of other less-known local heroes and heroines who literally risked their lives many times (see, for example, Zinn 1965; Chafe 1981; and Webb and Nelson 1980).

SNCC workers accompanied the McComb students when they marched to city hall, where they prayed on the steps. Refusing to leave, they were arrested and told by their principal to cease demonstrating. Their response was to stay out of school and turn in their books. "Nonviolent High" opened to provide them with an education. This came to be a model for Freedom Schools set up elsewhere. McComb was the city where Freedom Riders had been beaten at the Greyhound bus terminal; it continued to be characterized by virulent racism. Many other Mississippi communities resembled McComb.

The Kennedy Justice Department

On the basis of candidate John F. Kennedy's campaign rhetoric and highly publicized telephone call to Coretta King when her husband was in a Georgia prison, civil rights leaders had been overly optimistic about what Eisenhower's successor could and would do. Kennedy's encouragement of the voting rights project led them to expect far more support from the federal government than was forthcoming. He had appointed his younger brother Robert attorney general at the head of the Justice Department. Civil Rights was a division under this department, as was the Federal Bureau of Investigation. Since 1924, J. Edgar Hoover had ruled the Bureau with iron discipline, and no president or attorney general seemed ready or able to displace him. Hoover had acquired massive secret files on public officials, such that they usually had no wish to displease him. Bobby Kennedy had the usual problem of working around and trying not to offend Hoover, despite the Bureau's formal position in the organization charts. This was compounded by Hoover's unusual hatred for Martin Luther King and suspicion of any black protest group and the escalating need for FBI protection of civil rights workers. The specter of alleged Communist influence was one of Hoover's tools to gain the younger Kennedy's approval for wiretapping King's phones. Protection of his brother's interests influenced Bobby in his cautious dealings with the FBI. It appeared that the president's private life, including many telephone calls, could not bear scrutiny. J. Edgar Hoover kept a file on Kennedy's possible indiscretions.

In addition, both of the Kennedys had other major priorities at the beginning of the sixties, and it was not until 1963 that Bobby Kennedy developed the sensitivities that made him the most pro–civil rights member of his brother's cabinet (Navasky 1971). The attorney general believed in negotiation and behind-the-scenes maneuvering rather than public intervention and spent endless hours on the telephone trying to convince segregationists like Governor Ross Barnett of Mississippi to obey the law of the land. In Justice Department civil rights cases, "the sequence of preferences was clear: persuasion, negotiation, pressure, maneuver, litigation, court orders, enforcement of court orders via marshalls and, only in extreme extremis, troops" (Navasky 1971, 221).

Burke Marshall and other representatives of the Justice Department maintained that they could intervene only after acts in direct violation of civil rights had been clearly demonstrated—which usually meant after the fact. In one of the few cases where a Justice Department special assistant, John Seigenthaler, had tried to save someone from a mob, the FBI stood by and watched. The Bureau maintained that its position was to observe impartially and not become personally involved. But others gave testimony asserting that local FBI agents were anything but impartial. Here are the comments of three different civil rights workers from written affidavits (Navasky 1971, 129, 131):

When the movement came to Clarksdale, we encouraged the local people to talk to the FBI. We discovered that everything we told the FBI was told to the local police the next day. Our local people would be picked up by the police after they had spoken to the FBI, and the police would tell them everything they had said. (a SNCC fieldworker)

In February of 1962, after the Jimmy Travis shooting, my car was fired into three times while I was driving through the city of Jackson. I called the Jackson FBI. They refused to even consider an investigation. They said, "We don't have any proof that the shots were fired." (Mrs. Mattie Dennis)

In April, a big cross was burned on campus. It was part of a coordinated series of cross burnings held at that time. Several students on campus saw two vehicles leave the scene and that night they saw a dirty, greasy can of kerosene with fingerprints clearly visible in the grease near the cross. They brought it to me and I called the FBI. Nothing happened. . . . I won't talk to an FBI agent again. To talk to the FBI is to endanger yourself. I still have family in the South. (Reverend Ed King, chaplain, Tougaloo College)

Witnesses to violence, as well as the activists themselves, soon found that FBI agents would not protect them and might actually be in collusion with local sheriffs and chiefs of police (see Carson 1981, 48–49). Moreover, many incidents that took place in isolated areas could not draw the federal government's attention.

Escalation of the Movement and Counter-Movement

Extreme violence and even deaths seemed to be necessary before the attorney general's office would act decisively (Zinn 1965, 193; Piven and Cloward 1979). This made the need for massive, publicized confrontations even more apparent, bringing about the very situation that the Kennedys had hoped to avoid.

Their extensive experiences in local communities made SNCC members the most persistent critics of national policy. John Lewis, head of SNCC, wanted to make such views public in his speech on the occasion of the massive 1963 March on Washington (see chapter 7), but he was convinced by other black leaders, including the elder veteran Randolph, to tone down his remarks.

The activists' response to the dangers they faced was to persist and to bring in reinforcements. More communities joined the action. By the fall of 1963, SNCC workers were spread out all over Mississippi. Between the summer of 1963 and 1964, CORE, too, made extensive efforts to register black voters, expanding programs in Louisiana, South Carolina, and Mississippi. It also developed a new program in the rural counties of northern Florida and continued to be active in northern and western cities.

In June 1962, mobs had stormed the SNCC office in Greenwood, Mississippi, and two workers barely escaped. Others would not be so lucky. In October 1962, the supervisors of the county in which Greenwood was located (Leflore) used economic sanctions against local residents. It withdrew from a federal program that supplied surplus food to thousands of poor black people. Distribution was stopped, creating tremendous hardship. Northern Friends of SNCC groups collected food and clothing and brought it to Greenwood. According to Rothschild, this direct aid from SNCC and COFO gained even more support for voter registration efforts from the black community (1982, 16). The white community's response was increasingly to resort to violence. Incidents of shooting and other attacks were conveyed to the attorney general's office, which still seemed reluctant to interfere with local police.

The cities, too, experienced their share of violence. Jackson had been the scene of much protest and many mass meetings; Medgar Evers, the state NAACP president, was clearly becoming an influential leader. On 12 June he was murdered in the driveway of his home. Large demonstrations and jailings followed. Thousands attended the funeral. The murder of Medgar Evers occurred in the same month that John Kennedy sent a new civil rights bill to Congress. He himself would become the victim of an assassin before the end of the year.

Another city notable for mass involvement of local people was Selma, Alabama, where SNCC worker Reverend Bernard Lafayette started a voter registration campaign in February 1963. Selma was made more newsworthy by the actions of a sheriff often described as vicious, Jim Clark. Between 15 September and 2 October 1963, over 300 people were arrested in connection with voter registration activities, frequently for minor or imaginary offenses. Hundreds more demonstrators were brought into action including celebrities such as Dick Gregory and James Baldwin. Selma's "Freedom Day" was 7 October 1963. Three hundred and fifty local black folk stood in line that day from morning to night, asserting their right to register. When a volunteer tried to bring food to the people in the line, he was arrested and jabbed by cattle prods. Although Justice Department lawyers observed what took place, they took no action, but the media showed the event to the nation. The evening saw a packed mass meeting to culminate Freedom Day. Selma would again make national headlines in 1965 as the locale of the last major demonstration of the movement.

The litany of southern violence against black people trying to exercise their elementary rights seemed endless. When James Meredith sought to enroll in the University of Mississippi at Oxford in his native state, Kennedy's hand was forced, as Eisenhower's had been before him. In September 1962, Governor Ross Barnett persistently refused to allow Meredith to enroll, despite numerous efforts of the administration to effect a compromise and prevent a confrontation. Finally, President Kennedy had to send in federal marshals and federalize the Mississippi National Guard. For two days, white mobs fought the troops. The battle scene is captured in this account:

In the battle-scarred history of the Negro revolution since the 1954 Supreme Court decision, Oxford was a nightmare. For two horrible days—Sunday, September 30 and Monday October 1, 1962—the battle raged, with upward of 2,500 frenzied whites repeatedly charging the Federal marshalls, the federalized Mississippi National Guard and the Regular Army troops who protected the seething campus. . . . [The campus] trembled now to exploding tear-gas bombs and the screams of the whites: "Give us the nigger!" In the holocaust two men, a French journalist and a local Oxford resident, fell dead and at least 375 were injured. But in the end, defiant Governor Ross Barnett yielded and James Meredith entered the university. In 1963 Meredith was graduated. (Brink and Harris; 1964, 40–41)

As these confrontations became widely known, the nation reacted with increasing sympathy for the movement. A loose alliance of the major organizations was formed to create a giant mobilization of people—250,000—for an August 1963 March on Washington in support of proposed civil rights legislation. The SCLC's major Birmingham campaign (described in chapter 7) would precede the massive national demonstration. The Mississippi coalition for voting rights, COFO, was also planning events that would take it to the center of national attention.

COFO and the Freedom Summer

Although it was a coalition, COFO was dominated by SNCC and CORE; the two top administrators were program director Bob Moses of SNCC and assistant program director David Dennis of CORE. Aaron Henry, the council's president, represented the SCLC. But SNCC supplied the personnel in four of the five congressional districts of Mississippi, 95 percent of the staff headquarters in Jackson, and 90 to 95 percent of the money, according to one who was there (Holt 1965, 33). Through this uneasy coalition, several important events would challenge the exclusion of blacks from the Democratic party in the South.

First, a gubernatorial election was coming up, from which most blacks would be barred. So an unofficial Freedom Ballot was developed, with Aaron Henry as the candidate for governor and Edwin King, a native white Mississippi minister, as his running mate. State Democratic party rules would be followed in this parallel election, but no one would be turned away because of race. Ballot boxes were placed in churches and meeting halls all over Mississippi. Registration was open to all persons who met residency requirements, white or black. White lawyer Allard Lowenstein recruited about 100 college students from Stanford and Yale universities to help "Freedom Register" voters—the first large group of northern students brought into the Mississippi struggle. Many more had volunteered to come (Rothschild 1982, 20; McAdam 1988, 37). Eighty thousand black citizens participated in the vote—four times the number officially registered in the state at that time.[3] Clearly, black people were not indifferent to their exclusion from the official Democratic party.

White ministers and lawyers were increasingly entering the southern movement, but the federal government was still dragging its feet with regard to protection. The Justice Department had filed some lawsuits against county registrars and sheriffs, but only twice prior to passage of the Voting Rights Act of 1965 did the department take action to protect civil rights workers. Some movement leaders believed that it would be necessary to bring young white people and white church leaders into the danger scene in large numbers in order to get stronger action from Washington, despite growing resentment of the necessity. At a meeting in Greenwood there was much discussion and debate about the wisdom of bringing in another group of white students. The presence of trained white intellectuals was not seen as likely to encourage black people to develop their own indigenous leaders. Further, there was concern over the South's reaction to interracial groups, especially where white women were involved. In any context in which women are activists they are prone to be viewed in sexual terms, and white women volunteers would not only be subject to lewd insinuations from their enemies but, as part of any black male–white female couples, might possibly provoke greater violence. Key SNCC veterans Bob Moses, Fannie Lou Hamer, and Lawrence Guyot as well as Dave Dennis from CORE continued to argue for a massive influx of white students, for both ideological and tactical reasons. Moses and Hamer believed in working with positive whites and opposed self-segregation (Holt 1965, 36; Rothschild 1982, 21–22). Moses and Lowenstein felt that "national sentiments would not tolerate assaults against white students, especially those from leading colleges and prominent families" (Carson 1981, 98). This was the type of northern student to be invited. So "Freedom Summer" was planned for 1964, which aimed to bring 1,000 or more such students into the state to work in community centers, teach in freedom schools, and further voting registration. Approximately 300 of them would be women. Most would have backgrounds far removed from those of the poor African Americans of Mississippi.

A training center for northern volunteers was funded by the National Council of Churches at Western College for Women in Oxford, Ohio, in Spring, 1964. Student volunteers came, many from prestigious Ivy League schools of major state universities. They had to be at least 18 years of age and able to pay their own expenses; they would stay with local black families. Working with them were 100 paid SNCC fieldworkers, 40 from CORE, 400 ministers, priests, and rabbis, and approximately 150 volunteer lawyers from the NAACP Legal Defense and Educational Fund, the National Lawyers' Guild, and the Lawyers' Constitutional Defense Committee (McAdam 1988, 154). The lawyers would be kept tremendously busy trying the cases of arrested civil rights advocates, appealing to higher courts, and ferreting out valuable, still-applicable post–Civil War statutes that were originally intended to protect the rights of freed slaves (Kinoy 1983). A Medical Committee for Human Rights was formed by health professionals in order to provide needed medical and psychological services to both the workers and local Mississippians. About 100 doctors, nurses, and psychologists participated.

Mississippi also prepared for what it considered an "invasion" by the nonviolent youth. The mayor of Jackson expanded his police force, increasing its arsenal of vehicles and arms. The state hired 700 additional highway patrolman.

Unofficial violence did not wait. The summer of 1964 was inaugurated in flames—by the burning of six black churches, a number that would rise to 27 by the end of the season. The Klan took to night riding. The whites who had chosen to share the dangers of Mississippi blacks were not spared. A tragedy that rocked the nation occurred on 21 June, and the attention it drew seemed to prove COFO's assumptions about the importance of white lives.

On that day CORE workers James Chaney and Michael Schwerner, along with a newly arrived volunteer, Andrew Goodman, went to investigate the burning of a black church and the beating of three local black persons in the small farming community of Longdale in Neshoba County. Schwerner had previously brought voter registration efforts to the town and was targeted as an enemy by local segregationists. The station wagon of the activists was stopped by Deputy Sheriff Cecil Price near Philadelphia, Mississippi, and the three were taken to jail for "speeding." "Released" several hours later, they were never again seen alive.

On Saturday, 20 June, the first wave of recruits had left for Mississippi from their orientation site in Oxford, Ohio. Among them had been Goodman, a 20-year-old Queens College student from New York City. He arrived in Meridian with 24-year-old Schwerner, from Brooklyn, New York, and Chaney, a 21-year-old black Mississippian.

On the next day, the three had gone to investigate the burning of Mount Zion African Methodist Episcopalian Church. The staff at Freedom Summer headquarters immediately knew something was wrong when the men did not phone in at an appointed time. Mary King writes that she had just returned from the Oxford orientation sessions to her regular work—coordinating SNCC's communication offices in Atlanta—when she received a call from Mississippi about the disappearances. Posing as a journalist, she systematically phoned every jail and detention center in the counties surrounding Philadelphia to ask if they were holding the men. All denied this. One of those she spoke to was Cecil Price, the deputy sheriff later found to be centrally implicated in the murder plot. She also contacted the FBI, which let two days pass before its Mississippi agents took any action (King 1987, 378–79).

Rita Schwerner, wife of Mickey Schwerner, informed the volunteers she had been training in Ohio about the disappearances and flew to Meridian. She and the parents of the missing men appealed to the federal government to enter the search, and the national press highlighted the case. Sympathizers around the country joined in the effort to get officials moving. The White House ordered an investigation, but it was not until a month and a half later that the bodies were recovered from what had seemed a foolproof burial in an earthen dam, on 4 August—18 days before the start of the Democratic National Convention. Many black people had died anonymously in the South; James Chaney, the young CORE fieldworker, was not anonymous because he had been with two white companions when he was abducted and murdered. Even in her grief, Rita Schwerner called attention to this fact. President Lyndon Johnson dramatically increased the number of FBI agents in the state after the murders, but they were mainly assigned to this case rather than to protecting others.

Despite the shadow that the disappearance of Chaney, Schwerner, and Goodman cast, few summer volunteers left the project. Many of them, especially the women, were assigned to teach children in Freedom Schools. There they combined response to what the children wanted to learn with lessons in civics, citizenship, and rights. This traditional female occupation was welcomed by many of the volunteers; they less appreciated being assigned to the usual gender-stereotyped duties of cleaning up and typing. Male volunteers did more of the fieldwork and canvassing for voter registration. White women volunteers tended not to be sent to particularly dangerous towns for fear that their presence with blacks would further infuriate the local populace. As it turned out, the historic taboos against black male–white female liaisons also created powerful conscious and unconscious impulses to defy them (see McAdam 1988, ch. 3, for an informed interpretation of the historic and contemporary forces affecting the sexual behavior of the youthful volunteers and fieldworkers). In some cases, white women were seen as a divisive element, and they themselves faced dilemmas. They would be subject to criticism from someone however they handled the overtures of black males (Rothschild 1982, ch. 5). Despite sexual and racial tensions, the summer experience proved both memorable and radicalizing for the group of mainly middle-class white volunteers. For SNCC, it proved a turning point away from some of its founding principles. According to McAdam (1988, 33),

the logic of the project may itself have fueled the growing hostility toward whites in the movement. . . . [The veteran Mississippi staff] were being asked to depend on the importation of 1,000 sons and daughters of white privilege—with all their naivete and paternalism intact—to break a stalemate these veterans had been powerless to resolve.

The COFO-sponsored drive came to a head in an important action that had grave implications for the future of the civil rights movement. This took the form of a challenge to the seating of the lily-white regular Mississippi delegation to the Democratic National Convention in fall 1964 by the openly elected delegates of the movement-sponsored Mississippi Freedom Democratic party (MFDP).

The Mississippi Freedom Democratic Party

The South's black population, stimulated by the massive voter registration drive, was reaching a peak of political awareness. The number of African American registered voters in the region had increased by about half a million between 1960 and 1964. A highly militant local black leadership had emerged in Mississippi. Yet the state was sending an all-white delegation to the Democratic National Convention. The MFDP planned to challenge the seating of the regulars.

The strategy of COFO in summer 1964 was shaped by this goal. Efforts made to participate in the white Democratic local conventions met with failure. Four candidates who tried to run in the June Democratic party primaries were defeated. The MFDP had held its own statewide convention in April, selecting Aaron Henry as chairperson of the delegation. Modeled after the white political parties, it claimed to be the legitimate representative of the state. Its action appeared even more reasonable as the white Democrats threatened to support the candidate of the Republicans, Barry Goldwater. Meeting in August, the MFDP delegates pledged loyalty to the national party and its platform and selected their delegation. The leaders of the group were Aaron Henry, Fannie Lou Hamer, Victoria Gray, Ed King, and Annie Devine. SNCC's efforts to develop community leadership had paid off most dramatically in the persons of these Mississippi activists, who entered the center of American political life in fall 1964.

The national convention had to determine whose credentials were in

Fanny Lou Hamer, grass-roots Mississippi leader who played a prominent role in the Mississippi Freedom Democratic party. *Laurance Henry Collection, Schomburg Center for Research in Black Culture.*

order, those of the lily-white delegation or those of the MFDP candidates. Eleven votes were needed from the party's Credentials Committee to send the MFDP's request for seating to the convention floor. On the first day of the convention, the black Mississippians testified to the Credentials Committee about the difficulties they faced in trying to become part of the political process in Mississippi. Fannie Lou Hamer's moving testimony about the murders of civil rights workers, the daily terror, and the beatings and humiliation she had experienced for trying to register was being televised nationally. This clearly affected members of the Credentials Committee as well as the viewing audience. In an incident widely recorded (see, for example, Williams 1987, 241–42) Lyndon Johnson attempted to cut off the coverage of Hamer and the others by diverting the media to a hastily called presidential press conference. But the evening news carried Hamer's testimony once again.

At the same time, the Credentials Committee was being bombarded with derogatory information about Martin Luther King and his allies, and at least one author attributes this to the president himself. "Playing no-nonsense hardball with those Democratic liberals who initially had supported the MFDP effort, Johnson's men greatly eroded the MFDP's support inside the crucial credentials committee" (Garrow 1981, 119). The headquarters of the civil rights organizations at the convention were being surveyed electronically, and regular reports were going to the president. The FBI had taken a new tack in trying to disparage King; instead of alleging Communist influence, it was now casting suspicion on his personal morality.

The Democratic party still sought to pacify the regular Mississippi delegation, despite the latter's threat to bolt. A symbolic compromise was engineered by Lyndon Johnson, which envisioned several steps. It provided, first, that the regular Democrats would have to take an oath of loyalty to the party. Some seats would obviously be vacated by those unwilling to do so. There would then be two seats available as delegates-at-large, and these would be given to MFDP.

The civil rights leaders, their strength undermined by the behind-scenes surveillance and manipulation, had to consider the proposal seriously. The underlying disagreements that were threatening to split the civil rights coalition surfaced more openly. Various versions of positions taken differ somewhat, but King and leaders of the older established organizations seem to have been swayed by the pleadings of white liberals to accept the compromise. All were being pressed by important Democrats, such as Hubert Humphrey, to do so. Joseph Rauh, the MFDP's white legal counsel, appeared to back the administration's proposal. This action undoubtedly undermined future faith in white liberals, a rubric later applied indiscriminately to most of the movement's white allies. The position of James Farmer, head of CORE, seemed ambiguous. The younger people and the MFDP delegation itself were insulted by the compromise and rejected it. Later, SNCC and CORE members, led by Stokely Carmichael, staged a sit-in on the convention floor. It is interesting that, despite their disillusionment with national Democratic leaders, the MFDP members still recognized that the Republicans would be even less sympathetic to their goals and were among the few Mississippians to support Johnson over Goldwater, who won the state.

Despite their disillusionment, MFDP leaders returned to their home state ready to further challenge white hegemony. Indeed, they were back in Washington the next January to oppose the seating of congressional representatives from Mississippi. And in the summer of 1965 another contingent of student volunteers converged on the South, some to Mississippi to assist the MFDP and others to work throughout the Deep South under the SCLC's Summer Community Organization and Political Education (SCOPE) project.

The period between spring 1963 and fall 1964 witnessed the peak of the nonviolent movement. The nation's attention was focused on King's Birmingham campaign, the murder of the civil rights workers, and the successful interracial nonviolent March on Washington. The actions at the convention reflected a growing impatience with the compromises of ordinary politics and the feeling that successes were too dearly bought. The behavior of Democratic party leaders had underlined the growing criticism of white influence in the movement. The need to recruit relatively affluent white students for summer projects, and some of the problems caused by interracial dating, had been resented. Burnt-out and exhausted, many activists did not realize what their efforts had achieved. They had started in motion a significant increase in the number of black persons registered to vote in the South. The proportion of registered voting-age nonwhites would rise from 29 percent in 1960 to 62 percent in 1971 (Levitan et al. 1975, 177).

Both of the trends—the deep fissions among the major civil rights organizations and the rejection of white participants and allies—would increase. Developments that followed the Democratic convention will be addressed in chapter 8. First, however, chapter 7 focuses on other crucial movement events and demonstrations—the 1963 Birmingham campaign and the March on Washington, as well as the 1965 confrontation in Selma, Alabama, that led to the passage of the Voting Rights Act.

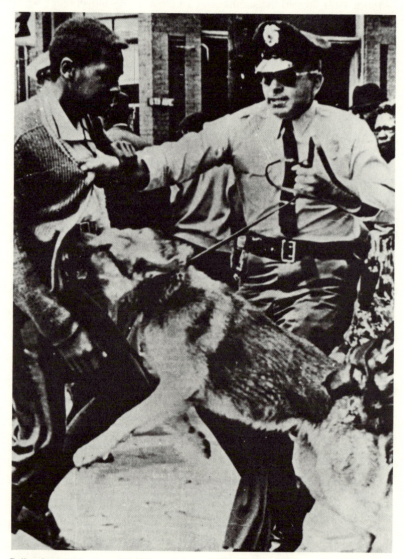

Police dog attacks a nonviolent demonstrator in Birmingham, Alabama. *Lloyd Douglass, Schomburg Center for Research in Black Culture.*

Chapter Seven

The Movement Peaks: Confrontations at Birmingham and Selma and the March on Washington

Nonviolent direct action seeks to create such a crisis and foster such a tension that a community which has constantly refused to negotiate is forced to confront the issue. It seeks to so dramatize the issue that it can no longer be ignored. . . . Any law that uplifts human personality is just. Any law that degrades human personality is unjust. All segregation statutes are unjust because segregation distorts the soul and damages the personality. It gives the segregator a false sense of superiority and the segregated a false sense of inferiority.

—*Martin Luther King, Jr.*

Southern reaction to the pursuit of voting rights had proven as harsh as the region's reaction to desegregation. And the black counterreaction had been to step up demonstrations rather than retreat. Nobody seemed more effective than Martin Luther King, Jr., in mobilizing national public opinion via television. He lent his presence to key voting rights campaigns at crucial moments, leading demonstrations, addressing mass rallies, and getting himself arrested. King's own writings attest to what those who knew him best claim—that he was beset by doubts, concerns, and misgivings. At the same time, he clearly had a sense of divine mission that propelled him on into renewed dangers. This was so obvious in his presentation of self that some of the more rebellious, less formal activists (young Turks) labeled him "de Lawd." Despite or possibly because of his successes, SNCC people who had spent many months organizing communities were sometimes miffed at the publicity King was able to draw. Local leaders who had pioneered in resisting racism and who had prepared the way for more widespread confrontation tended to be ignored by the press and the federal government when King entered the scene. Montgomery had strong leaders in E. D. Nixon and Jo Ann Robinson; Birmingham had Fred L. Shuttlesworth. Countless others like them whose names are lesser known had inspired, organized, and mobilized their communities (see Raines 1977).

King came off powerfully on the television screen as he intoned moral principles to justify nonviolent mass actions that often had the effect of inviting violent responses from the opposition. His capacity to inspire blacks and whites of varying backgrounds was unmatched by other leaders and would be exemplified in the SCLC's Birmingham campaign and in the March on Washington.[1] In Birmingham, as in Albany, Georgia, earlier, the battle against segregation was to continue on a massive scale, and the SCLC was the organization that could best create major citywide confrontations.

When southern clergymen publicly voiced their opposition to King's tactics, he responded with his famous "Letter from Birmingham Jail," an excerpt from which opens this chapter. It was written during one of the many times that he was incarcerated, usually with his loyal friend Ralph Abernathy. King was also able to hold together a group of aides who were powerful men in their own right and many of whom had constituencies of church members and supporters. This group knew that inspiration and intention alone would not win the battle; hence they continually reassessed their strategies. Some of King's earliest arrests were not planned, but he soon learned when going to jail would be the best way of dramatizing the nature of the opposition. Because of his importance and because his life was truly in danger, the federal government was much more likely to intercede with local authorities than in the case of more ordinary arrestees. Yet perhaps because of the very strength of his leadership, FBI director J. Edgar Hoover called him, at one time, "the most dangerous man in America."

The Albany Movement

Albany, Georgia, was one of the places where King and the SCLC moved in after the groundwork had been laid by other organizations. It was the fifth largest town in Georgia and had a large black population. It would become the site of the first large-scale community uprising since the Montgomery boycott and would involve thousands. The aim was an all-out assault on segregation in all its forms. In hindsight, some movement analysts felt that the objectives had been too diffuse.

When SNCC workers Charles Sherrod and Cordell Reagon established a headquarters in Albany in late 1961, the conservative adult NAACP leadership viewed them with alarm (Williams 1987, 165). But they did find an active NAACP youth chapter at Albany State College that was interested in testing transportation facilities. Together with the Baptist Ministers' Alliance, the Federation of Women's Clubs, and other local groups, SNCC and the Youth Council formed a coalition of African Americans called the Albany Movement. It was decided to test the recent Interstate Commerce Commission ruling (the result of the Freedom Rides) that outlawed segregation in terminal facilities. An action was planned for Thanksgiving weekend, starting 22 November 1961, when many students would be returning home for the holidays. Members of the NAACP Youth Council entered the Trailways bus terminal and proceeded to the restaurant, whereupon they were arrested. The Albany State College administration took a dim view of the students' behavior, and by afternoon, as hundreds of others arrived at the terminal, an on-the-scenes college administrator guided them to the "colored" waiting room. Two students who had been working with SNCC defied this official and entered the "white" facility. Their arrest and confinement to jail helped mobilize the black community, which demonstrated its support at a large mass meeting. When the two were expelled from Albany State, other students led a protest to the president's house.

Since the federal government showed no sign of enforcing the ICC ruling, another test of transportation facilities was arranged for 10 December. On that date, an integrated group of SNCC workers arrived at Albany from Atlanta and went to the white waiting room, whereupon they were arrested. There followed a week of rallies, protest marches by high school and college students, and mass arrests. Civil rights organizations converged on the city as the action escalated. But a relatively polite police chief, Laurie Pritchett, did not get the negative press that would have increased sympathy for the demonstrators. Pritchett had studied the nonviolent movement and would prove to be a formidable opponent—one who tried to avoid violence and its attendant publicity, and who used his intelligence to outwit the movement strategists.

While 200 people had been released on $100 cash bonds, another 300 were still incarcerated. The financial drain was beginning to cause concern. At this point, it was decided—not unanimously—that King should be invited by Albany Movement president Dr. William G. Anderson to lend his presence to the scene. Albany Movement secretary Marion

Page had been against inviting SNCC "outsiders" to the city and now applied the same reasoning to oppose King's presence. Most others disagreed.

King had just returned from London. There seemed to be crises everywhere that demanded his attention, and he stayed "mostly in transit between airport and rostrum" (Branch 1988, 538). King agreed to make a stop in Albany. On 15 December he addressed a meeting at the Shiloh Baptist Church and was drafted to lead a prayer vigil to city hall the next evening. This led to his first arrest in Albany—for parading without a permit—along with Abernathy, Anderson and the other marchers. The number arrested now stood at more than 700—the largest number of civil rights demonstrators ever arrested up until that date. By the end of the Albany campaign, some 2,000 persons—about 5 percent of the total black population of the city—would have gone to jail for the cause.

Twice in Albany, King would have to accept bail despite his wish to remain in jail. (A third arrest, for disorderly behavior—in actuality a prayer demonstration outside of city hall—would result in more than two weeks of incarceration.) A fact known to very few at the time of the first arrest was that Anderson was beginning to crack under the pressure of confinement and was hallucinating. Still, he refused to leave the jail before King, and so in deference to his precarious health, the two were bailed out together. Meanwhile, the SCLC's Wyatt T. Walker had entered the Albany scene full steam, antagonizing longtime SNCC activists and their local allies. The split among the organizations became public knowledge as Walker's assumption of leadership was decried. King remained patient and nonretaliatory, despite SNCC's frequent criticism of him and his organization; through these confrontations as well as their cooperative efforts, a number of SNCC's leading members developed cordial—even warm—relations with King.

The struggle raged through the spring and summer of 1962. The presence of King and the large number of arrests had made Albany a hot news item, but success eluded the movement. A December truce, which promised desegregation, had proven unstable. Consequently, an intensified boycott of city buses took place, forcing them out of business. King and Abernathy returned to stand trial in July 1962 and were sentenced to 45 days in jail. Their plan to serve their terms, along with the many local residents who had been arrested, was thwarted when they were unexpectedly released. Officials would only say that "an unidentified, well-dressed Negro male" had put up the bail. Years later, it became known that the release was engineered by Police Chief Pritchett, with the collaboration of Albany mayor Asa Kelley and other white officials

(Branch 1988, 605–6). King recognized this as a trick but could do little except denounce the tactic. Protests continued in Albany, but desegregation was still a long way off.

Less than an overall success, the Albany Movement was widely criticized. A number of factors had worked to its disadvantage. U.S. District Court judge J. Robert Elliott, a Kennedy-appointed segregationist, had made further mass action problematic when he issued a restraining order, ruling that black protest marches denied Albany's white people equal protection of the law. A frequently negative press, public squabbling among organizations, King's need to go to jail three times, and Chief Pritchett's cunning and restraint (along with his use of an informant in the civil rights ranks) were some of the negative factors. Nonetheless, the Albany Movement is considered an important milestone in the development of the SCLC's strategies and tactics and in the evolution of black consciousness. Youth had proven to be a major force in galvanizing a community into action. The movement now encompassed all segments of the population. Many had experienced the "bridge-burning act" of going to jail, their ability to confront this danger making them stronger and more committed. As King assessed the Albany Movement, he counted as a gain, too, the facts that thousands of black people had become registered voters and that many lessons had been learned. The SCLC sought another target for major confrontation that would profit from tactical errors now understood. The results would be different when the SCLC chose its own place for action—Birmingham, the citadel of segregation.

Birmingham entered the nation's headlines in 1963. But in the same year, 1962, that the Albany Movement flourished, actions were taking place in northern communities. Though the major national leaders did not conduct campaigns in the North, local leaders were very active. Northern black people began to file suits against local school systems. Chicago was one scene of action, where demonstrators staged wade-ins and sit-ins as well as campaigns against de facto segregated schools. In the summer of 1962, SNCC started an Albany-type campaign in Cairo, Illinois. In the South, voter education work was proceeding, under the direction of newly recruited Andrew Young and veteran educator Septima Clark.

Birmingham

Birmingham was the largest industrial city in the South and the turf of powerful segregationists. In fact, King called it the most segregated city in America. It had experienced 17 unsolved bombings between 1957 and

1964 and was the scene of Fred Shuttlesworth's rescue of Freedom Riders from armed mobs. But now Shuttlesworth, whose organization was affiliated with SCLC, thought the time was ripe for confrontation.

King and his advisers carefully planned the Birmingham campaign—a contrast to Albany, where they had been brought in as a rescue effort. Trying to keep the plans secret until the time was ready, King called for a summit meeting of his closest advisers, to be held at a retreat in the town of Dorchester, Georgia, early in January 1963. This hand-picked group of 11 included top officers of the SCLC and the two northern advisers and fund-raisers, Stanley Levison and Jack O'Dell, upon whose association with King the FBI based its allegations of Communist influence (Branch 1988, 688). Through its surveillance, the FBI had found out about this meeting and actually photographed the 11 as they entered the airport for their return trip. Hoover had never documented his charges against Levison and O'Dell, claiming such evidence was classified information. King, in response to warnings from the Kennedys, minimized their official role in SCLC.

This meeting—and the presence of Levison and O'Dell—fueled Hoover's campaign against King. Deke DeLoach, one of Hoover's key lieutenants, sensed this was an appropriate time to send an "inflamed" memo to his boss about King's failure to respond to a phone message he had left the previous November. Taylor Branch, whose monumental work on the King years is based on careful study of all available documents, quotes the DeLoach memo as follows:

I see no further need to contacting Rev. King inasmuch as he obviously does not desire to be given the truth. . . . The fact that he is a vicious liar is amply demonstrated by the fact that he constantly associates with and takes instructions from Stanley Levison who is a hidden member of the Communist Party in New York. (Branch 1988, 692)

According to Branch, Hoover wrote, "I concur," on the bottom of the memo. Branch's own comment is worth quoting in full:

With that, on King's thirty-fourth birthday, the FBI officially wrote him off as unfit for mediation or negotiation. Thereafter, upon receiving intelligence that someone was trying to kill him, the Bureau would refuse to warn King as it routinely warned other potential targets, such as Shuttlesworth. The FBI assigned full enemy status to King, who had staked his life and his religion on the chance that enemy-thinking might be overcome. That an intelligence agency took such a step in the belief that King was an enemy of freedom, ignorant of the reality that King had just set in motion the greatest firestorm of domestic liberty in a hundred years, was one of the saddest ironies of American history. (Branch 1988, 692)

Not only would the FBI not protect King and civil rights demonstrators; now, under the guise of national security, it did its best to discredit him and disrupt the movement. Only the Bureau's later pursuit of the Black Panthers would equal the intensity of this campaign. Indeed, it would be hard to exaggerate the degree of involvement of the nation's leading law enforcement agency—often with the tacit consent of Presidents Kennedy and Johnson (and later the enthusiastic encouragement of Richard Nixon)—in counter-movement "intelligence" activities.

The extent of Hoover's personal vendetta against King and the FBI's involvement in such activities only became clear many years later, when previously classified material became available (see especially O'Reilly 1989). Ironically, the FBI's massive collection of files on African American activists and its volumes of information gleaned from wiretaps and bugs (in homes, offices, and hotel rooms) now provide incontrovertible evidence. Certainly, King had no inkling of the depth of the campaign against him as he prepared for the Birmingham confrontations.

Forty percent of the city's citizens were black, and they were becoming important economically. Boycotts could hurt white business. Though Shuttlesworth had a strong base in the community, there were other important black people who disagreed about bringing the movement to their front door. Black militance frequently had the boomerang effect of getting rabid segregationists elected. And Birmingham was in the midst of a mayoral election in which Eugene "Bull" Connor was pitted against a more moderate candidate. The SCLC waited until the election was over and Connor had been defeated before going on with its campaign, although it was anxious to affect Easter shopping. The election was contested, and Bull Connor remained commissioner of public safety.

King spoke to many local groups and conferred with local black leaders in order to convince them that the Birmingham campaign should take place without further delay. Most finally agreed that the solid segregation of the city had to be attacked head-on. The SCLC was also aware that a reputedly vicious police chief, who could be expected to meet nonviolence with violence, was unfortunately a necessary ingredient in gaining sympathy and publicity. Indeed, that proved true in Birmingham.

The city's white supremacist practices were challenged on many fronts, with boycotts of the downtown area, marches, meetings, and voter registration efforts. April 1963 was a momentous month. Lunch counter sit-ins began on the third of the month and continued. Since

Connor obtained an order directing the people to cease demonstrating until their right to do so had been decided in court, the actions were now illegal. For the first time, a court decision was disobeyed, inviting arrest.

King personally led the demonstration defying the order and was jailed. His wife Coretta became alarmed when he was held incommunicado for 24 hours and she called the president. Kennedy, whose election had been helped by his earlier well-publicized phone call when King was in jail, again intervened on his behalf. But many others were also behind bars, and northern supporters came to the rescue to help supply bail money. Harry Belafonte raised $50,000. Eight days after their arrest, King and Ralph Abernathy accepted bond.

The black business community was unhappy with the unrest, and some elements of the white clergy were also pressuring for an end to demonstrations. Movement strategists felt it was necessary to escalate the action instead. It was decided to bring in youth and children for a "children's crusade," a proposal attributed to Andrew Young. High school students did not have jobs and bills to pay, as did black adults, and they could afford to go to jail. High schools and colleges were visited by the SCLC, and student leaders were contacted. James Bevel recalls that young women were the first to volunteer, stating:

The first response was among the young women, about thirteen to eighteen. They're probably more responsive in terms of courage, confidence, and the ability to follow reasoning and logic. Nonviolence to them is logical. . . . Then the elementary students, they can comprehend that too. The last to get involved were the high school guys, because the brunt of the violence in the South was directed toward the black male. The females had not experienced that kind of negative violence, so they didn't have the kind of immediate fear of, say, white policemen, as the young men did. So their involvement was more spontaneous and up front than the guys. (Hampton and Fayer 1990, 132)

Children as young as six years of age participated when, in April, they came out by the thousands. The children marched on city hall, paraded in the streets, and picketed stores, all in an orderly fashion and usually singing freedom songs. Many people who had never before shown concern about the rights of black schoolchildren criticized the SCLC for this action. Mass arrests of children started to take place, and the movement escalated. Thousands of adults took to the streets in demonstrations. Then Bull Connor made his move. On 4 May he set his men to using clubs, police dogs, and pressure fire hoses on the demonstrators, some of whom were women and children. The scene was captured by the

Unidentified woman demonstrator is arrested by agent of law enforcement. *Schomburg Center for Research in Black Culture.*

newspapers and hit the front pages across the nation. More than one agreed that "Connor blundered into the hands of the Negro demonstrators by using tactics . . . that went beyond the 'polite repression' America had become accustomed to" (Bennett 1966, 238).[2]

The brutal treatment of the demonstrators also enraged black spectators. Untrained and uncommitted to nonviolence, people on the sidelines responded to the police action by throwing rocks and bottles at them. Their action reflected a growing mood in the country.

Not only had Birmingham become a media event, it had also gained the personal intervention of Burke Marshall of the Justice Department. Pressure was put on store owners by influential national business leaders and on the SCLC by the federal government. Marshall was almost able to convince King that the demonstrations were hurting chances of negotiation. In this instance, as in others, the SCLC leader was considered by some to be too cautious. Shuttlesworth, just out of the hospital and not fully recovered from injuries sustained during an earlier action, refused to go along with an almost-agreed-upon cessation of further demonstrations. His stance led to a stronger position and a more favorable compromise.

The protesters had officially demanded four things:

1. The desegregation of lunch counters, restrooms, fitting rooms, and drinking fountains in variety and department stores
2. The upgrading and hiring of black people on a nondiscriminatory basis in business and industry
3. The dropping of all charges against jailed demonstrators
4. The creation of a biracial committee to work out a timetable for desegregation in other areas of Birmingham life

Many imprisoned demonstrators were set free, this time on bond money raised by Robert Kennedy. On 10 May, in what was considered a significant victory, an agreement was signed. Birmingham store owners agreed to desegregate all facilities.

But here, as in many other cases, the official gains of the movement elicited extremist reaction. The form it took this time was the bombing of the home of Martin King's brother, A. D. King, a Birmingham minister. Then the black-owned motel where the movement had made its headquarters was bombed. This was too much, and adults who had held themselves in check through many phases of the Birmingham events finally exploded. Blacks rioted for hours in an eight- or nine-block area of their own neighborhood. Although little damage was done in this first riot on 11–12 May, the action was a prototype of others to come. Nonviolence was becoming increasingly unpopular as a principle, although it had served well as a tactic.

The bombings were by no means over. After what some called a high point of "gladness"—the 28 August 1963 March on Washington—the movement would descend to a low of sadness the very next month. In September, a bombing at the Sixteenth Street Baptist Church would take the lives of four young girls and injure 20 others.

Through its Birmingham campaign and Martin Luther King's famous "I Have a Dream" speech at the March on Washington, the SCLC held the limelight in 1963. But the other organizations were also extremely active. CORE engaged in a major campaign in Plaquemine, Louisiana, where its demonstrators were assaulted by mounted troopers with cattle prods. Protests were massive and many community leaders were arrested. James Farmer, CORE's head, came to lend his presence and his own formidable charisma. Still, this campaign did not gain proportionate media attention or the intervention of the president.

CORE had also held a William Moore Memorial Freedom Walk, following the route the white CORE member from Binghamton, New York, would have taken had he not been cut down. Moore, a mailman, had planned a one-man walk from Chattanooga to Jackson to protest southern segregation. He was murdered on 24 April. CORE's response was to continue the march, and SNCC joined the action. The marchers were harassed with stones and bottles and were arrested, beaten, and attacked with cattle prods when they reached the Alabama state line.

Another significant site of protest was Danville, Virginia, where demonstrations began at the end of May. Although located in the upper South, Danville's die-hard segregation history was more typical of the deep South. The response of white authorities to black protest there has been called "a case study in legal repression" (Fairclough 1987, 145). Movement leaders were indicted for conspiracy, marches were banned, and pickets limited to six. Huge bonds were required for those arrested, and long prison sentences meted out. Defense lawyers were ill-treated and harassed, and the police used clubs, fire hoses, and tear gas against peaceful demonstrators. A two-day visit by King did little to aid morale this time; the legal battles would continue for a decade. Only in the area of voting registration did the SCLC have some success.

These and many other events in 1963 involved hundreds and thousands of people, jailings, and police brutality. But particular combinations of people and places were more likely than others to draw the media's and hence the nation's attention. Somehow, Birmingham upstaged other significant efforts. Another bloody confrontation with another sheriff unhesitant about using force against unarmed demonstrators, Jim Clark, would have to be flashed across the nation's television screens before the voting rights of people in Mississippi and Alabama could be assured. That would take place much later, in terms of the pace of the movement, in 1965 in Selma, Alabama.

The March on Washington

The March on Washington, a culminating event of the movement, drew the largest number of people to the Capitol than ever before—about a quarter of a million. Estimates are that 20 to 30 percent of them were white; many interracial northern groups attended. The 28 August 1963 march was a peaceful demonstration, a rally—perhaps an extension of the thousands of packed mass meetings that had taken place in black churches all over America and especially in the South.

Civil rights leaders had felt that the events of 1963 required a significant climax. It was the veteran A. Philip Randolph, the originator of the threatened World War II March on Washington, who now proposed one that would really take place. A main objective was to demonstrate to Congress that public opinion was on the side of desegregation and voting rights and that a considerable number of whites strongly supported these goals. The consistently higher unemployment rates of black people were being viewed with increasing impatience, but the employment issue was played down in the interests of getting a strong civil rights bill passed. Still, the concern with jobs—always a priority for the conference's main organizer, Bayard Rustin—was reflected in the buttons produced for the day depicting the march as one for "jobs and freedom."

Rustin coordinated and synchronized the efforts of local leaders in lining up people, buses, trains, and cars for the march and the subsequent rally at the Lincoln Memorial. Probably most of those who attended were part of or had linked up with organized groups—civil rights organizations, churches, union locals, and others. Ancient school buses were put back into service as more and more people signed up for the historic mobilization. President Kennedy had, at first, opposed the march, but relented in the face of the determined activists. All the major churches finally supported the event, and their representatives showed up in great numbers. But the white labor movement, as usual, lagged behind. The National Council of the AFL-CIO maintained a position of neutrality.

Nonetheless, a number of international and local unions participated in force.

The mobilization faced other issues. The program for the day had to meet the desires of the allied groups—the relatively conservative Urban League and the NAACP as well as the increasingly radical SNCC and CORE. Meetings were held to iron out disagreements and develop a program that all could support.

John Lewis of SNCC was a respected believer in nonviolence; his original speech represented the considered views of his constituents. The speech, distributed in advance, unsettled the more conservative participants because of its harsh assessment of the federal government's role. Indeed, Archbishop Patrick O'Boyle threatened to withdraw from the march if the speech were not modified. Moments before delivery, under pressure from the other movement leaders but most touched by the venerable A. Philip Randolph's request, Lewis rewrote it with the aid of James Forman, Courtland Cox, and Joyce Ladner. Forman recalls doing the revision out of a spirit of unity and producing what was still the most militant speech of the day (Hampton and Fayer 1990, 166–67). Said Lewis, "By the force of our demands, our determination and our numbers, we shall splinter the segregated South into a thousand pieces, and put them back together in the image of God and democracy" (Williams 1987, 202). Omitted was his penetrating question, "Which side is the Federal government on?" Unity and goodwill prevailed for the day, at least on the surface, as noted entertainers, black and white, performed and a series of leaders addressed the crowds. The program was long, but the final speaker, Martin Luther King, Jr., provided an inspirational ending that outdid any of his previous oratory.[3]

Some critics felt that, although King depicted it as the greatest demonstration for freedom ever seen in the United States, the march had accomplished little. Still, "never before had leading representatives of the Catholic, Protestant, and Jewish faiths identified so closely and visibly with black demands" (Fairclough 1987, 153). The religious leaders persisted in their commitment over the next 10 months, actively lobbying for passage of the civil rights bill and influencing a number of U.S. representatives. And despite the behind-the-scenes disagreements, the march presented an image of civil rights unity and strength.

Before the march, Kennedy's civil rights bill had been stalled in Congress, and he had seemed reluctant to utilize the services of Lyndon Johnson, his vice president, in efforts to sway the lawmakers. The peacefulness of the day, its enormous numbers, and its interracial char-

Writers, artists, and performers support the civil rights movement. Shown are James Baldwin and Joan Baez marching with activist leader James Forman. *Laurance Henry Collection, Schomburg Center for Research in Black Culture.*

acter may have succeeded in convincing the chief executive that he might be able to push the bill through. Whether he could have, and whether a strong bill would have emerged, will never be known. The events of the year had moved Kennedy to a stronger public posture in favor of civil rights, but the year's violence tragically took his own life as well. Kennedy was assassinated on 22 November in Dallas, Texas; thus, fate decreed that it would be up to Johnson to push Kennedy's legislative program forward. The former vice president, who had been languishing in his lesser role, immediately placed the highest priority on the civil rights bill. A definitive voting rights bill was still to come.

Following the March on Washington, the SCLC debated where its next action should be. Along with SNCC, it demonstrated against segregation in Atlanta. Various other actions were considered and ruled out. The SCLC did move into St. Augustine, site of previously well-publicized demonstrations. Although results were mixed, television coverage of hostile attacks against black protesters may have spurred undecided senators to help speed passage of the 1964 Civil Rights bill (Abernathy 1989, 286), which was then being delayed in the Senate by a southern filibuster. Too, the pervasive influence of the Klan in St. Augustine was openly revealed, prompting vigorous action by Judge Bryan Simpson to halt the Klan's intimidation of businesses. The renewed demonstrations showed that poor race relations could hurt the tourism-based economy of St. Augustine.

Elsewhere there were signs that future protest efforts might not be so peaceful. June demonstrations in Cambridge, Maryland, "degenerated into open warfare and the imposition of limited martial law. In the same period, there was a bloody brawl in Philadelphia where pickets protesting union bias used their bodies to stop work on construction projects" (Bennett 1966, 239). Gloria Richardson of the SNCC-affiliated Cambridge Nonviolent Coordinating Committee and Cecil Moore of the Philadelphia NAACP were militant leaders who were able to mobilize the black masses through appeal to economic issues. Some felt that the March on Washington was a diversionary tactic, intended to forestall more aggressive demonstrations.

The 1964 Civil Rights Act

Many attribute Johnson's success in engineering a strong civil rights bill through Congress in 1964 to the man's consummate skill and political knowhow. At his first presidential appearance before Congress after Kennedy's assassination, he invoked the memory of a predecessor whose actions in civil rights had not always matched his promises, with these eloquent words:

No memorial oration or eulogy could more eloquently honor President Kennedy's memory than the earliest possible passage of the civil rights bill for which he fought so long. We have talked long enough in this country about equal rights. We have talked for one hundred years or more. It is time now to write the next chapter—and to write it in the books of law.

I urge you again, as I did in 1957 and again in 1960, to enact a civil rights law so that we can move forward to eliminate from this nation every trace of discrimination and oppression that is based upon race or color. There could be no greater strength to this nation both at home and abroad. (Miller 1980, 339)

The House of Representatives passed the administration's bill, 290–130, on 10 February, 1964. The Senate passed it on 2 July by a vote of 73 to 27. Johnson had invoked all his skills, personal persuasion, political knowhow, and the Kennedy name to engineer this major victory for the movement.

But it was far from easy. The law is now history, and few are aware of the tortuous process involved in gaining bipartisan support and agreement between the House and the Senate. Hostile amendments had to be defeated and filibustering brought to an end (Whalen and Whalen 1986). Republican help—particularly that of Representative William McCulloch of Ohio and Senate minority leader Everett Dirksen of Illinois—was key in gaining votes at crucial times and defeating the southern Democrat-Republican conservative coalition. One amendment offered by the chairman of the House Rules Committee, Howard Smith, in an effort to defeat the bill had historic consequences. He proposed that the word *sex* be added to the list of discriminations. According to analysts of this legislation:

By adding the word "sex" to the list of discriminations (race, creed, color, and national origin) prohibited in employment, it would give all women—black and white—their first equal job rights with men. It would affect every employer, labor union, governmental body, and employment agency in the country. It would be one of the most radical civil rights amendments in U.S. history. (Whalen and Whalen 1986, 117).

Smith had counted on making the bill so controversial that it would be voted down. Five congresswomen rose to support the Smith amendment and convinced others to pass it.

The bill was the most comprehensive civil rights measure ever passed by Congress. Kennedy's original version was strengthened in its enforcement provisions, and it prohibited discrimination in employment. Several specific issues were addressed regarding voting rights (see Figure 1).

Figure 1. Provisions of the Civil Rights Act of 1964

Title I — Strengthened the voting law of 1870

Title II — Reenacted and augmented the public accommodations laws of the 1875 Civil Rights Act

Title III — Authorized suits by the attorney general of the United States to desegregate public facilities

Title IV — Authorized authority as in Title III with respect to public schools

Title V — Authorized the attorney general to bring suit for individuals incapable of doing so themselves and established a four-year Commission on Civil Rights

Title VI — Prohibited discrimination in federally assisted programs and provided for withdrawal of federal funds where noncompliance persisted

Title VII — Prohibited discrimination in employment by employers, employment agencies, and labor unions and established an Equal Employment Opportunity Commission

Title VIII — Required compilation of registration and voting statistics by the secretary of commerce

Title IX — Permitted the attorney general to intervene in any civil rights lawsuit of general public import that is begun in a federal court

Title X — Established a Community Relations Service to assist communities or persons involved in civil rights disputes

Title XI — Provided for jury trials and penalties for criminal contempt arising out of enforcement of the act

(Adapted from Masotti et al. 1969, 31–32)

Police violence in Birmingham, the death of the four children in the Sixteenth Street Baptist Church, the peaceful march on Washington—all had contributed to a climate of public opinion favoring the legislation. Passage of the civil rights measure illustrates what must already be apparent: that the legislative approach and the direct action approach went hand in hand, supplementing each other. Johnson's skills and determination were vital, but so were the massive demonstrations throughout the country that followed Birmingham and engulfed almost 1,000 cities. The term *contagion* is sometimes used to describe the spread of a movement, but that has a superficial, nonrational connotation. Personal and organizational contacts, reinforced by widespread media coverage, informed black people all over the nation that the time had come for them to act. Black leadership was no longer in an accommodationist mood; if it were, activist youth would defy it. Not only were their own churches and celebrities supporting the movement, but white clergy and liberal leaders were increasingly lending their voices and their bodies to the furtherance of civil rights goals.

Selma's Struggle

Even in 1963, as public opinion polls showed more white people to be sympathetic to the goals of the movement, divergent tendencies had surfaced among the activist groups. Generally speaking, the most militant of the civil rights organizations were SNCC and CORE. The conservatives were represented by the Urban League and parts of but not all of the NAACP. Centrist positions of various sorts were expressed by King, Randolph, and Rustin, who felt that coalition politics held promise. The most militant in the civil rights groups were critical and cynical about the role of white liberals and white labor. The nationalist rhetoric of the Black Muslim leader, Malcolm X, was striking a responsive chord, as he stressed black pride, self-defense, and self-help (see chapter 8).

Few black leaders remained unaware that the problems of the ghettos, which had been virtually neglected during the direct action campaigns, required attention. CORE had stepped up its battles in the North, using innovative and frequently criticized nonviolent but disruptive tactics. But there was one more significant test of the SCLC's methods even after the march and the passage of the 1964 civil rights bill. The demonstrations in Selma, Alabama, reflected the momentum of the southern movement still at work, despite the doubts of some strategists.

King had made a speech in Selma early in January 1965, stressing the power of the vote, and he obviously was much revered by black people there. The events that followed King's appearance are graphically and movingly described in retrospect by two young women who joined the Selma movement at the ages of eight and nine.

Sheyann Webb, age eight, had heard King's speech and knew his lieutenants were in town. She slipped into a meeting at Brown Chapel AME church and pondered the words of Hosea Williams. This is her recollection: "I kept thinking about the words Hosea Williams had said about if you can't vote, then you're a slave. So many black people not only could not vote, but they were even afraid to *try* to register. I knew that night that being a part of that nonviolent army Dr. King had spoken of was going to be the most important thing in my life" (Webb and Nelson 1980, 11).

Sheyann and her friend Rachel West did indeed become regulars in the movement, which meant that they frequently attended the meetings at Brown Chapel and took part in the marches and prayer vigils that were so numerous that cold and rainy winter. Local leaders and SCLC staff treated the children with respect, knew them well, and protected them at crucial times when danger was greater than usual. Sheyann and Rachel frequently led off the singing of freedom songs at the chapel. Songs and singing had been an important part of the movement from the first; the young girls wondered if white people could understand how very important a song like this could be to black folk:

> O freedom, O freedom,
> O freedom's over me, over me,
> And before I'll be a slave,
> I'll be buried in my grave,
> And go home to my Lord
> And be free.

The children knew how great a role singing played in group morale, in binding the people together, and in "bringing out what courage we had when things looked bleak." A song like, "Ain't Nobody Gonna Turn Me 'Round" lent itself to local situations, where lyrics could be added to fit the occasion, as in this example:

> Ain't gonna let George Wallace turn me 'round,
> turn me 'round, turn me 'round,
> Ain't gonna let George Wallace turn me 'round
> I'll keep a-walkin', I'll keep a-talkin',
> Marchin' up to freedom lan'.

There was need for courage and unity in the months of January through March 1965 as the intensity of the campaign in Selma escalated. King was in and out of the city, confident that the SCLC's Hosea Williams and local leaders did not need his constant presence. Alabama public safety director Al Lingo and Sheriff Jim Clark were determined to prevent demonstrations by using Alabama's traditional methods of force and intimidation, and injuries and even deaths were not ruled out. Scenes of beatings, use of tear gas, and armed horsemen riding into peaceful demonstrators could hardly escape the notice of the press. These tactics would bring to Selma hundreds of sympathizers, including many nuns and ministers, to join with local black citizens.

Similar demonstrations were taking place in Marion, Alabama, and on one bloody night there, 18 February, troopers attacked civil rights activists as they were coming out of church, in a well-planned and officially condoned action. Reporters were beaten and cameras destroyed or sprayed with black paint. Streetlights were dimmed to conceal the violence. A local youth, Jimmie Lee Jackson, was shot in the stomach by a trooper as he was protecting his mother; he later died. The opposition had made sure that no television record would be available to show the nation what had happened. King spoke to 3,000 mourners at Jackson's funeral which was held on 3 March. The injured man had lingered on for a week after the shooting. The national and even the state press spoke up in condemnation of Alabama officials.

Meanwhile, the Selma movement was given renewed impetus by the courage of more than 100 black schoolteachers—vulnerable local employees—who marched from Brown Chapel to the courthouse, prodded and pushed along the way. Only two days a month were set aside for voting registration, and on each of these days, the demonstrators would line up to wait for a chance to register. On 1 February, King returned to lead the bimonthly ritual. He, Ralph Abernathy, and hundreds of others were arrested. That afternoon 500 students marched to protest the arrests and were themselves jailed. The rallies grew in numbers.

Another white reaction on 10 February further increased the resolve of the community. On that day, a group of marching teenagers were pushed and prodded by deputies into a forced march toward the prison road camp. This went on for several miles, with a number of children becoming nauseated and ill. The next registration day was 15 February, and several hundred local residents came out for the effort. A few days later, they heard of the brutality at Marion and the shooting of Jimmie Lee Jackson.

A march from Selma to Montgomery—50 miles—was then conceived as a protest against police brutality and the denial of voting rights. Governor Wallace first agreed to provide trooper escort, then reversed his position and banned the protest. At first, no one thought the action would be more than a routine effort, like those that went on almost continually. But Hosea Williams conveyed to SCLC headquarters the news that thousands were preparing to participate. The day of this march, 7 March 1965, would live in the memories of Selma people as "Bloody Sunday."

Some members of SNCC, alienated from the more moderate members of the movement, did not think the organization should participate. But one of its longtime leaders, John Lewis, played a prominent role. As the marchers, led by Lewis and Hosea Williams, arrived at the Edmond Pettus Bridge, heading toward Montgomery, they were met by armed troopers. Horsemen with gas masks headed directly into the marching group. Here is Sheyann's account as she remembers it, having been the youngest in the battle lines that day:

I looked and I saw the troopers charging us again and some of them were swinging their arms and throwing canisters of teargas. And beyond them I saw the horsemen starting toward us. I was terrified. What happened then is something I'll never forget as long as I live. . . .

I saw those horsemen coming toward me and they had those awful masks on; they rode right through the cloud of teargas. Some of them had clubs, others had ropes, or whips, which they swung about them like they were driving cattle. (Webb and Nelson 1980, 96)

Hosea Williams lifted her up and ran with her out of danger as fast as he could. Everyone was running from the tear gas and the clubs, openly pursued by Sheriff Jim Clark and his men. Seventy-eight marchers required medical attention. Unfortunately, it took outright brutality like this on the part of legally constituted authorities to gain a national audience for people who were merely trying to assert their right to register as voters. This time the cameras caught the action, and supporters flew in from all over the country. One of them was James Reeb, a Unitarian minister from Boston. The next day, he was hit by a club-wielding segregationist as he was leaving a black-owned restaurant. Although many prayed for his recovery, he died.

Temporarily demoralized, the Selma movement regained its resolve and set about to reschedule the 50-mile march. U.S. District Judge Frank M. Johnson, Jr., had been asked to rule on the right of black people to engage in the protest march. The judge advised the SCLC's lawyers to postpone the next march until formal court hearings could be held, beginning on 11 March. King agonized over whether to comply. He believed in obeying the federal courts, and he knew Judge Johnson's record on civil rights was excellent. A march before 11 March would not have federal protection. Judge Johnson then handed down an injunction against the march. But other leaders as well as the mobilized community were unwilling to wait. LeRoy Collins, an emissary of President Johnson, arrived in Selma with orders to stop the march, but assessing the mood of the demonstrators, he proposed a compromise instead. King was asked to stop the march at Pettus Bridge and return to Selma after a symbolic confrontation. Cooperation was requested from and given by the law enforcement officials to allow the march to proceed up to the point of the previous Sunday's attack.

About 1,500 marchers were assembled at Brown Chapel, ready to defy the injunction if necessary. King started the march, with only a few aware that he had tacitly agreed to the compromise. At the designated spot, he halted the march for a brief prayer, then turned the group around. While his action prevented further bloodshed and showed respect for the federal courts, it was considered treacherous by some, weak by others, and disappointing to the brave assembled activists. King's tendency to compromise was not appreciated, even when the results were positive. Meanwhile, another Johnson, the president of the United States, took to television to assert the nation's obligation to protect voting rights. Propelled by the events at Selma, he would soon be able to get the strongest voting rights bill in history through Congress.

But at the moment, the highly important court order by Judge Johnson was issued. On 17 March the judge proclaimed the right of black people to march from Selma to Montgomery with these words: "It is recognized that the plan as proposed . . . reaches to the outer limits of what is constitutionally allowed. However, the wrongs and injustices inflicted upon [blacks in Selma] have clearly exceeded—and continue to exceed—the outer limits of what is constitutionally permissible" (Webb and Nelson 1980, 116).

Lyndon Johnson ordered the Alabama National Guard federalized, and thousands of sympathizers flew in to make the historic march. It took place on 21 March, two weeks after the first debacle. There would be two more deaths of white volunteers, the ugly recurrent response by extremists to every civil rights victory. Viola Liuzzo was shot in the head after a high-speed chase because she was a white woman transporting marchers between Selma and Montgomery. On 5 August 1965 the voting rights bill was signed into law by President Johnson, but the same month a young seminarian who had endeared himself to local families, Jonathan Daniels, was killed while doing voter registration work.[4]

The Voting Rights Act of 1965 had finally enabled blacks in the Deep South to vote and to elect black and liberal white candidates. The act's provisions were as follows:

> It suspended literacy tests and similar devices in all states or counties in which less than 50 percent of voting age residents were regis-

tered to vote on 1 November 1964. Initially this clause affected 26 counties in North Carolina and the entire states of Alabama, Georgia, Louisiana, Mississippi, South Carolina, and Virginia.

It provided for the appointment of federal examiners to register persons in these areas to vote, thus taking power away from arbitrary local officials.

It directed the attorney general to institute court action against the enforcement of poll taxes as a prerequisite to voting in state and local elections. In 1966 the federal courts upheld efforts to carry out this provision, truly outlawing the poll tax in all elections. The numerous devices invented over the years to prevent black citizens from exercising their right to vote had been stricken down at last.

The Selma demonstrations can be credited with hastening the passage of Johnson's voting rights bill and with insuring that a measure this strong would be passed at all (Fairclough 1987, 251). The Selma action was the last major black-and-white together, SCLC-style protest to be effective on a national level. Only four days after the voting rights bill went into effect on 11 August 1965, a major civil disturbance took place in the Watts area of Los Angeles. Riots in Rochester and Harlem in the summer of 1964 had preceded Watts, but the devastation of four days of burning and looting that left 34 people dead, most of them black, was a sharp indicator that protest was entering another stage.

The marches, meetings, economic reprisals, and physical suffering that nonviolent demonstrators had encountered was not yet over, as CORE continued its voter registration work in rural Louisiana. But the willingness to risk lives and not fight back was showing signs of wearing thin. The slogan of black power would take the headlines away from the more familiar and now increasingly questioned "black and white together" rallying cry, once so inspiring that it had been built into the movement's anthem, "We Shall Overcome."[5] The next chapter examines this transition from civil rights to black power, a trend first evident in SNCC and expressed most powerfully in the oratory of the Muslim leader, Malcolm X.

U.S. Rep. Adam Clayton Powell, Jr., confers with Malcolm X and comedian-activist Dick Gregory. *Laurance Henry Collection, Schomburg Center for Research in Black Culture.*

Chapter Eight

The Transition to Black Power

> *The concept of Black Power . . . is a call for black people in this country to unite, to recognize their heritage, to build a sense of community. It is a call for black people to begin to define their own goals, to lead their own organizations and to support those organizations. . . . Before a group can enter the open society, it must first close ranks.*
> —*Stokely Carmichael and Charles V. Hamilton, 1967*

Stokely Carmichael and Charles V. Hamilton, in a small book, *Black Power: The Politics of Liberation in America,* spell out the meaning of this elusive and, to some, frightening term. Carmichael first proclaimed the slogan publicly on a 1966 march through Mississippi that was a continuation of one initiated by James Meredith. Meredith, it will be recalled, was the first black person to gain entry into the University of Mississippi. Now he had chosen a new project: he set off alone on a "march against fear" through his home state of Mississippi. On the second day, he was injured by a sniper and hospitalized. Civil rights leaders rushed to his bedside and, with his acquiescence, gathered to continue the march. In Greenwood, Carmichael gained the attention of the press with his public call for black power, rivaling the rhetoric of nonviolence and purposely drawing Martin Luther King into a debate over their differing philosophies.

During the march, King continued to assert his values. But the press and the public were more geared to Carmichael's contrasting pronouncements, which he had planned as a direct challenge to the older leader. The positive response of many young people to Carmichael's words seemed to prove that the civil rights revolution had shifted and was getting out of hand. There is a tendency to think in generalities—to believe that all blacks immediately gave up integrationist aims and favored the switch to black power and self-defense, that all whites were frightened by the new directions of black protest and withdrew their support. Actually the nonviolent integrationist stage had given rise to the black power stage; the two periods overlapped. One phase of the black freedom struggle had reached its peak as the other was in ascendancy. The SCLC, the NAACP, and the National Urban League disagreed with separatist philosophies, but their leaders as well as most black people could hardly object to other values stressed by black power proponents—like racial pride and unity. The foremost proponent of nonviolence, King, was hesitant to criticize those with whom he disagreed, writing in his last book, "I should have known that in an atmosphere where false promises are daily realities, where deferred dreams are nightly facts, where acts of unpunished violence toward Negroes are a way of life, nonviolence would eventually be seriously questioned" (1967, 26). Whites too were not monolithic in their responses to the new developments and did not secede from the movement en masse.

Many nation-shaking events occurred in the momentous years of 1964–68, which were related to and interacted with the civil rights and black power movements. One was a major series of urban disorders, or riots, that left many black neighborhoods looking as if they had been under siege. Another was the growth of other significant social movements, many of them inspired by the vanguard efforts of the civil rights activists. These drew attention and resources away from the black freedom movement and absorbed the energies of many of the no-longer-comfortable and less-welcome whites. Probably most important was the escalating, undeclared war in Vietnam and the massive antiwar movement that embroiled the country. Many agree that with the 1968 election of Nixon black protest declined. The exception was a new surge of student activity centered on the campuses—the black studies movement, which started in 1966 but gained its main impetus after Dr. King's death.[1]

The black power slogan attracted immediate attention when Carmichael openly flaunted it in the company of more moderate civil rights leaders. The young SNCC leader had popularized a rallying cry that captured the direction that many of his peers would take in the second half of the 1960s. A number of interrelated elements were part of the black power doctrine, and few were really new. Nor was a specific, agreed-upon program set forth by its proponents. But all black power groups agreed with the values proclaimed in the excerpt opening this chapter. These values took shape in various black nationalist philosophies that declared the claim of black people to be treated as a legitimate ethnic group seeking their share of power and material benefits. Jews, Poles, and Italians were not questioned when they maintained separate clubs, schools, and associations; blacks now asserted the validity of their own African American culture and their right to create and develop their own institutions. Cultural nationalism, one wing of the black power movement, became a strong force.

The Shift in Goals

These claims as such did not seem to warrant extreme opposition. But what drew the disturbed attention of the white public were three additional elements that departed from the norms of the civil rights movement. The first was rejection of the goal of integration and interracialism, the second, rejection of the practice of nonviolence. The third was a growing critique of capitalism by some of the black power groups.

White integrationists who had insisted on the insignificance of racial differences were frequently puzzled by the new emphasis on cultural distinctiveness. In contrast, few black people had trouble drawing a line between the wish to celebrate their own culture and identity and the enforced segregation to which they had so long been subjected. Their quest for cultural autonomy did not deprive others of basic opportunities, only that of freely associating with black people—a choice that many whites had never exercised but that white integrationists valued.

Worse, insistence on the right to self-defense conjured up images of black men with guns. Very perceptively, Bell has suggested that behind the civil rights movement's "pronouncement that 'no man should use violence' lurked the popular notion that 'the Negro should not use violence'" (1968, 170). Black power advocates did not agree and counseled response in kind to white aggression. Their endorsement of self-defense could easily be twisted into visions of black assaults against whites. As the black power groups modified and evolved their philosophies, some of them did adopt revolutionary perspectives. The civil rights groups had sought inclusion in the ongoing political and economic structures; the black power groups questioned these very structures.

Historic Roots of Black Power

Historically, black protest had swung between integration and separatism, with each new period being heralded as an advance over the previous one. Booker T. Washington's public emphasis on separate racial development and his seeming apoliticism were viewed as accommodative and self-defeating or, alternatively, as the only possible response to the age of lynching and terrorism. Du Bois, Trotter, and others were able to move protest into a more active form, taking advantage of the changed national conditions described earlier. Du Bois believed in strengthening the black community, but insisted upon political protest and struggle.

Some sociologists and political scientists view black separatism as a reaction to disappointment and despair, a product of disillusionment after rising expectations. The post–World War I experience supported this theory. Minor gains had been made during the war, but these were followed by job losses and a rise in racist violence. As their economic plight became extreme during the Great Depression, the urban black masses were attracted in numbers to Marcus Garvey's United Negro Improvement Association with its self-pride and emigrationist themes. "Making it" in the United States seemed hopeless, therefore undesirable.

The Disappointments of Reformist Politics

The new black power advocates borrowed heavily from Garvey in asserting racial pride. But the other dynamic fostering a rejection of integration was related to disillusionment with white allies. Though two major civil rights bills had been passed, the more militant leaders felt betrayed by the Democratic party's moderation. Through the Mississippi Freedom Democratic party, black people from the deepest South had tried to take what they considered their legitimate place in the government. The Democratic party's need to compromise was understandable from the vantage point of normal politics and reformist views. But its certification of the disloyal all-white Mississippi delegation at the national convention constituted a sellout by white liberals from the point of view of the black revolt; some turned to the idea of a third party.

Paradoxically, it would seem, a liberal executive—Lyndon Johnson— was highly vulnerable to criticism; the later administration of Nixon would stifle hope with its law-and-order themes and outright rejection of black interests. In actuality, movements surge forward when there is belief in the possibility of change and that is what Johnson had provided.[2] Yet he and John Kennedy before him had been concerned both with the effects of their actions on the electorate and the pacification of southern white Democrats. The liberal alliance they had tried to forge was facing serious challenges.

A conference on civil rights sponsored by President Johnson gave evidence of the split between the movement and the administration. A November 1965 planning meeting was set up to precede a full conference in June of the following year. According to sociologist Lewis Killian who attended, "The famous Moynihan Report, *The Negro Family: The Case for National Action,* was both the stimulus for the calling of the conference and almost the cause of its cancellation" (1975, 102). Black social scientists as well as activists strongly objected to Moynihan's targeting the problems of the black family rather than their societal causes. However, when SNCC boycotted the June 1966 conference, it gave another reason; its unwillingness to support a government involved in the Vietnam conflict, a war directed against colored people. Despite warnings that this would weaken the civil rights cause, Martin Luther King, too, felt morally impelled to take a position against the war. Somehow his views did not gain widespread publicity until 1967. However, the Johnson administration was aware of them and limited King's role in the conference. States Lewis (1978, 312), "The role of Martin King was carefully minimized. His antiwar position had now completely alienated Lyndon Johnson." Later in 1966, CORE officially opposed the war.

Johnson's last year as president became a painful one as "all the people who were for him on the civil rights issue were against him, mostly, on the war issue" (Miller 1980, 489). The antiwar movement escalated. When it succeeded in pushing Johnson out of the presidential race, Robert Kennedy entered the Democratic party primaries. There are grounds to speculate about what might have occurred had the second Kennedy brother not been assassinated. Bobby had grown in his allegiance to black goals over the years, and he had come out against the Vietnam war. If he had been elected, the federal government's civil rights alliance might have been rekindled. But to the nation's horror, he was shot down on 4 June 1968, immediately after winning major primary victories. Although most black voters supported Hubert Humphrey, the Democratic candidate, the more radical black activists remained disillusioned with the administration and its Vietnam policy. But there were other forces leading to the reassessment of nonviolence and integrationist goals.

The southern roots of black power: Lowndes County, Alabama. *Laurance Henry Collection, Schomburg Center for Research in Black Culture.*

Self-defense as a Response to Southern Terrorism

The notion of self-defense, of every person's right to protect himself or herself against attack, is a well-established legal principle. The black power doctrine did not call for unprovoked aggression against whites. What was decisively rejected was the notion that blacks should remain nonviolent in the face of white violence. This was a major break with the accepted rule governing demonstrations—whether they were simple marches, sit-ins, or some of the more dramatic disruptions organized by northern CORE units. Nonviolence had functioned well in gaining sympathy for the movement, but only King, his followers, and the early CORE people had elevated it to an unshakable moral principle. Tactically, as pointed out earlier, it would have been suicide for the early protesters to meet their attackers head-on. When blacks and their white allies were bloodied and martyred in the name of civil rights, they were considered noble and committed. In contrast, those who suggested that people should arm themselves against attack were labeled militants.

Slaves had been required to bear the lash without defending themselves, but occasionally their anger had burst forth. Black retaliation might well have been feared by racist whites (the principal purveyors of interracial violence) as they sensed the unexpressed rage of their victims. Even in early stages of the movement, some black people in Deep South areas had been talking of arming themselves for self-defense. Robert F. Williams, Malcolm X, Stokely Carmichael, the Black Panther party, the Nation of Islam, and other groups all publicly criticized the principle of nonretaliation for physical suffering unjustly inflicted. But Williams's pronouncements antedated the others; his position was so out of joint with the times that he was forced into exile.

Williams, a North Carolina official of the usually moderate NAACP, was eventually suspended by the national office of his organization. He had taken over the leadership of the NAACP in Monroe after the branch was all but destroyed by Klan intimidation. In the summer of 1961, a crisis occurred that eventually led Williams to flee to Cuba. Involved in nonviolent demonstrations by former Freedom Riders, he voiced his belief that blacks should defend themselves against attack. He was accused of kidnapping a white couple and holding them hostage; in his version, the whites, Klan members, had driven into the armed black community and he was trying to protect them. Williams went into exile. He then expounded upon his revolutionary views in newsletters and a book, and spent time in China as well as Cuba. He was considered especially dangerous because he integrated the black nationalist position of the Nation of Islam with a critique of the capitalist economic order.

Similarly, many members of CORE were to have strong reactions to harrowing situations such that they questioned the policy of nonviolence. According to James Farmer, his narrow escape from a Mississippi mob on 1 September 1963 had such an effect (Bell 1968, foreword).

CORE had worked with small-town residents in some of the most oppressed areas of Louisiana. In the summer of 1964 it sponsored a major registration campaign which, despite the involvement of local black people, achieved little concrete success. Cross burnings by the Klan, armed pursuit by carloads of whites at high speeds, and similar ventures were added to the usual forms of intimidation for those trying to register. Some folks in West Feliciana Parish had earlier responded to white violence by arming themselves. Now in Jonesboro, a small industrial town near Monroe (and the seat of Jackson Parish), an organization called the Deacons for Defense and Justice was formed. Its purpose was to protect civil rights workers and the black community. Local people had decided to arm after 50 hooded Klansmen with burning torches, headed by a sheriff's patrol car, marched through Jonesboro's black section. One hundred armed whites converged on the jail where two civil rights workers were being held on trumped-up charges; they were dispersed only when the federal government intervened. In this case, armed self-defense was a protective reaction to widespread and life-threatening Klan activity tacitly or openly supported by local white officials.

The Urban Roots of Black Power: Malcolm X

There were northern and urban roots, too, for believing in the right to self-defense. Malcolm X proclaimed this stand during the height of the passive resistance stage, when his views were running against the tide.

Like King, Malcolm was dedicated to his people and was cut down in the prime of his life. He was assassinated while giving a speech at the Audubon Ballroom in Harlem on 21 February 1965.[3] Malcolm's parents were active in the Marcus Garvey movement, and the son reflected many of the ideas of this important black nationalist. Highly intelligent and a top student in junior high school, the then Malcolm Little was discouraged in his aspiration to become a lawyer because of his color. Dropping out of school, he began to lead a street life, moving on to burglary and eventually being sentenced to 10 years in prison. It was there that he became acquainted with the philosophy of the Nation of Islam (the Black Muslims). He joined this growing religio-political sect and was made minister of its Harlem mosque in 1954 after his release. Nationalist in ideology, the Muslims combined a strong psychological message with practical and successful economic development ventures. Emphasizing pride in blackness, self-help, and separatism, it created many black-owned businesses. The urban-based Nation of Islam stressed the type of puritanic virtues that had enabled white Americans to succeed—stable marriage, fidelity, abstinence from alcohol, controlled diet, good working habits, and industry. Whites, themselves, were "blue-eyed devils," to be avoided. The group was able to rehabilitate ex-criminals and drug addicts as no medical or psychological approach had.

For approximately ten years, Malcolm spoke in the name of Elijah Muhammad, the group's spiritual leader, but he was clearly gaining a major following among the young and disinherited blacks of the urban ghettos. After being suspended by Elijah Muhammad because of remarks made upon the death of President Kennedy, Malcolm decided to set up his own organizations—a religious group called the Muslim Mosque, Inc., and the secular Organization for Afro-American Unity. The Nation of Islam had refused to take part in politics, but Malcolm was now beginning to develop a political platform.

Malcolm was a spellbinding speechmaker and influenced others mainly through his oratory and ideas rather than through specific programs. The media found him an audacious and exciting personality, and television helped bring his ideas to the public. Moderate blacks were at first critical of Malcolm, and most whites were frightened by what sounded like antiwhite rhetoric. In contrast, his analyses of white racism and hypocrisy struck responsive chords in the hearts of poor black urban dwellers, ex-convicts, and street people, who had directly experienced the contempt of white society. Malcolm asked why black people would want to integrate into a corrupt white society. The poet Sonia Sanchez explains his appeal in this way: "He says, 'I will speak out loud what you've been thinking'" (Hampton and Fayer 1990, 254). To Sanchez, Malcolm epitomized the strong black male that black women hoped for.

The foremost proponent of black power and black nationalist philosophies, Malcolm gradually made sense to some of the black middle class, especially the young. He had a significant overall impact on the civil rights movement in several ways. First, he directly influenced a number of black leaders and organizations, such as Stokely Carmichael and SNCC as well as many youth. Second, he was able to reach members of the lower socio-economic class as no other contemporary leader could. Finally, in contrast to the civil rights leaders, he provided a radical, anti-white position. On balance, persons like King appeared to epitomize reason and gained a more receptive audience. Lawmakers and presidents were more likely to welcome the voice of brotherly love, once there was an aggressive, effective spokesperson on the scene opposing integration.

In the opinion of sociologist Alphonso Pinkney, Malcolm X might have been the most important black leader in American history (1976). After a visit to Mecca in which he noted the insignificance of color in Islam, Malcolm stated that he had modified his views about the possibility of working with whites and would turn away from racism. Reconciliation with the civil rights leaders he had so often opposed became a possibility, especially as they were now switching their focus to poverty, urban, and class issues. Indeed, Malcolm himself suggested this in an interview. The notion was echoed by Clarence Jones, an associate of King (see Warren 1966, 263). Writing before Malcolm's assassination, an author who had interviewed the major black leaders maintained, "With his change in views Malcolm X is in a position to enter into any centralized grouping of the various elements in the Movement that may be managed. He will, in fact, be in a position to be the center of such a centralized grouping" (Warren 1966, 263).

Malcolm's death was a tremendous loss to the African American community. Like that of Martin Luther King, Malcolm X's stature and significance grew after his death, despite quite different treatment of the two men by the media. The noted actor Ossie Davis's touching eulogy at Malcolm's funeral focused on the man's personal warmth and grace and his love for his people.

The Black Panthers

New black nationalist groups that arose in the second half of the 1960s reflected the mood of urban blacks and the early rhetoric of Malcolm X. They were both a response to and a cause of the growing split between the two races as attention focused on the heretofore neglected and deteriorating economic status of black Americans and the ubiquitous problems of the huge urban ghettos. Over time, SNCC and CORE transformed themselves into nationalist groups and ejected their white members. A variety of new groups arose: the Republic of New Africa, the US Organization of Ron Karenga, the Black Community Development and Defense Organization of Imamu Baraka, the Black Panthers, and others (see Pinkney 1976 for a thorough analysis of these groups).

The Black Panther party, a self-defense group, was founded in Oakland, California, in 1966 by Huey Newton and Bobby Seale. It soon gained attention and media coverage out of proportion to its actual numbers. The Panthers asserted their right to monitor police actions as a way of inhibiting the unnecessary use of force. Carrying guns for self-defense and dressed in military attire, the Panthers became easy targets for the police and the FBI. Their weekly newspaper blasted police brutality, racism, and the unfair justice system. Each week it printed the group's 10-point program, which demanded trial by a jury of one's peers, decent housing, full employment, and control by black people over their own communities. Community control would be an objective espoused by many local groups.

A number of famous cases became showpieces for the Panthers, as their members were arrested and jailed. "Free Huey" became a popular cry, referring to the incarceration of Huey Newton. George Jackson, who was killed in prison, became a hero on the basis of his sensitive writings about the justice system and his development of a political perspective while imprisoned. Similarly, the Panther Eldrige Cleaver wrote a best seller, *Soul on Ice,* which explained his personal deviance in terms of black-white political realities. Such books were influential and widely read, as had been James Baldwin's searing indictment of white society in *The Fire Next Time.*

The Panthers underwent a number of ideological transformations as they critiqued capitalism and imperialism and attempted to reconcile their nationalism with an international third world perspective. For a time Carmichael attempted to create an alliance between SNCC and the Panthers, but the two groups did not agree about working with white allies. Eventually, both experienced serious internal splits, partly fostered by the active intervention of the FBI in its Counter-Intelligence Program (COINTELPRO). "On August 25 (1967), Hoover ordered FBI field offices to begin a new effort 'to expose, disrupt, misdirect, discredit, or otherwise neutralize the activities of black nationalist, hate-type organizations and groupings, their leadership, spokesmen, membership and supporters, and to counter their propensity for violence and civil disorder'" (Carson 1981, 262). Agents infiltrated black protest organizations in large numbers, and some took an active part in planning and decision making. They were encouraged to foster feuds and dissension within and among black groups, coming up with such ploys as sending fictitious notes from one group to another, creating rumors about the infidelity of husbands and wives, and portraying loyal members of black organizations as government informers. The thoroughness of the FBI's action against the Panthers is evident in the fact that, by 1969, it was investigating every one of the 42 Panther chapters and all of its members and sympathizers (O'Reilly 1989, 298).

The neutralization of black power organizations was taken seriously by other agents of law enforcement. One lawsuit that resulted from a pre-dawn raid on the Chicago headquarters of the Panthers was, in 1982, settled for almost $2 million (*New York Times,* 14 November 1982). In the courts for 10 years, the suit accused law enforcement agents of vi-olating the civil rights of Black Panther members. On 4 December 1969, fourteen Chicago policemen had raided the headquarters, carrying with them a warrant authorizing a search for illegal weapons. In the ensuing "gun battle," the police fired between 80 and 100 times, killing Mark Clark and Fred Hampton, and injuring four other persons in the apart-ment. Only one bullet had been fired from a weapon belonging to one of the apartment's occupants, and it turned out to be one fired into the floor by the dying Mark Clark. "Bullet holes" in the door proved to be fake, evidence that the authorities had tried to cover up the facts of the raid. (For an eyewitness account, see Hampton and Fayer 1990, 534–35.)

While the Panthers were the group most subject to official control efforts, other black power groups were targeted as well, in an effort to destroy the black power wing of the movement (McAdam 1982, 219).

The International Roots of Black Nationalism

Anticolonial struggles abroad were increasingly seen as linked to those of African Americans. Third world peoples had rejected the domination of the white European powers, and their revolutionary literature found a responsive audience among black nationalists. Frantz Fanon's powerful book about the Algerian revolution, *The Wretched of the Earth,* stressed the absolute duality of the colonizer and the colonized, and the impossi-bility of their coming to terms. Fanon saw class struggle as an inevitable next stage once the white colonizers were ejected. In the United States, however, blacks were not a numerical majority and were not in their land of origin. Nonetheless, the problems of colonization and powerlessness were strikingly similar for subordinated people of color everywhere; race was a sharp dividing line between the colonizer and the colonized. The successful revolutions in other parts of the world provided inspiration for African American theorists who tried to develop their own analysis of the interrelationships between race and class in the United States. The country's pursuit of the war in Southeast Asia was seen as further proof of its imperialism.

The Contribution of the Nonviolent Movement to Self-pride

Within SNCC, Stokely Carmichael—or Stokely, as he was widely known—echoed Malcolm's emphasis on self-pride and self-direction. This aspect of the black power doctrine, like the idea of self-defense, was a natural consequence of the transforming effects of rising up against oppression. Carmichael, one of the first of the civil rights leaders to worry over white participation, pointed out that unlike most ethnic groups, black people had been denied their heritage and degraded as inferior. The effects on black consciousness and black pride had sometimes been devastating.

Ongoing experiences in the struggle provided an antidote, modifying the consciousness of thousands. Many African Americans were able to stand straight for the first time and to take pride in their community. The adults who had persevered in line for hours in the hot sun and pouring rain in order to exercise their right to register, the students who had been pulled off stools, reviled, and dragged off to jails had returned again and again. Indigenous black leadership had come to the fore, and white participation was less needed. At the same time, the conscious furtherance of pride in self and community became a major goal of cultural nationalists. The black revolt became, in part, a cultural movement, as it tried to rediscover black history and express the African American experience.

Racial isolation and adaptations to life in America combined with and drawing upon African cultural elements like religion, music, and family forms had created a new culture, a phenomenon called ethno-genesis. Accounts of the successes and failures of the black power movement tend to focus on political gains, or lack of them, sometimes overlooking the important changes in American culture brought about by this expressive part of the movement. The term *black* was turned around from a negative contrast conception (everything black is bad, everything white is good) to a positive affirmation of self. "Negro" hair, it was found, could be styled in many ways, utilizing its natural qualities instead of being straightened and set into "white" styles. The white hair-fashion world later boldly imitated the Afro look. College campuses all over the country faced demands that their curricula be made more relevant to African Americans, that the study of African and Asian cultures be placed alongside that of Western civilization. There was a creative flowering in the arts, akin to the Harlem Renaissance, involving theater, poetry, dance, and the visual arts (see, for example, C. Drewry 1971; Jones and Neal 1968). The nationalists sought not only a transformation of culture but transformations of self, as the "black is beautiful" theme flowed naturally from pride in heritage. The long-range impact of these aspects of the black power movement has yet to be fully assessed, but Pinkney provides some interesting facts about changes in black self-esteem:

Many studies conducted in the 1950s showed that in experimental situations black children invariably expressed a preference for white dolls over brown dolls . . . Recent studies, however, show that since the spread of nationalist ideology among Afro-Americans, anywhere from 70 to 82 percent of black children express a clear preference for brown dolls. . . . The interpretation to be drawn from these studies is that the black children (as well as Afro-Americans in general) are experiencing an increase in self-pride and group pride as a result of the changed political and social climate. (1976, 219)

The Decline of Interracialism

Frederick Douglass had made the point many years before that people could not rely on others to hand them their freedom and that blacks should lead their own movement. This position, in SNCC and CORE, led to the conclusion that whites should leave the predominantly black organizations. Support for this sentiment arose at the grass-roots level in bitter response to the extreme southern backlash that had met the assertion of equality. Black activists knew that they had not changed white hearts and minds by appeal to conscience despite the rhetoric of nonviolence. Creative disorder was the force that had influenced the white South. Very simply, business people disliked the repeated demonstrations and boycotts that cut into their profits; politicians, too, found it in their interest to end the continued disruption.

The movement now drew from a wider spectrum of people of both races; the initial closeness and unity of highly selected and disciplined cadres was modified. There were growing problems with interracialism within civil rights groups, some of them reflecting the society that had made the movement necessary. Carmichael and a faction in SNCC maintained that white freedom fighters should use their talents in their own communities. John Lewis, the southern-born leader of the group and a veteran of numerous campaigns, did not agree and, in 1966, was replaced by Carmichael as the organization's president. There would be many agonizing decisions as disagreements split some of the civil rights groups, and experienced and dedicated workers lost favor. The rhetoric of black power would increasingly be used as a weapon in the black leadership struggles that took place in SNCC, CORE, and many local communities in the late 1960s (Carson 1981, 236–37). These battles were not only draining for long-term activists, many of whom were already experiencing burn-out, but were harmful from a broader perspective. "Once effective insurgent organizations were rendered impotent by factional disputes that drained them of the unity, energy, and resolve needed to sustain protest activity. The growing divisions within the movement not only reduced the possibility of cooperative action *between* movement groups but further diminished the organizational strength of insurgent forces by stimulating disputes *within* these groups that reduced their effectiveness as autonomous protest vehicles" (McAdam 1982, 189–90).

At the end of 1966, after much debate, SNCC voted to exclude whites. Bob Zellner, a native Alabamian who had been through dangerous and bloody times as the group's earliest white field secretary, was one of those finally forced out—even though a black fellow worker, Cleveland Sellers, named Zellner as "one of the few whites who commanded the unqualified respect of everyone in the organization" (Carson 1981, 242). In May 1967, Zellner and his wife Dottie petitioned SNCC for recognition and full voting privileges with regard to a planned project of organizing the poor white community in New Orleans. Their request was refused (Cagin and Dray 1988, 441). According to Mary King, the organization was now dominated by newcomers rather than veterans.

Progress toward making CORE an all-black organization occurred gradually with each national convention accelerating the trend. It was still the most interracial of the organizations in 1963–64, but by spring 1964, James Farmer was urging white members to step back into secondary leadership roles or limit themselves to providing technical assistance.

Alan Gartner, a white member, was so central to the organization that he was a possible candidate for national director. At Farmer's suggestion, he stepped aside and did not oppose black candidate Floyd McKissick. When McKissick became national director, he stressed the need for community control and self-determination by black people, but he did not altogether exclude alliances with whites.

Experienced black civil rights workers had developed close relationships with particular white activists and appreciated their sacrifices. Whatever their contribution, the latter had undoubtedly gained a great deal personally in acting out felt beliefs. But personal feelings were put aside as the strong swing toward black self-determination gathered momentum. Everywhere whites were being told that they would have to play different and lesser roles, and in some cases, they were told to withdraw from organizations altogether.[4] While the less-committed might easily find other causes among the burgeoning movements, there were other longtime activists for whom the loss was painful. One of these, Mary King, described feelings of disorientation, of having to find a way to go back to a society "from which I felt dislocated," of knowing that nothing in her life would ever replace SNCC, and of a three-year mourning period (King 1987, 516).

It is probably difficult for some people to really understand how central the civil rights movement was to some whites. The sociological concept *reference group* may help. Although we are all born into *membership groups* of various kinds, such as being black or white, being a northerner or a southerner, we often develop strong positive sentiments about other groups that we admire—and guide our behavior in terms of the ideals of these groups rather than our own membership group. Thus, for example, a small number of southern whites, early on, rejected the segregationist norms of their region and looked to interracial, integrated groups as their reference group. People who can may switch out of old membership groups in order to join a new group that embodies what they believe in. The early SNCC represented the ideals that young integrationist whites valued. In addition, the white veterans in SNCC had experienced the strong camaraderie of combat, of shared dangers. Despite her sense of loss, Mary King concluded that the move to exclude whites had probably been inevitable, citing emotional exhaustion, the effects of sophisticated young people from the North on southern blacks, the rising black nationalism in the cities, and the disillusionment with white allies experienced by SNCC in its own political efforts. Still, she could not help but speculate about whether the FBI had infiltrated her organization and brought about some of the developments.

The national trend toward all-black organizations worked out differently in local chapters, with some whites continuing to participate well past the general decline of interracialism. Many other whites had contributed to the movement mainly financially. The changed posture of the SNCC and CORE led to a sharp withdrawal of this support; the integrationist NAACP, and the SCLC while King still lived, then received the bulk of the funds available from white sympathizers. This did not affect the policies of the more militant organizations, which eschewed dependence on whites; anti-McKissick forces at CORE's 1967 convention demanded the ouster of remaining white members. In the summer of 1968, Roy Innis was elected national director, and CORE became a black nationalist organization. By that time, the financial support of whites had virtually disappeared and the group was facing bankruptcy (Meier and Rudwick 1973). The SCLC had always been a predominantly black organization, but its leaders continued to consult with white government officials and certain trusted white advisers such as Stanley Levison.

Majority Involvement in Minority Movements

Marx and Useem maintain that the rejection of white participants in the movement follows a pattern that is true of other situations where majority, or dominant group members have been involved in minority movements (1971). In the earlier stages of a movement, it is low in power resources; outside support is welcomed. Later stages have a different dynamic. When civil rights gained respectability as a national issue, its leaders were able to make their own direct ties with federal officials and were not as dependent on white go-betweens. Government programs began to supplement the financial resources that movement organizations had formerly obtained from white donors.

Different stages of a movement also draw upon members with different types of commitment. The initial inner core of true believers tends to consist of idealists who devote all their time and energy to the cause. But when a movement reaches out to mobilize the support of large numbers, it gives up its selectivity. Some, though not of course all, of the later white participants came when it was a liberal rather than a radical thing to do. The increasing number of lower-economic-status black people now entering into protest were less integration-oriented than had been the middle-class leaders of the movement. Many southern blacks had welcomed the white civil rights workers and opened up their homes; in the North and West, black urban dwellers were often not only alienated from whites but also tended to reject the self-appointed middle-class leaders of their own race.

The problem of the acceptance of white allies can also be put into social psychological context as an issue of commitment. A relevant analysis deals with the role of "the wise"—the ally of a stigmatized person or group who, through identification, voluntarily takes on the stigma (Goffman 1963). The commitment of the wise is subject to question because the possibility of escape always exists. Of course, the stigmatized—in this case, the blacks—cannot lose that identity. Thus, minority activists tend to feel that they are more committed and more daring than associated outsiders; there is no question about the primacy of their own liberation. Allies may be interested in several causes, diverting their attention from that of the specific minority.

Questions of commitment are also raised within the stigmatized or minority group—with the constant evaluation of one's loyalty and dedication, the accusation that certain individuals are selling out, are Uncle Toms, or that they want to be white. People like King and Rustin, who believed in coalitions or who negotiated with the white power structure, were constantly being accused of conservatism, as of course were the less mass-action-oriented NAACP and National Urban League. Attempts of black power organizations to work with white new leftists ran into difficulties and were ultimately abandoned. While the white left supported black insurgency, the nationalist mood of the black organizations made them suspicious of even the most radical whites.

How the Movement Mirrors Society

The relationships of dominant and minority-group members within interracial organizations exist within the broader context of the society. An obvious but important truth is that "even with the best of intentions race has a persistent relevance that is hard to overcome. Traditional social forms and etiquette, as well as stereotypes, facilitate (or at least do not directly counter) usual patterns of dominant-subordinate relations, even among those committed to a more equalitarian society" (Marx and Useem 1971, 95–96). Divergent backgrounds reinforced typical racial patterns. The more privileged whites almost always had advantages over

southern black peers, frequently being better educated and more artic-
ulate. The tendency of whites to assume leadership might unconsciously
surface even among the most dedicated. On their part, southern blacks
in the movement sometimes had trouble "shaking loose from deferential
tendencies," a problem that has also been observed in some studies of
interracial learning groups. Sometimes southern blacks were more im-
pressed by the white worker than the black one, a factor that could not
have desirable long-term effects. Black role models were needed.

Efforts by white volunteers to overcompensate by being solicitous or
deferential did not work either. Interracial dating was a way of flaunting
custom, but many black people were critical of its divisive effects. It was
hard to create a normal dating situation in the case of black men who
were challenging a taboo and white women confused by conflicting motivations. Some might lend themselves to exploitation in their efforts to
prove loyalty. Such dating was not crucial to the black revolution and
created extra dangers in the South where black male–white female sexual relations were officially prohibited. (For a feminist view of male-
female relations within the civil rights movement, see Ferree and Hess
1985, 45–47. See also the section in chapter 10 of this book entitled
"Competing and Complementary Movements.")

Similarly, some minority group activists could not help but displace
antiwhite feelings onto the white volunteers—the most accessible sur-
rogates for white society. That society continued to impinge in harmful
ways. White students had been deliberately brought in to gain publicity
in 1964 and 1965. Yet the greater attention accorded to the death of
whites proved that their lives were valued more than those of blacks.
The crushed bones in the body of James Chaney, the black CORE member killed with Schwerner and Goodman, showed that he had suffered an
unbelievably severe beating. And while searchers were combing the riv-
ers for the three missing civil rights workers, they came upon a number
of unidentified black bodies—local residents whose deaths had passed
unnoticed. Thus did the society's racism poison relationships within the
movement.

Yet one cannot generalize about "black-white relations" in the movement without noting their variations. Much of what has been written in
criticism of white volunteers deals with the college student recruits of
the summers of 1964 and 1965. Pinkney (1968) and others have shown
that many whites around the nation were part of the movement much
earlier than that, entering when it was less popular and more deviant an

act for whites. For many years, interracial groups in northern and western CORE chapters and in fair housing groups carefully utilized racial identification to its best advantage, using black and white teams to test discrimination or to negotiate. Many whites acknowledged that they had much to learn from their black peers. Even when black organizations no longer wanted direct white participation, white support groups formed to provide what they could in terms of resources and influence (see, for example, West 1979).[5] Local interracial councils and committees, unattached to the national organizations, continued to operate. In the wake of the urban riots, some northern civil rights activists attempted to provide relief supplies and legal aid to ghetto inhabitants.

While there was a loss of white support during the black power phase, not all white supporters could be classified as shaky liberals. The author's study of white women who were core activists in the northern phase of the movement showed that, by and large, they understood the black power mood and the need for whites to play lesser roles (Blumberg 1980a). Their dedication did not decrease because the movement was in the North, for these were the same people who led battles against de facto school segregation in their own communities and who had gone door-to-door with fair housing petitions. The committed looked for ways to support the movement when white roles began to change. Still, as longtime integrationists, many found it difficult to accept the fact of the increasing racial polarization that was occurring.

The Response of the Public

The core activists discussed above did not represent the views of the majority of the white public. Nor did support of traditional civil rights aims make whites (or black leaders such as Kenneth Clark and Bayard Rustin) uncritical of certain positions of the black power groups. Those who had supported the early SNCC and CORE saw the original purposes of these groups transformed. Jewish people, in particular, had been represented in the movement in disproportionate numbers. The Jewish conductor Leonard Bernstein had been subject to extensive criticism for his promotion of dialogue between members of the Black Panthers and potential white donors. Now many Jews began to see their own interests as a group compromised by some of the new directions, and they withdrew financial support. SNCC and CORE had begun to speak out against the state of Israel after the Six-Day War, and some black urban activists showed a willingness to exploit a residue of anti-Semitism in the ghettos, where many storekeepers were Jewish. Incidents of public black anti-Semitism were blown up by the press, even when they had been repudiated by black leaders.

In certain local situations, too, Jewish people were disproportionately affected by black demands. The Oceanhill-Brownsville dispute over control of the school system in New York was a case in point. Community control, a replacement for failed integration plans, provided that parents and community leaders would have a say in the governance of local schools. A bitter battle between the powerful teachers' union, the United Federation of Teachers, and the community board started gradually in 1966, went on for over two years, led to a major teachers' strike, and involved charges and countercharges about anti-Semitism. Jews were on both sides of the struggle, but since Jews made up a good part of the membership of the UFT they were sometimes seen as the enemy. (For a presentation of many of the original documents and a chronology of events in this power struggle, see Berube and Gitell 1969).[6]

The mood of white America with regard to the black revolt began to show a marked change. According to opinion polls, whites thought that blacks wanted to go too fast—but blacks were dissatisfied with the tokenism that substituted for significant progress. Polls reflect how broad samples of the population react to hypothetical situations, but nonetheless, when distinct differences occur by race, they validly reflect the disparity in perceptions. A series of Gallup polls between 1962 and 1971 asked the public what was the most important problem facing America. "From its peak in the years 1963–65, the issue of civil rights experienced a general decline in salience during the late 1960s and early 1970s" (McAdam 1982, 197). The percentage of the people surveyed who felt that race relations was the country's most important problem fell from 52 to 7 between 1965 and 1971. During these years, the war in Vietnam overshadowed civil rights as an issue.

The visibility accorded tokens seemed to convince others that African Americans were really getting ahead. As a discriminated-against group the latter were more sensitive to the purposes behind tokenism—the providing of minor concessions in order to prevent significant change (Phillips and Blumberg 1983). In the North, increasingly a scene of black demands, much of the support for the movement, especially financial, had come from people whose own lives were not disturbed by it. The change in public opinion was only one of the factors that influenced the national government in its dual policy toward black power advocates and its attempts to contain urban disorders. Repression and neutralization of militant groups was combined with Great Society Programs designed to ameliorate some of the problems of the poor. The next chapter will look at this more closely.

Focus on the Cities

Both successes and disappointments propelled civil rights organizations to reexamine their objectives. Desegregation of public accommodations had come to most of the South. Many blacks had been registered to vote, and the Voting Rights Act would increase this number. Attention now turned to the more deep-rooted urban problems, which were national in scope. The building of black institutions, community organizing, and community control would prove to be the new thrust.

Tactically, the South as first target had not been a mistake; financial resources had been poured into the movement not only by the black community but by liberal northerners. Some of the latter's sons and daughters had been inspired to spend a summer in the Deep South. But civil rights organizations had not penetrated the serious problems in the nation's cities, such as unemployment, discrimination, union bias, de facto segregated housing, and precarious police-community relations. These were brought sharply into focus when a major conflagration broke out in Los Angeles in 1965, the Watts riot. The acknowledged, educated, black middle-class leaders found that they had little influence on angry urban masses as other ghettos went up in flames.

The movement had shown what black power, even when nonviolent, could do. Black power leaders had provided justification for black rage and for seeing the white system as the enemy, sentiments that came easily and naturally to the ghetto dweller. Civil rights leaders could only react by using the riots as reasons for demanding needed programs and by trying to make the country understand the root causes of the problems. More radical leaders like Stokely Carmichael and H. Rap Brown went further—they justified the rioting. The press played up their speeches.

The conditions of blacks in the cities had been deteriorating during the major thrust of the movement in the early sixties. The government's official riot studies competed with those of independent social scientists and on-the-scenes participants in efforts to explain what had gone wrong.

The next chapter places the urban rebellions in the context of the black revolt and analyzes the decline of effective civil rights activity in the second half of the sixties. The forces leading to the black power transition, its objectives, and some of its manifestations have been presented here, but the black power movement was so complex and many-faceted that to do it full justice would require another book.[7]

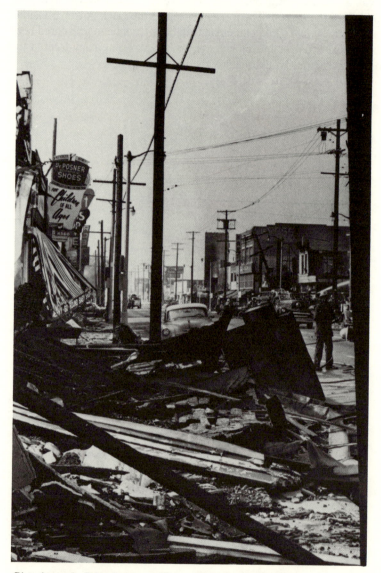

Riot aftermath: Sabbath scene in Watts. *Wide World Photos, Inc.*

Chapter Nine

Urban Rebellion

Violence is as american as cherry pie.

—H. Rap Brown

Widespread and spontaneous attacks on property occurred in the black ghettos of northern and western cities between 1964 and 1968. Stores were broken into, looted, and burned. This series of urban rebellions, more popularly referred to as riots, were a response to racial oppression that ran parallel to and interacted with nonviolent civil rights campaigns and black power activity. Labels have tremendous implications, especially when they refer to emotionally charged events such as the civil disturbances that shook American cities during these years. The term *riot* suggests out-of-hand expressive violence with little social meaning, whereas the term *rebellion* implies reality-based mass protest.

Despite the efforts of local and national movement organizations, the government's Great Society programs, and southern civil rights gains, the black poor of the North and the West had experienced deterioration in the conditions of their lives. The nationally acknowledged civil rights leaders were troubled and upset by the death and destruction of the riots but found themselves powerless to influence the participants. The more militant black power leaders interpreted the mass action as welcome rebellion; their rhetoric, however, provided little direction for channeling the expressive energy of the people toward long-term goals.

Rebellion

Some analysts agree with the black power leaders in their use of the term *rebellion,* interpreting it as action that lies somewhere between re-

159

form and revolution. When a group aims to overthrow an existing social order completely through the use of violence, it is revolutionary. Davis, a student of revolution, conceptualizes the urban disorders of 1965–68 as having "involved a widespread joint commitment to rather fundamental change among all segments of black society: change in the political power structure of the country in all political units—cities, counties, states, and nation. And these changes, involving all blacks and all parts of the political community, were accompanied by the violence that is a universal element of revolution" (1979, 429). Then why does the author not call the black rebellions a revolution? Because those frustrated—blacks—constitute a small proportion of the total population, and because discrimination based on race is not generally condoned by the nation's constitutions and laws (1979, 429). He suggests, then, that black people were not trying to overthrow laws that contained some protections. They were insisting that the laws be applied fairly.

The Precipitating Factors

A final precipitating factor can usually be discovered that sets off active expression of long-smoldering grievances. The issue of police bias and brutality was surfacing over and over again as almost totally white police forces walked the streets of the almost totally segregated ghettos. "Accidental" killings of black males by offical law enforcement agencies symbolized—then and still—white disregard of black life. In a fateful case, one more Harlem youth was shot in July 1964. CORE led a group of demonstrators from a rally to a police station and sat-in in front of it. The police pushed some people back, scuffles ensued, and the officers arrested the CORE leaders who had been maintaining discipline. What ensued in New York City was the beginning of the major riots. The protesters threw bottles and bricks at the police, and the police responded, setting off four nights of intermittent violence between them. That same summer, riots flared in Rochester, Jersey City, Elizabeth, Patterson, and Philadelphia—all related to police issues. No wonder the colonial analogy would surface: one group was the master and the other the colonized, which was controlled and policed by the other race (see Blauner 1972). But it would not be until the following summer, when a major ghetto went up in flames, that racial problems would be recognized as national rather than regional in scope.

The growing polarization between the two races was evident in their reactions, available to us through polls and postriot studies. Black riot participants and nonparticipants tended to see the eruptions as spontaneous and unorganized protest against disintegrating conditions. Many white people accepted the pronouncements of local officials and police chiefs and viewed them as the behavior of criminal elements responding to outside agitation or communist conspiracy.

Urban Problems

What were the deteriorating conditions of the ghettos? First of all, there was massive segregation in poor housing, related both to the low economic position of most ghetto residents and to the fact that aspiring middle-class families were not permitted to join other ethnic groups that had escaped to suburbia. Immigrant groups had voluntarily concentrated in city areas—ghettos—as a way station to individual mobility and pursuit of the good life. Fulfilling the demand for unskilled labor, many had made it well enough to move out of the center cities. But most urban black people were now locked into the deteriorated, almost totally segregated ghettos.

Efforts by fair housing groups to break the solid patterns of exclusion in most white neighborhoods had been relatively unproductive. New public housing was hard to get off the ground, in spite of the availability of funds, because of the opposition of white residents and the recalcitrance of public officials. Urban renewal, touted as a way of removing slum housing, had acquired the label "Negro removal." The poor were displaced as these areas were rebuilt to benefit business and industry. The obligation to relocate them to other housing sometimes translated into a series of moves from one condemned dwelling to another soon-to-be-torn-down site.

De facto school segregation was a related problem. Efforts to find a remedy were at least as difficult as they had been in the South. Segregation statutes were not on the books in the North, but housing patterns achieved the same results. Racial separation was also created by the location of schools; judicious selection of sites for new ones could help relieve imbalance. But white school boards, which made these decisions, could often be accused of preferring to bolster existing segregation patterns. Although many plans had been advanced for desegregation, the opposition focused on one of them—busing—and made this the code word for resistance. The black power movement had an alternative—community control. If black students were to continue to be taught in de facto segregated schools, the community itself ought to have a say about their education. This, too, became a subject of controversy.

Schools affected residential patterns. Housing segregation intensified as whites sought homes in areas served by good (white) schools. Black people were grossly underrepresented in local governance, with token conservative or moderate figureheads occasionally sitting on school boards or other agencies. The stores in the ghetto were owned mainly by whites, who could take advantage of the residents' lack of transportation facilities or need for credit by overcharging or selling inferior merchandise. The landlord and the social worker were, of course, white. The experience of powerlessness, of not being in charge, was overwhelming.

Probably the most important issue for black people was that of jobs and unemployment. Income provides an index of the general well-being of a group. And because of inflationary factors that raise average gross income over the years, the best way to understand *real* income is by comparison. A high point was the year 1951, when black median income was 62 percent of white median income (Brink and Harris 1963, 54). By 1962, black income was reduced to only 55 percent of white earnings. Brink and Harris, writing in 1963, bring out the worrisome fact that "the Negro's wage is showing an alarming tendency to decline, relative to whites" (54). More than half of their nationwide sample of black people believed that they would be paid less than a white for doing comparable work.

The unemployment rate of black youth had actually increased in disproportion to that of white youth during the years of extensive civil rights activity. In 1954, this black teenage rate was only slightly higher than that of whites (Wilson 1978, 89). Since 1966 it has been greater by a two-to-one ratio, according to official statistics. These rates do not include the discouraged, who no longer seek employment.[1] Long-term shifts in the economy had played havoc with the job prospects of relatively unskilled blacks. The modernization of agriculture had pushed black farmworkers off the land and to the cities. The change from an economy dominated by production to one dominated by services then decreased the number of available jobs. Better jobs in service industries require more education than the unskilled possess. Industrial growth has occurred in the suburbs rather than in the cities, where most blacks now live, and public transportation is often inadequate. Furthermore, business has been dominated by white males, so that until affirmative action attacked this hegemony (supported by minority groups and womens' groups) few blacks found the means of entry to white-collar occupations.[2]

Many of the urban problems, which have only been sketched in broadest outline here, could not be solved by a head-on assault, such as was possible in the case of segregated public accommodations. These problems were highly interrelated and formed a pattern of institutionalized racism, one in which government at all levels was involved. Blacks had been barred from union training programs and hence kept out of the skilled trades. Now seniority systems assured that they would continue to be the last hired, first fired. Tests for municipal police and firefighting jobs were so written as to virtually ensure continued racial exclusion. Ghetto education was not preparing black youth for college, let alone white-collar jobs. Even as blacks increased in educational level, the disparity between their income and that of whites with comparable education also increased. Municipal services were deteriorating, given blacks' lack of power and representation. Black business could not compete with white where all the major financial and credit institutions discriminated against them. Only in a few areas, confined to serving the black population, was black enterprise able to flourish.

The Watts Revolt

Sears and McConahay (1973) have given us a perceptive analysis of the first major urban rebellion, which took place in the section of Los Angeles known as Watts in August 1965. In the words of Killian, "Watts marked the point at which the violent black crowd entered the black revolution" (1975, 89). The riot had erupted on 11 August, four days after the new voting rights law went into effect. A member of the administration noted that warnings had simply not been seen as the nation concentrated on southern racial problems (Miller 1980, 435). Half of the nation's black population was now in the North.

The scope of the Watts riot took the nation by surprise. It started with the arrest of a young black man for drunk driving—and escalated into a confrontation between police and a crowd of onlookers. The crowd grew and became a mob, overturning cars and looting shops. By dawn, the police announced, incorrectly, that the outbreak was over. The precipitating incident had suddenly unleashed a massive amount of repressed anger against the police and the internal colonialism of the ghetto.

The rioting lasted six days and spread over a wide area of territory that came to be called the Curfew Zone (an area sealed off by the National Guard and the police). This zone was more than 80 percent black and covered 46.5 square miles—an area one and one half times as large as Manhattan. Thirty-four persons were killed, 31 of them black, and more than 1,000 persons were injured seriously enough to require treatment. Almost 1,000 buildings were damaged, burned, looted, or destroyed. A half million blacks were said to have participated in the disorders (Sitkoff 1981, 200). A huge number of National Guard troops, police, and sheriff's deputies were needed in order to restore order.

As public officials made their pronouncements condemning riot particiipants, many of them reflected wishful thinking—that those who took part were newcomers to the city, criminals, or persons unduly influenced by "outside agitators." These officials generally refused to admit that conditions in the cities they governed might in some way be responsible for the reaction of the black population.

The urban disorders that had occurred in Rochester, Philadelphia, and Harlem the year before were similar but had not drawn as much notice. Both the Harlem and Watts riots were instigated by conflicts between white policemen and black residents; all had involved attacks on property and violent response to the police. White areas generally went untouched, but the property of ghetto merchants was destroyed or their stores looted. Inevitably, whenever deaths were involved, more blacks than whites were killed, many of them bystanders.

Since the Watts riot was the prototype of ones that would follow, it is instructive to examine research findings about those who participated. Sears and McConahay interviewed two samples of black respondents, called (1) the Curfew Zone sample, representing people in the large area of Los Angeles cordoned off during the riot, and (2) the arrestee sample, 124 residents of the Curfew Zone who had been arrested during the rioting. Both were interviewed during late 1965 and 1966 by black interviewers. The research found that approximately 20 percent of the residents of the Curfew Zone actually participated in riot activities—far more than the 2 percent estimated by the official McCone Report. Many more persons were involved as close spectators.

The official report had concluded that participants were marginally related to the community as drifters, that they were unemployed or school dropouts and mainly newcomers to Los Angeles from the South. This interpretation robbed the actions of any political significance. In contrast, the two independent researchers found that sample members who were natives or long-term residents of Los Angeles were significantly more involved than recent migrants. Those most active as participants and as spectators were young males under the age of 30. No differences in educational status were found between them and young males who did not take part. Participants in the later Detroit and Newark riots had a higher level of education than comparable others. These factors throw into serious question some of the assumptions of the McCone Commission about the type of person who participated.

Indeed, the people who became involved appear to typify the new urban blacks who now populate the cities in large numbers. They are younger, are more likely to have grown up in the North, have more education than their older counterparts, and tend to compare their own achievements with those of whites. This finding supports the relative-deprivation hypothesis, which stresses the tendency to rebel among those who feel that they are deprived compared to significant others. It also confirms that revolutions are not started by the most deprived and impoverished of the population. Others say that the relative-deprivation hypothesis focuses mainly on individual psychology and depends on the chosen measurement indices. Sears and McConahay's "new ghetto man" data refute the notion that rioters were the most marginal people, people unattached to groups, or recent migrants experiencing disorganization. As Feagin and Hahn (1973) point out, the riots were group actions engaged in by people connected in interpersonal networks. Knowledge of them spread rapidly by word of mouth.

In contrast to the theories of the white officials, most of the interviewed area blacks perceived the Watts riot as "(1) a purposeful symbolic protest (2) against legitimate grievances, (3) designed to call attention to blacks' problems" (Sears and McConahay 1973, 159).

Relationship of the Urban Rebellions to Civil Rights

Some social scientists view the riots as a group response that attempted to take the black revolt a step further than the civil rights movement had. Killian sees them as part of the long-term struggle of blacks for equality that has been manifested in so many different ways over black history (1975). Similarly, Feagin and Hahn interpret the riots as a type of political action related to what had gone before:

Rioting was probably occasioned less by the impersonal, anomic or psychologically stressful conditions of urban life than by the concentration of large numbers of black residents in distinct sectors of the city, by their frequent interaction, by their developing cohesion and political consciousness, and ultimately by their mobilization for militant political action. (1973, 48–49)

The riots were related to the nonviolent movement in a number of ways. For one thing, although they had shared in the growth of black pride and black aspirations, the urban lower classes had not profited materially from southern desegregation and voting rights gains. The highly publicized violence and racism of sheriffs and their men in the South only reinforced already-held opinions about the all-white urban police forces. Demands for civilian review boards reflected citizen distrust. Often seemingly routine police action would touch off the underlying tensions and grievances of the urban populations. Furthermore, civil rights groups had been organizing in the black communities, trying to use the tactics of negotiation and nonviolent demonstrations to attack the problems of jobs, housing, and de facto segregation.

The usual southern techniques had been used even more aggressively in the North. For this effort, CORE vied with NAACP chapters, frequently recruiting workers from disaffected members of the older protest organization. Even when engaged in its greatest efforts at voter registration in the South, CORE was also highly involved in northern campaigns. Brooklyn, New York, CORE was a vanguard group. It had attempted a stall-in, a disruption of traffic, on the opening day of the New York World's Fair, 22 April 1964, which was controversial even within the organization. Chicago had experienced a school desegregation fight in which protesters also disrupted traffic by lying down in the street. Milwaukee, Wisconsin, and Springfield, Massachusetts, had gone through school desegregation battles that saw the use of innovative CORE techniques—the blocking of buses and sit-ins at a school superintendent's office. But no major northern campaign had attracted the united force of the southern campaigns or the sympathy of the white public. CORE had won some urban victories, but not enough to stave off the destruction of the 1964–68 riots. City political machines were strong, and long-term interest groups had carved out their areas of patronage and entitlements.

The actions of the masses were also related even more directly to experiences of the civil rights movement. Recall that the first of the property riots occurred in Birmingham in 1963, following the bombings of black-owned buildings after an official victory. The rampage that lasted for hours was a response to the white lawlessness. Participants in the nonviolent resistance movement had pledged and practiced not to retaliate, but black onlookers were not so constrained. In the early days of Montgomery, when his home was bombed and partially destroyed, Martin Luther King had made an eloquent and successful plea to the crowds not to resort to violence. But now the ghetto residents of Watts were not in a mood to listen to him as he attempted persuasion. Even during the nonviolent stage, the time-honored right to self-defense had been claimed by some activists in the Deep South when lives were threatened (see Raines 1977, 115).

The urban rebellions reflected the mood of protest and the new self-assertiveness; no studies have been able to discover any plot or plan by individuals to foment them. Black power leaders, notably H. Rap Brown, actively endorsed the riots and hence were accused of instigating them.

Looking at the timing of the riots and the rise of black power groups, Feagin and Hahn posit a reverse causation. A number of disturbances, including Watts, had occurred before Carmichael's black power pronouncement. The ghetto residents sought self-determination, a restructuring of power arrangements so that they would share in decisions affecting their lives. Black power proponents such as SNCC activists recognized this underlying direction and articulated it in their speeches (Feagin and Hahn 1973). But SNCC, now beset by internal divisions, lacked the cohesion and persistence that had characterized its community organization efforts in the South. For King and the SCLC, the violent disorders were a challenge demanding that the nonviolent movement respond to the needs of the nation's urban population. The year after Watts, they set up headquarters in Chicago to do just this.

Response to the Riots

Following the riots, official agencies of law and order gradually began a massive effort to improve their riot-proof hardware, electronic communications, and ability to put down a revolution. The FBI increased its infiltration of black organizations and developed plans to counter any future insurgency. Nonetheless, urban riots of serious proportions occurred in 1966, 1967, and 1968. No major city was spared. By the end of 1968, police reported that some 50,000 arrests, over 8,000 casualties, and nearly 300 race riots and disturbances had taken place since 1965 (Sitkoff 1981, 200). The Newark riot had been predictable, but the Detroit situation had seemed somewhat better. Nonetheless, the Detroit riot was so severe that Governor George Romney was forced to request federal troops. Thirty-seven black people and three whites had been killed and more than 2,000 injured. Property damage was estimated at $350 million. The president and various governors appointed prominent people to riot commissions to investigate the causes and propose remedies. Their official reports all had similar conclusions (see, for example, National Advisory Commission on Civil Disorders 1968 and Governor's Select Commission on Civil Disorder, State of New Jersey 1968). In thousands of words, they pointed to discrimination and deprivation in jobs, housing, education, and welfare, to police action, segregation, and the institutionalized racism that alienated ghetto residents.

The report of the New Jersey Commission unequivocally stated, "The evidence presented to the Commission does not support the thesis of a conspiracy or plan to initiate the Newark riot" (Governor's Select Commission on Civil Disorder 1968, 144). Despite similar lack of proof for the theory in other cities, polls showed that a significant proportion of whites believed that the riots had been due to leftist agitation. These views were symptomatic of the wide gap between the two races.

Indeed, the National Advisory Commission on Civil Disorders (the Kerner Commission) cautioned, in an oft-quoted statement, "This is our basic conclusion: our nation is moving toward two societies, one black, one white—separate and unequal. Reaction to last summer's [1967] disorders had quickened the movement and deepened the division. Discrimination and segregation have long permeated much of American life; they now threaten the future of every American" (1968). President Johnson and Vice President Humphrey did not seem pleased with the report of the commission and virtually ignored it.

The official reports recommended programs to ameliorate the negative conditions and also improvement in police control of riots. A new civil rights bill in 1968 reflected the government's two-pronged thrust: besides stronger strictures against housing discrimination, it contained an antiriot provision. Harsh penalties were set for persons found guilty of crossing state lines or using interstate communications facilities to incite riots. A number of black power leaders would be prosecuted on these grounds. The Omnibus Crime Act of 1968 was also passed. It provided for the establishment of a national training center in riot control techniques and for financial aid to local law enforcement agencies. The latter was supported with massive federal funding.[3] Federal funding of poverty programs also increased in riot areas. Federally sponsored school desegregation efforts "increased sharply during and immediately following the peak period of urban rioting" (McAdam 1982, 221). A number of national corporations expanded their activities directed toward minorities.

At first, many black residents believed that more attention might be paid to their problems. Later this view declined, as many of the burnt-out areas were not rebuilt. The temporary relief provided by charity organizations to neighborhoods in which services were disrupted was a short-run measure. Many blacks had been arrested and were awaiting trial. The split between the races sharpened. The urban disorders had alienated many whites and brought out the underlying racial divisions that already existed. Many northern whites, if not positive about black rights, were at least neutral so long as they were not affected. But now the spotlight on northern inequities was creating widespread reaction. Formerly subtle forms of racism became more blatant. Communities mobilized in citizens' groups to oppose school desegregation or the building of housing projects in their neighborhoods. Urban ethnic groups, once the backbone of the Democratic party, were defecting, making the civil rights cause increasingly unpopular with politicians.

A strong white backlash and an emphasis on law and order was evident, but local black leaders picked up on the theme of community control more aggressively. After the 1967 riot in Newark, for example, there was a significant amount of new organizational activity; by 1968 a black united front was attempting to establish control over the city. Eventually a black mayor, Kenneth Gibson, was elected, as occurred in a number of other cities.

Black people were asserting themselves as an identifiable interest group that would seek representation in the ongoing institutions of the society. The urban rebellions were but one example. This thrust took many forms: the demands of black students for their own black studies programs, the black caucus movement in professional organizations, black protest in prisons and the armed forces, and the seeking of electoral office. African Americans now sought entry into the mainstream in the name of the group. Nonetheless, appointments and admissions were made on an individual basis. Once entry had been gained to formerly de facto segregated settings, the black person was expected to resist assimilation to white values and work for the interests of the group. The dilemmas of individuals placed in these roles and the paradoxes of, for example, running a black studies program in a predominantly white institution have been analyzed by participant observers in these scenes (see the statement of a former black studies director, Thomas Slaughter, in Albert, Goldstein, and Slaughter 1974, 137–57, and Phillips and Blumberg 1983).

Absorption into the Institutional Structure

Black people had migrated to states that were strategically important in national elections. The Democratic party had become overwhelmingly favored by the black population, and it intended to maintain this advantage. A federal strategy for the cities, the War on Poverty, had been initiated by President Kennedy as early as 1961. Johnson's Great Society program continued it. The aim was to get more black votes while not alienating whites. It was felt that state and city governments had not been responsive to their new growing constituency.

The War on Poverty and its continuation in the Great Society legislation initiated a large number of projects for the inner cities. In 1961, $10 million was appropriated for youth development projects intended to stem juvenile delinquency. A Community Mental Health Centers Act was passed in 1963 which provided $150 million for setting up the centers. In 1964, Title II of the Economic Opportunity Act allocated $350 million to community action programs designed to deal with poverty problems. Other measures followed—a model neighborhoods program in 1966 and a neighborhood services program in 1967. Head Starts were providing preschool education, meals, and health care to children usually disadvantaged when entering the public school system. Participation of the poor was mandated in the acts. In all these programs, the executive branch created a direct relationship between the national government and the ghettos, bypassing the traditional state and city agencies. Altruism was not the motivating force; the Democratic party was reviving "the traditional processes of urban politics, offering jobs and services to build party loyalty" (Piven and Cloward 1972, 261). But their clientele was volatile, as the new agencies frequently warred with the bureaucracies of local government. Poverty agencies were often run by civil rights or black power activists whom the federal government could not control; there was a considerable amount of turbulence. The riots had reflected the new political consciousness and activism. Nonetheless, the government experiment was successful in integrating many into the political system. Despite their militancy and resistance to cooptation, those running community agencies became dependent on government funds. Assessing the overall effect, Piven and Cloward assert:

If civil rights workers often turned federal dollars to their own purposes in the short run, in the longer run they became model-cities directors, or community-action executives—that is, they became government employees or contractors subject to the constraints of federal funding and federal guidelines. In many cities the Great Society agencies became the base for new black political organizations whose rhetoric may have been thunderous but whose activities came to consist mainly of vying for position and patronage within the urban political system. . . . From the perspective of integrating blacks into the political system, the Great Society was a startling success. (1972, 274, 276)

Indeed, the same authors maintain that the seemingly radical black power ideology was very much suited to the needs of the black leadership stratum attempting to grasp new opportunities for official public roles. The increase in numbers of black voters in the Deep South was dramatic. By July 1967, the Department of Justice indicated that more than 50 percent of eligible black votes had been registered in the five states of the Deep South. Black gains in the South raised the overall black registration rate to nine-tenths that of whites by 1972 (Levitan, Johnston, and Taggart 1965, 177). "In virtually no time at all the movement had been incorporated into the electoral system" (Piven and Cloward 1979, 254). By 1970, black people were the majority in 13 cities. This increased concentration assured the election of many black city officials.

Another means of pacifying the urban poor was through a modification of the welfare system. Here, too, local agencies that had restricted relief giving were bypassed. New services were established that provided information about welfare entitlements and expert assistance to help the poor obtain what they were entitled to by law. The National Welfare Rights Organization emerged to press their claims, a grass-roots movement of predominantly black women which also drew upon the civil rights movement for leadership (West 1981). Applications for welfare rose sharply after 1964, and many were granted. This was one more evidence of government's need to forestall further disorders. Giving relief was certainly simpler than correcting the persistent causes of black poverty.

Despite some gains for middle-class African Americans, and the election of a number of black mayors, the acute problems of the urban poor remain. Poverty, unemployment and underemployment, teenage pregnancy, drug addiction, and the related scourge of AIDS (often the consequence of intravenous injection) all take a terrible toll. Mental illness, suicide, and black-on-black crime increase as frustration turns inward toward oneself or one's group. A "shoot-to-kill" policy seems to be nationwide police practice when it comes to young black males who fall under suspicion (as almost any are likely to). Such victims are most often shot in the back and assumed to have a weapon. Periodically, black communities are inflamed by yet another killing and its justification by authorities—pushing them to act out their grief in anger.

It is generally agreed that the government's effort to control through force was successful. The loss of black life in the riots and the new military antiriot measures effectively prevented further major disturbances after 1968. The environment had become less conducive to protest. This changing political and societal atmosphere also affected nonviolent civil rights efforts. The movement went into a period of decline, affected by multiple interrelated developments—just as its rise had been. The next chapter examines the efforts of King to modify and revitalize the movement during the turbulent period of the escalating Vietnam conflict.

Martin Luther King, Jr. *Laurance Henry Collection, Schomburg Center for Research in Black Culture.*

Chapter Ten

Movement Decline

Well, I don't know what will happen now. But it really doesn't matter
with me now. Because I've been to the mountaintop. I won't mind. Like
anybody, I would like to live a long life. Longevity has its place. But I'm
not concerned about that now. I just want to do God's will. And He's
allowed me to go up to the mountain. And I've looked over, and I've seen
the promised land. I may not get there with you, but I want you to know
tonight that we as a people will get to the promised land. So I'm happy
tonight. I'm not worried about anything. I'm not fearing any man.
"Mine eyes have seen the glory of the coming of the Lord."
    —*Martin Luther King, Jr., sermon at Mason Temple,*
                    Memphis, Tennessee, 3 April 1968

Many take the year of Martin King's death, 1968, as the end of the civil
rights movement, that is, the nonviolent direct action thrust of the black
freedom struggle. Movement demise is not as sudden as this, and nonviolent protest activities continued with less frequency and less publicity.
King's popularity had suffered a decline with his outspoken antiwar activities, the upsurge of black power, and the urban riots. He had learned
from and reassassed his experiences and was now entering a new phase
in his growth. His strong antiwar stance, opposed by many traditional
black leaders, eventually became the will of the country. He had begun
to attack the basic economic problems of workers and the poor. In the
words of one of his biographers, King "was killed at the climactic point
at which he might have helped to create a coalition of racial, populist,
intellectual, and national groups" (Lewis 1978, 393). Eliminating his voice
greatly reduced the possibility of such a coalition.

The Effort to Revitalize the
Civil Rights Movement: Chicago

King had found himself ineffective in trying to cool the Watts rebellion. Open rejection by young people of his race troubled him, and he tried to create a dialogue with youthful black power advocates. The urban disorders made it abundantly clear that the movement would have to be made more relevant to the current problems of the lower socioeconomic classes. Two of the three original nonviolent action organizations, SNCC and CORE, were now in the black power fold. The national NAACP, despite the contributions of some of its more militant branches, had stood for legal methods and lobbying rather than direct action. The NAACP Legal Defense and Educational Fund, a separate body, had provided essential legal aid. The SCLC remained as the main national organization dedicated to nonviolence in an increasingly violent atmosphere.

The organization had been seeking a target for a new major campaign that would once again prove the effectiveness of nonviolent confrontation. This time it focused on a northern city—Chicago—and the results were debatable. Chicago seemed a logical site not only because of its severe de facto housing and school segregation and job discrimination, but because local civil rights organizations sought the movement's support. The year after the Watts riot, King was invited to Chicago by its black protest leadership. Although they by no means agreed on all issues, the SCLC and the other major and locally based civil rights groups were formally allied in the Coordinated Council of Community Organizations (CCCO), headed by Al Raby. Jesse Jackson, in charge of the SCLC's Operation Breadbasket[1] in Chicago, was also anxious for his organization to come to that city.

On 26 January 1966, King and his family took up temporary residence in Chicago's Lawndale ghetto area. Southern experience would prove to be insufficient preparation for this crucially different northern campaign. Chicago was the second largest city in the nation. Demonstrations brought out unexpectedly vicious white mobs that sometimes numbered in the thousands, and black urban dwellers were in a mood to retaliate. Their anger had been recognized and articulated by Malcolm X; similar grievances had been given violent expression in the Watts riot. Support could not be expected from the Democratic administration because of both King's anti-Vietnam stand and Mayor Daley's power in the party. As a big-city boss, Daley also knew how to use his power of patronage to buy off key black politicians.

The atmosphere conducive to nonviolent protest had changed. Goals were now more complex as they sought to corrode entrenched institutional discrimination in the job and housing areas. The following statement summarizes this:

Even if the Vietnam issue had not strained relations almost to the breaking point, there was virtually no possibility of White House assistance in Chicago. The political power of the Daley machine within the Democratic Party, the socio-economic thrust, as opposed to the formerly legalistic, of the SCLC's Northern campaign, the complex interrelationships of Eastern finance, Midwestern industry and labor, and federal power—all these constituted built-in restraints upon pro–civil rights intervention by Washington outside the South. . . . Meanwhile, in Congress legislation was introduced to curtail civil rights demonstrations by Representative Roman Pucinski, an Illinois Democrat and formerly a consistent supporter of civil rights legislation. (Lewis 1978, 343)

These factors affected the nonviolent movement in general. Civil rights forces felt that 1966 was a crucial year in which they needed to counter the rising black power mood. King focused on housing discrimination in its various forms: exploitative slum housing and de facto segregation created in collusion with real estate interests. Not only would the SCLC confront a strongly entrenched mayor able to control black voters, it would be pitted against the powerful Chicago Real Estate Board (Fairclough 1987, ch. 11). Black income, severely lower than that of whites, became another target. Operation Breadbasket pressured firms that had been slow to hire or promote black people. Drives against slum landlords were undertaken. The usual methods of marches and rallies were employed to mobilize the community, and efforts were made to negotiate with city officials.

To add to the problems, King's attention was divided among Chicago, his ministry in Atlanta, and the Vietnam war. Even before the SCLC took an official position against the war in 1967, its top leader was speaking out and publishing articles questioning the war's morality. Such an article appeared in the 1 January 1966 *Chicago Defender* but aroused little public notice. In the same month, King defended former SNCC member Julian Bond, deprived of his elective seat by the Georgia legislature because of an anti–Vietnam war position. These activities not only demanded King's time and energy but had interacting effects. The peace effort was displacing civil rights as the most important public issue, drawing many of the funds that civil rights organizations relied upon (Fairclough 1987,

287). As the SCLC's prime fund-raiser, King frequently had to interrupt other activities to go on fund-raising tours. His posture about the war had sharply alienated President Johnson.

As the civil rights forces drew attention to the problems of slum dwellers, Daley countered with his own expressions of concern about the issue. He met with the civil rights delegations, assuring them of good intentions. On the same day, 26 May 1966, that King announced plans for a march on city hall, Daley was able to announce the successful negotiation of a federal loan for housing renovation. The significance of the day for civil rights forces was heightened by another tragedy. Jerome Huey, a 17-year-old black youth, was beaten to death on a streetcorner by four white youths in the de facto segregated suburb of Cicero (Lewis 1978, 321). This was the kind of hateful incident that had galvanized thousands in the South, and the Chicago Movement intended to utilize it. Mass demonstrations were to be held.

Meanwhile, another major event drew Martin King away from the Chicago scene at this crucial time. On 6 June, James Meredith was gunned down at the beginning of his one-man "journey against fear" in Mississippi. King rushed to join other leaders for the memorable Meredith march described earlier. The violent resistance encountered on that march did nothing to aid the civil rights cause, as black power advocates proclaimed the right to strike back. It was a dangerous journey for the national leaders of the black movement. Marchers were attacked, their campsites were fired upon, and they encountered such racial extremists as Cecil Price, the same deputy sheriff under whose jurisdiction Schwerner, Chaney, and Goodman had met their deaths, and who was then suspected of direct involvement in the murders. State officials had declined to prosecute the case, but the following year, Price was found guilty of the federal charge of conspiracy to violate the civil rights of the three activists (Cagin and Dray 1988, 441–52).[2] Another person who harassed the marchers was Byron de la Beckwith, "known by thousands as the unconvicted killer of Medgar Evers" (Garrow 1986, 482). Meanwhile, the Chicago campaign had to wait.

During the Meredith march, the growing disagreements among the major civil rights organizations had become more overt. First, the NAACP and the Urban League were goaded into withdrawing from the march by SNCC (Garrow 1986, 476–78). SNCC's leader, Stokely Carmichael, had decided he would manipulate the press attention that always accompanied Martin Luther King, Jr., to showcase the organization's new slogan, "black power." For a while, SNCC and CORE proponents of black power attempted to outshout the "freedom now" chants of SCLC marchers. This march poignantly illustrates the dialectics of social movements—the ever and ongoing attempts to maintain internal unity while coping with the changing movement environment (see the Appendix). The urgency of the Meredith march had temporarily interrupted King's concentration on the Chicago campaign, but such emergencies were nothing new. King continually shuttled between Mississippi, Chicago, Atlanta, and wherever else he was needed (Garrow 1986).

The experiences of the Meredith march convinced SCLC leaders even more that they needed a success in Chicago. A huge rally was held in Soldier's Field on 10 July, followed by a march. The Chicago Movement presented the city with eight demands, which involved a many-pronged attack on segregated housing and the real estate practices accompanying it, several proposals that would increase the number of jobs available to black people, establishment of a civilian review board by the police department, and other related issues.

It seemed, however, that the anger and frustration of Chicago's African American community would not wait: 1966 became a riot summer in the city. A police-related incident eventuated in a major three-day conflagration. The rivalry between nonviolence and other forms of black revolt was heightening, as was white backlash. The racism of northern white citizens became more overt as they gathered in huge numbers to threaten and jeer nonviolent demonstrators. At an August rally in Marquette Park, King was stunned by a rock thrown at him, and only the police presence held back mobs ready to kill. Racism was virulent in Chicago, but unlike southern officials, Daley and Chicago dignitaries continued to meet with King and his CCCO allies. More marches and demonstrations were held, while the city responded by announcing additional plans to eradicate slums.

Movement leaders decided that they had to embark on a dangerous mission—a march through the antiblack suburb of Cicero. The major victories had been won in the South after vicious confrontations that forced the hand of the federal government. Mobilization for this march was successful, and even the most radical black groups prepared themselves for it. Two days before it was to take place, a controversial compromise was reached with the city administration and the business community, for "the Selma bridge syndrome was embedded in the psychopolitical constitution of the SCLC" (Lewis 1978, 346). That syndrome was a willingness to compromise, to accept the opposition's promises in good faith.

The organization's leaders had held off a proposed march at the Pettus

Bridge in Selma against the wishes of its followers. But the Selma march had gathered additional forces and then taken place. An unsatisfactory compromise had almost been accepted in Birmingham before Fred Shuttlesworth's last-minute veto. As in Randolph's threatened World War II March on Washington, the mobilized masses were disgruntled about the cancellation. A small group of blacks, led by CORE, SNCC, the Brothers for Afro-American Equality, the League of Labor and Education, and other organizations, did march through Cicero on 4 September. They were attacked by white mobs even though National Guardsmen and police tried to protect them. King's Chicago campaign and the compromise were severely criticized, although major concessions had been promised. Later, when the city failed to live up to its agreements, King told his staff, "I look back over [it] and wish we'd gone to Cicero" (Fairclough 1987, 307).[3]

The Assassination

King's internationalism, like Malcolm's, had been gaining in strength, and his increased concern with the poor of all races was symbolized by a proposed Poor People's campaign in Washington, to take place in 1968. According to some accounts, the idea had first been suggested by Mississippi activist Marian Wright Edelman.[4] While key advisers such as James Bevel, Jesse Jackson, and Bayard Rustin opposed the plan, King believed that a "tent city" of the nation's poor—later named "Resurrection City"—would focus congressional attention on poverty. Poor people from all over the country would be encouraged to camp out on public ground to dramatize their plight and to join delegations to government departments and legislators.

Planning and preparation for this campaign were interrupted when King was called to Memphis. His last major action was to support striking sanitation workers in that city, a move that can be seen as class as well as race oriented. Broad-based support of the strike by Memphis African Americans also indicated that jobs were viewed as a civil rights issue (Beifuss 1985). At the time of King's death, the Poor People's campaign was distastefully anticipated by the FBI and official Washington. Criticism of a class system that created poverty alongside of plenty smacked of revolution rather than reform, of attempts to change the economic system rather than become integrated into it. Though he never abandoned nonviolence, King's belief in the need for more radical change had increased. It was widely known that King's life was in danger, and the now-

troubled man seemed to live at a more hectic pace than ever in antici-
pation of what might come. Sleep was a rare commodity for him. But his
last sermon (part of which heads this chapter) reflected a calmer, fatal-
istic, premonitive mood.

On 4 April 1968, King was shot and killed by a powerful rifle blast as
he stood unprotected on the balcony of the Lorraine Motel. Official inquiries followed, but many questions remain unanswered about the killing, such as the reason for so little police protection and the conduct of
the hunt for the assassin (see, for example, Lane and Gregory 1977).
According to polls, a majority of Americans believe that the person convicted, James Earl Ray, was not a lone killer motivated to plot or execute
the act. Soon after the shocked nation heard of the assassination, Lyndon
Johnson went on public television to express the country's grief.

For many black folk, this was white hypocrisy, and they acted out their
feelings. Grief turned into rage. Crowds rampaged to protest King's
death; the champion of nonviolence was linked to those among his people
who loved the man and understood his significance but who could not
accept his tactic. Looting, rioting, and fires occurred in 125 cities in 28
states. Forty-five people were killed, 40 of them black. Six days later,
Congress, prodded by Johnson, moved on a languishing civil rights bill,
which the president dedicated to the fallen leader. Although it prohibited
discrimination in the sale or rental of about 80 percent of all housing, it
also included antiriot provisions.

Three years earlier, Malcolm X had been killed as he was evolving a
political philosophy and program that might have proven highly significant. The black revolution was stopped at least in part by the two murders and the ensuing disarray among black leadership. The death of
charismatic figures always presents problems of succession, and this was
true for the SCLC. In addition to the assassinations and arrests of militants, other leaders of potential national scope, such as Carmichael (and
earlier Robert Moses), had removed themselves from the running. Carmichael went into temporary exile in Africa. Ralph Abernathy had been
personally selected by King as his successor, even though others, such
as Andrew Young, appear to have played a much more critical intellectual
role.[5] Abernathy, more of a companion and friend than a strategist or
unifier, could not mobilize the same following. His major effort, to go
ahead with the Poor People's campaign after King's death, turned out to
be chaotic. The Poor People's campaign brought thousands of poor—
mainly blacks and some poor whites, Indians, and Mexican Americans—
to Resurrection City. They camped out in hastily constructed shacks and

tents on Lafayette Square across the avenue from the White House and joined delegations to public officials. But the weather did not cooperate: it rained every day, bogging everyone down in the mud. Some young street people could not be controlled, discipline was difficult to maintain, and fights broke out. Three weeks after the opening of Resurrection City, Robert Kennedy was assassinated—reviving the pain of King's violent death. Gradually, many of the people decamped. Ultimately, those left in the camp were evicted by police.

Although Malcolm and Martin were great leaders who appeared at a propitious time in history, the question remains about whether or not national and international events would have permitted a continuation of the civil rights movement on center stage. Great men respond to their historical times. Not only was loss of leadership great and internal movement divisions strong, but the external movement environment had changed.

The years 1966–70 have been called the declining years of black insurgency. This trend occurred despite the widespread incidence of urban rebellion, for "if the riots of this period conveyed an image of escalating racial conflict, they also masked a series of more subtle processes that were simultaneously at work undermining the efforts of insurgents to develop the organizational and tactical forms needed to sustain the leverage attained by the movement during the mid-1960s. The result of these processes was dramatic and quickly felt. By 1970, the movement as a force capable of generating and sustaining organized insurgency, was moribund, if not dead" (McAdam 1982, 182).

The nation became involved in another major divisive issue, its economy dipped, white backlash was translated into votes, and the black struggle was relegated into the background.

The War in Vietnam and the Peace Movement

When Johnson outlined his Great Society program on 4 January 1965, he had just won a major electoral victory. His advisers and the American people in general still supported the undeclared war. Johnson proposed and pushed through major legislation: Medicare, Head Start, aid to education, all of them programs that attacked poverty and were intended to help the poor of all races. As the war escalated and with it the antiwar movement, funds were directed to military needs, and less were available for domestic programs. Johnson failed to act on the Kerner Commission's recommendation for greatly increased financial assistance to the cities. Martin King's outspoken opposition to the war had its expected effect on the government's support of SCLC campaigns and Johnson's posture toward him. Instead of being judged by history as the greatest presidential ally of the civil rights movement, Johnson now merited an unflattering postscript to his record: he wrote off the one civil rights leader who might have stemmed the tide of racial polarization (Lewis 1978, 330).

On 25 April 1968, in the same momentous month of King's death and passage of the new civil rights bill, the nation's largest antiwar demonstration occurred in New York. Several hundred thousand people marched through the streets, and later 89,000 gathered for a rally (Miller 1980, 519). The pendulum had swung away from concern with racial inequality to concern with an undeclared Asian war.

Johnson decided not to run for reelection at the last minute, because of both failing health and the antiwar movement. Peace candidate Eugene McCarthy, Hubert Humphrey, and Robert Kennedy vied for the presidential nomination. On 4 June 1968, Kennedy was fatally shot in Los Angeles and Humphrey became the official Democratic candidate. Another candidate, segregationist governor George Wallace, drew unexpected support from white trade unionists. He received 14 percent of the popular vote, a pivotal group whom the Republicans hoped to capture in the future. At the moment, Wallace votes were a Democratic party loss. Humphrey was defeated by Richard Nixon, and in 1968 a new administration, which had no obligations to black voters, took office. Now the direction away from support for civil rights and the Great Society programs was official. "Law and order" became the code words for containing black insurgency. Other movements gained the attention and resources of the public.

Some national black leaders had linked the conflict in Asia to oppression at home, but the interracial peace organizations did not attract their people in large numbers. At first the civil rights leadership was split between pro- and antiadministration positions. Roy Wilkins of the NAACP and Whitney Young of the National Urban League openly criticized King's antiwar stance, while others thought quietly that joining the two causes was a tactical error. Many white activists agreed with King's position and participated in both peace and civil rights. But at the same time that they experienced a restriction of roles in the civil rights movement, white people found increased avenues for peace activity. When a social movement becomes unavailable to some of its members, they tend to seek another similar one (Weiss 1978, 230), and many whites drew the same connections between peace and civil rights that King did.

The two movements were not united on the campuses of the nation's universities. Students, black and white, had rebelled against the bureaucracy and alienating procedures of their colleges. Now the campuses became the site of much antiwar agitation. Young white people created a counterculture, the hippies, but also the New Left—radical critics of capitalism. They applauded the black liberation effort but were forced by the black nationalist mood to do it from the sidelines. Some of the radical whites had come out of the civil rights movement.

In the second half of the sixties, the nation's previously all-white universities had begun to open their doors to the children of the ghettos in much larger numbers. The major changes in the complexion of American universities and colleges were a direct outgrowth of the racial struggle that was taking place in the society. More black students were demanding entry to college. Allowing them in and providing financial aid so that they could come appeared to be a way to prevent further urban riots. Special programs and financial aid mechanisms were set up to attract minority students, led by the Ivy League colleges and supported by the government and foundations.

As the new students attempted to avoid cooptation—"brainwashing" that would rid them of their black consciousness—black power was the clear orientation of black student leaders in 1967 and 1968 (Edwards 1970). The students pressed for cultural programs and academic courses geared to their needs (see Wilkinson 1969, 129–46). Originating in the predominantly white colleges outside the South, the movement spread throughout the nation to include the traditionally black schools. Demands for black studies programs and the revision of racially biased curricula escalated after the murder of King. Exposure to traditional offerings demonstrated the neglect or distortion of black life that flowed from the society into its social sciences. Reviewing some of these biases, Edwards reproduces textbook citations to black people that speak for themselves (1970, 137). He writes:

In three sociology textbooks currently in wide use the word "negro" is indexed as follows:

(1)   Negro, p. 314
           see also:
                crime
                delinquency
                illegitimacy
                illiteracy
                deviate family structures

(2) Negro, p. 219
    see also:
      racial problems
      race riots

(3) Negro, p. 112
    see also:
      etiquette
      illegitimacy
      illiteracy
      "passing"
      prejudice
      race riots

Black students frequently found themselves out of place among the middle-class whites. Although some of the African Americans were of that class themselves, they emphasized the folk culture of the lower classes. There was often a highly separatist mood, and demands were made for separate black dormitories and autonomous black study programs controlled by black people.

Serious confrontations occurred between student groups and university authorities at the major universities of the country (Pinkney 1976, ch. 9, Edwards 1970).[6] The overreaction of forces of law and order were more vicious than they had ever been in the streets: black students were gunned down at Jackson, Mississippi, and Orangeburg, South Carolina, as were white students at Kent State. For a while, campus revolt was a media event and a concern to educational administrators throughout the country, and they shared accumulated wisdom regarding ways of disciplining deviant students and preventing further disruptions. The quiet, serious campuses of the 1970s replaced the volatile ones of the 1960s after several tumultuous years, seeming to follow student activism's pattern of decadinal contrast in America.

Competing and Complementary Movements

The civil rights movement fed into and affected a number of other movements that surfaced in the late 1960s. The organized protests of Chicanos, Native Americans, and other racial/ethnic minorities escalated. Welfare rights and prison reform were closely allied to the black struggle. Defense committees had been formed after the riots, aimed at seeing that black participants were not unjustly convicted.[7] The Plainfield, New

Jersey, Joint Defense Committee, like other similar groups, absorbed many white former civil rights activists of the area in its long-term efforts to obtain justice for black defendants accused of murder. Prisons were disproportionately filled with members of racial minorities; prison riots highlighted the overcrowding and inhumane conditions in many of them. It was natural that interest would turn to the state of the prisons.

The women's movement emerged as a stronger, more enduring, and a more significant movement than many others. The leaders of the newly resurgent women's movement recognized the extent of psychological subjugation among women and the need for consciousness-raising. African Americans had taught them the importance of creating self-pride and of countering the effects of early socialization.

Many of the young white women in this movement had developed a feminist consciousness out of their experiences in civil rights and the New Left. Mary King and Casey Hayden first raised the issue of women's oppression in a position paper written for discussion at a SNCC conference. Their later "memo," directing attention to women's unequal position in all spheres of life, was circulated to women around the country and had a profound influence on other white activists. The civil rights movement reflected the patriarchy of the larger society in some ways; it also gave these women the opportunity to develop themselves, find strengths, and become sensitized to all forms of oppression.

The civil rights movement took place prior to the resurgence of the renewed women's movement and gave it impetus. At that time, few people were consciously examining gender inequality, although they might be aware of it. In the 1980s, the women's movement acted back on the civil rights movement, as participants and scholars reexamined it from the perspective of gender. For example, Septima Clark told her autobiography to Cynthia Stokes Brown when she was 81 years old. One of the few women ever on the executive staff of the SCLC, she recalled that "the men" didn't listen to her very much (Clark and Brown 1986, 77). Ella Baker openly criticized elite leadership and male pomposity. Although she set up the first office of the SCLC, its officers were reluctant to name her executive director (Morris 1984, 102–4).

SNCC was, at first, relatively egalitarian. However, as indicated in chapter 6, there were serious concerns about bringing white women to Mississippi for the 1964 Freedom Summer. McAdam, who was able to locate and study the original applications to the project, noted a definite sexist bias in the treatment of women volunteers. Females were asked more questions about their views on sex than were men, and their attractiveness or lack of it was often mentioned by interviewers (McAdam 1988, 58–60).

In the main, male leadership went unquestioned, especially in the SCLC, despite women's major role in mass mobilizations. For many reasons—not least that the civil rights movement faced a very male-dominated power structure—men were given most of the formal leadership posts in the movement. Another reason was African American males' self-conscious quest for manhood and their women's encouragement of male strength. Manhood was a strong theme of the movement, made very explicit in the signs of striking Memphis garbage workers that said, "I am a man."

While aspects of the women's movement consciously emulated the civil rights movement, the two struggles were not united. Black women tended to see feminists as middle-class oriented at a time when sensitivity to the problems of the poor was needed. Few white women would agree that racial equality was more important than sexual equality, and few black women took the opposite position. They saw the existing system as oppressive to both black men and black women. The feminist goal of increasing access to paid work made little sense to those who had always had to work out of economic necessity. Inadequate pay and marginal jobs forced many lower-socioeconomic-status women onto the welfare rolls. The welfare rights movement was also primarily a women's movement—one of poor black women—and more relevant to the special problems of the race. But it was short-lived (see West 1981). Only much later did African American women openly criticize the male chauvinism they had encountered in the civil rights and black power movements (see Giddings 1984, White 1984). Today a key group of black feminists are developing feminist theory that encompasses analysis of the interrelationships of race, gender and class (see, for example, D. King 1988).

Black people and white women frequently saw themselves as competing for the same scarce goods—affirmative action spots in universities and corporations. Women constituted over half the population, and they were voters. Without the two important groups utilizing affirmative action procedures and pressing the government to pursue them, both might have lost out. Affected individuals tended not to view it in these terms. Another group of discriminated-against persons, lesbians and gays, began openly to mobilize to demand equal rights.

Affirmative action was first mandated in a presidential executive order in 1963, and in 1967 women were added to the groups protected. Because selection procedures for jobs and schools tended to work against

Martin Luther King, Jr., marches with community leaders in support of the Memphis Sanitation Workers' Strike. *Ernest C. Withers.*

members of minorities, the affirmative action orders proposed that spe-
,cial efforts be made to recruit them. Each institution was asked to set
goals and timetables for the attainment of minority representation that
fairly reflected the available pool of such applicants. In the 1970s, there
was considerable controversy over the application of these rules, as government, business, and university functionaries were charged with the
enforcement of minority rights.

Affirmative action measures can be seen as an institutionalization of
civil rights goals. They were an effort to counteract the longstanding,
previously institutionalized racism that automatically ensured normal
discriminatory behavior—such as recruiting from all-white schools or all-
white networks. In the case of women, they sought to provide an antidote to everyday sexism which automatically eliminated women from
competition under a variety of pretexts. Black women, faced with double
jeopardy, were at the bottom of the job ladder. Working through established institutions on a case-by-case basis came to replace nonviolent
protest and black power pronouncements as a mode of action, especially
on the question of jobs for educated or skilled black people.

Unfortunately, the 1980s—the Reagan years—saw an open assault on
the principles of affirmative action by the federal government, exemplified in such actions as the appointment to the U.S. Civil Rights Commission of persons who opposed affirmative action and the selection of
conservative federal judges who would construe laws narrowly. This
trend continued under President George Bush (*New York Times*, 10 April
1990, A1, A19).

Why the Civil Rights Movement Declined: A Summary

The first chapters of this book explained the conditions conducive to the
rise of the movement. Transformations in those conditions led to its decline.[8] At the beginning, the southern movement could build upon preexisting social networks created by the major black institutions: the
churches, black colleges, and civic and fraternal organizations. Important
and charismatic race leaders came out of these groups. The movement's
ideology rested upon established national and religious values. A tactic
was adopted that made the enemy seem wrong and the protesters right.
The regional emphasis and regional goals provided clear-cut issues that
many northern whites could support. The Kennedy and Johnson administrations, interested in black votes and representing the party of social
concern, could be forced into action on behalf of the movement. Violence

against unarmed demonstrators received wide media coverage and drew additional support. Legislation was passed and federal troops brought in at crucial times.

As at the outset, the interaction of internal factors with the movement's external environment was crucial in determining its demise. The meaning of many of the concrete events and controversies described can be understood in terms of social movement theory (see the Appendix). The psychological state of black people predisposing them to seek change does not disappear. But their belief in the possibility of advances is crucial to the upsurge or continuance of the movement at any particular time. Various opinion polls support the notion that, by the end of the sixties, African Americans were disillusioned and less optimistic about the value of continued demonstrations. Civil rights organizations were unable to establish the strong community base in the North that they had in the South. The movement was now fragmented and decentralized, weakening its overall impact. Ideologies competed, and the media found the black power movement more newsworthy and exciting than the message of nonviolence. Despite the revolutionary rhetoric, the cultural nationalist wing deflected attention from political goals. But the perception of black power was that it was dangerous. It did not rely upon the accepted ideologies of the country that had made the nonviolent movement morally unassailable.

Once official desegregation and voting rights had been won, the civil rights movement also needed new goals. These were more national in scope and at the same time more threatening to the official economic system—capitalism. Where the FBI had made unfounded allegations about communist influence in the early stages of the civil rights movement, it could now point to the open verbal challenges to capitalism and imperialism made by black power advocates. In the name of national security and anticommunism, all kinds of illegal activities could be justified to eliminate black power and civil rights leaders. Opponents made few fine distinctions among the black protest organizations and saw all but the most moderate as antigovernment (Garrow 1981). Undercover and infiltration activities already in practice could be and were heightened. Various lawsuits charging the government with illegal entry, harassment, and violations of civil rights continued into the 1980s. Ignored was the fact that radical rhetoric did not appear to translate into comparable political strategies. The Panthers, for example, used a free breakfast program for poor children as one of its most successful efforts.

Probably there was little chance that radical blacks would combine with white Communists at this time. Some black leaders were trying to evolve their own form of socialism, coupled with a separatist mood and sometimes pan-Africanism. But others were trying to develop black businesses and to gain better access to income under the current economic system.

Perhaps more threatening than black power advocates whose anti-white, antiestablishment posture made them ready targets was the changed position of Martin King. His antiwar position and concern with economic issues before his death were a greater challenge than desegregation had been. Lacking the support of the federal government, isolated from other black organizations because of his anti–Vietnam war position and loyalty to nonviolence, King's potential for bringing black people together was still viewed as real. Until his death, white liberal funds flowed to the SCLC. Afterward, they were diverted to the moderate NAACP. A disunited, financially impoverished movement was confronted by powerful, increasingly hostile agents of social control, who capitalized on the internal discord.

The African American people recognized that the environment of the 1970s, with its law-and-order themes, was not conducive to further open protest. Cities that had experienced the death and destruction of major riots did not repeat them. Such tendencies to violence that remained were successfully repelled by the government. SNCC and CORE were defunct and SCLC weakened by internal disagreement after King's death. Indeed, King had mediated over its many internal conflicts for years, holding the group together.

It was left to government functionaries, working within schools, businesses, and local communities to administer the laws and executive orders that had eventuated from the movement. In this, they would be prodded by militant individuals and the traditional black organizations. Black caucuses in trade unions, professions, and other settings pushed for adequate representation of their interests and served as specialized pressure groups. The new African American officeholders throughout the nation worked through electoral politics rather than confrontation, while intellectuals from the group debated the relevance of class analysis to racial problems (Wilson 1978, 1987; Willie 1979).

Progress in a cause is not continuous. The civil rights and black power movements had created significant changes, although much remained to be done. It would require another book to analyze the progress (or lack of it) of African Americans in the years since the late 1960s. However, it is clear that in the 1980s, economic depression and the policies of the Reagan administration threatened to wipe out the victories that were so dearly won. A rallying of forces prevented Ronald Reagan from scuttling the Voting Rights Act in 1982, demonstrating that strength can still be marshaled to support elementary rights.

Social movements do not die while their grievances remain: they experience peaks and ebbs, maintaining holding actions until the environment once again becomes conducive to open protest. The bipolarization of blacks and whites noted by the Kerner Commission is still evident in many walks of life—including the nation's colleges. Against this trend, Jesse Jackson tried to rebuild the civil rights coalition (this time a "rainbow" coalition) to support his 1988 bid for the Democratic presidential nomination. Appealing to all population groups and building a strong base in the black community, Jackson came in second in a field of seven candidates. His use of electoral politics as a route to fighting inequalities represents only one approach, but one that a number of former civil rights activists have embraced. As long as grievances continue, the struggle will resurface. The question is: when, and in what form?

Appendix: Civil Rights as a Social Movement

*My job was to go into the towns and break the hold that the power struc-
ture had on the people and get them aroused and get them to marchin',
picketin', demonstratin', and goin' to jail. That's how I ended up in jail
ninety-six times, 'cause that was my job. Dr. King saw in me that part
of me that I could arouse others and get others to stand up.*
                                       —Hosea Williams, SCLC field staff director

The historical details of a movement can be fascinating to the interested
person, but in themselves they do not answer all the whys that arise.
Sociology has developed social movement theory in an attempt to explain
individual cases—such as civil rights or the women's movement—in
terms of general principles. This theoretical appendix presents the ori-
entations that are implicit in the body of the work.

Social Movements and Collective Behavior

A social movement is a type of behavior in which a large number of participants consciously attempt to change existing institutions and establish
a new order of life. A new order of life, in this case, would be a system
in which African Americans have an opportunity to share all the country
has to offer on an equal basis with others. A broader definition of social
movements would include not only persons who engage in group action
for a cause but also those who agree with them on the need to change
(McCarthy and Zald 1977, 1217–18).

Collective behavior directed toward changing some aspect of the social
structure involves people who are aware of the issues and of one another, not necessarily members of formal groups. People less prone to
join a movement organization may be willing to take part in large demonstrations, where they swell the numbers known to favor the cause. Or

they may watch from the sidelines, applauding or jeering. The issue of mobilizing support among those who share beliefs is a major one for social movements.

While much collective behavior, such as that of crowds, is relatively spontaneous, social movements are more formalized, and when they are large, they are made up of many local, regional, and national movement organizations. Each tries to formulate ideologies, attract members, develop strategies and tactics, gain the support of the uncommitted public, and counter the forces of opposition. These are the characteristics of social movements that have been used to analyze the civil rights struggle.

How Movements Develop

What should we look at in trying to understand the course of the movement? Society is complex and social occurrences are sometimes random, accidental, unpredictable, or "disorderly" (Perrow 1979). A movement is not a monolithic, preplanned event. Thousands of individuals and organizations of varied class and racial backgrounds became involved in civil rights activities. Plans and strategies were continually formulated, but the movement had to respond to unpredicted events, the strategizing of the opposition, and the wishes and desires of constituents. Nowhere was this more evident than in its first major event, the Montgomery bus boycott. This event set the tone for much that would follow, but at first the leadership was unsure of how effectively their people could be mobilized and how much endurance they would have. Even leadership is sometimes a matter of chance. Martin Luther King, Jr., was selected to head the group organizing the Montgomery movement partly because he had been in Montgomery for only two years. He had not had time to become involved in any local factional disputes nor to be subjected to attempts at cooptation by white leaders. Given King's superior education, strong family background, and impressive oratorical style, he became the choice of more experienced community activists such as E. D. Nixon.

As chapter 2 shows, a buildup of events sets the stage for the explosion of a social movement. Once begun, movements feed back into themselves, affecting the people and organizations involved. Tactics are modified, new kinds of people are recruited, opposition grows or fades, and the movement in turn must adjust to these changes. In modern times, the mass media have come to play an important role. The attention of newspapers and television to various events helps to create their importance; other occurrences, for whatever reason, appear to be less newsworthy. History is then written in terms of the boldest, most noted undertakings, and much of the quiet, persistent, often locally originated action gets overlooked.[1] For example, CORE had many daring and hard-working chapters in the North and West whose civil rights demonstrations were overshadowed by the media's attention to the South. The movement was assisted in the latter region by a couple of vehemently racist sheriffs whose brutal actions were captured by excellent photographs.

Systematic explanations flow more logically after a movement has occurred than when one is trying to predict its future direction. A given movement often provokes the creation of new theory to better explain it, and that is true of the one under study. Scholars are sifting through the mass of information now available and are reexamining so-far-accepted interpretations (see, for example, Branch 1988; Fairclough 1987; Garrow 1986; McAdam 1981, 1988; Morris 1979, 1981, 1984; and Weisbrot 1990).

Theorists tend to agree about the kind of interacting factors (variables) involved in the development of social movements, but they show less unanimity when assessing the importance of each. Are underlying dissatisfactions or grievances the main element to study, or is the ability to attract and mobilize people, money, and public opinion most crucial? Earlier theories concentrated on the origins of movements and the psychological states of their participants (Smelser 1962; Blumer 1951). Resource mobilization theorists pay less attention to the characteristics of the group seeking change than to the forces that limit and control it from the outside (Zald and McCarthy 1979, 1–2).

The society as it is, the established system, has the stamp of legitimacy and stability; it is backed by the official power of government and police forces. Change will bring disruption to those currently privileged, and hence resistance is inevitable. The term *social control* has been given to all the factors that operate against or inhibit the progress of the movement from the outside. The movement environment—the general society in which it operates and especially those parts of the society that will be affected by change—provides one set of dynamics that must be taken into account. Another interconnected set of dynamics is, of course, the volatile inner life of the movement: its beginnings, concrete expression in organizations, manner of attracting followers, and the strategies and tactics used to attain its objectives. Parts of the environing system will be hostile, parts neutral, and parts sympathetic. Movement leaders try to grasp the opportunities that seem available; they seek to sway decision makers, appeal to public opinion, and use any pressure at their command.

Of course, both interacting systems are important. The civil rights movement was clearly shaped by the determined efforts of the protesting group. But it was also influenced by those in power, as well as the changing national and international scene.

This point of view is shared by McAdam, who employs what he calls a political process model: "Neither environmental factors nor factors internal to the movement are sufficient to account for the generation and development of social insurgency. . . . The political process model rests on the assumption that social movements are an ongoing product of the favorable interplay of *both* sets of factors. The specific mix of factors may change from one phase of the movement to another, but the basic dynamic remains the same" (1982, 39–40).

Figure 2 depicts these two interacting systems, the social movement and its environment. The movement and its varying internal aspects are presented at the left in column A as a thrust for change penetrating the surrounding environment, column B, the society. All elements on both sides interact with and are affected by the others, but the connections between some are more direct and obvious. For example, it is relatively easy to point to a precipitating incident (point 3 of B) which serves as "the last straw," a final act of insult or injustice that triggers response from an aggrieved group already prone to action (point 3 of A). Actions originate on both sides of the line, as do responses to actions. In fact, the borders fluctuate, as some people and resources shift from one side to the other.

Let us look at each of these points briefly.

1. Many terms have been used to describe the psychological aspects of strain; all refer to the felt discomfort, upset, and maladjustment of individuals who feel unfairly disadvantaged. Here, so-called maladjustment can be a healthy response to an intolerable situation, pushing the group to seek change. King wrote of the experiences of the early civil rights protesters as being psychologically liberating. Black citizens were acting out long-suppressed feelings about the injustice of segregation. Similarly, there are many analyses of the kinds of environmental situations that produce a sense of grievance. For example, a gap between expectations and realities, or between actual conditions and official standards may cause anguish. The American legal system is supposed to operate fairly but frequently does not in the case of racial minorities.

Figure 2. The Movement and Its Environment

A. Movement	B. Environment
1. Psychological state of constituents predisposing them to seek change	1. Situations that create strain, dissatisfaction, dissonance
2. Belief in the need for and possibility of change	2. Structures and processes providing avenues for change or making change more possible
3. Group reaction to immediate incidents that trigger readiness to protest	3. Precipitating incidents that trigger onset of movement
4. Mobilization of constituents and other resources through preexisting social networks, other means of communication	4. Potential resources that may be mobilized, e.g., sympathetic persons, votes, the uncommitted or uninformed public
5. Ideology explaining goals and rationale of the movement	5. General societywide principles that can be drawn upon
6. Formation of various movement organizations which cooperate and compete with each other; emergence of leaders	6. Support of or opposition to various movement organizations and leaders
7. Changing strategies and tactics	7. Opposition and control; governmental role; counter-movements

"Usual" discriminatory practices may become more offensive under wartime conditions, when minorities are called upon to prove patriotism. High occupational status combined with low racial status may cause a sense of conflict or dissonance.

2. Unfair conditions or other sources of strain need to be viewed as social rather than personal problems. The situation of strain "must be made meaningful to the potential actors" (Smelser 1962, 16). A generalized belief identifies the source of strain, its characteristics, and what is needed to correct the situation. This belief must include the idea that success is possible (Wilson 1973, 48–49; McAdam 1982, ch. 3). Within the movement environment, there may be shifts in power, economic conditions, or culture that are conducive to change. A series of Supreme Court decisions, culminating in the historic 1954 school desegregation case (*Brown* v. *Board of Education*) made change through legal structures seem more possible. Wartime and the need for full population uti-

lization constitutes an emergency that tends to work to the advantage of minorities. In contrast, opposition to the Vietnam war drew attention away from domestic civil rights issues.

3. Given the other factors creating readiness to protest, an immediate incident, such as an unfair beating or arrest of a member of the aggrieved group, can bring on group reaction. A precipitating incident, a specific event, is needed to set into motion initial movement activities. For example, the arrest of a well-known black woman, Rosa Parks, ignited the Birmingham bus protest. Leaders of the black community had been waiting for such an incident to dramatize their complaints (Lewis 1978, ch. 3).

4. Communication about and sharing of group grievances must take place. These are facilitated by the presence of preexisting social networks: groupings of and connections among people who have previously interacted with one another in positive ways (Gerlach and Hine 1970, ch. 4). The very oppression of segregation had reinforced the maintenance of a separate black social world, held together by an intricate network of kinship, religious, fraternal, and social groups that were wholly black. A separate African American press had flourished, to provide fuller and unbiased coverage of news about the black community. Information could and did spread quickly once the civil rights movement started. There are also potentially mobilizable resources within the larger society. These include people who are neutral, uninformed, or even sympathetic, and who may be swayed by arguments and events to donate time, money, or votes. Such potential support might be drawn from the national government and the court system, the foundations, and white liberals and radicals. The first major event in Birmingham was supported by donations that came in from around the world, as well as collections regularly taken at local mass meetings.

5. Every movement develops a system of ideas explaining and justifying its goals. Ideology is geared toward both the movement's members, or constituents, and potential outside allies. It draws upon society's values and principles, such as those embodied in the Constitution, Bill of Rights, and Judeo-Christian humanitarian ideals. Members are given hope and a sense of noble purpose. Those opposing the movement compete in terms of ideas as well as actions.

6. Many organizations, local and national, take form, some more radical and some more conservative. Leaders of various kinds emerge. Their groups compete for members, publicity, and public support, but together they form the movement. The environment's response to dif-

ferent organizations and leaders varies. Preferences develop for particular leaders, who may role-play effectively for the good of the movement.
When there is too much dissension, they may be unable to contain their
disagreements. Outside forces respond to and sometimes foment disunity within the movement. The major civil rights organizations were
able to cooperate up to a point, when extreme disagreement finally ended
joint efforts.

7. Long-run plans are developed—for example, the use of nonviolent
direct action in the quest for moral victory. Tactics are everyday tools
and actions based on the general strategies. Both are modified in response to unfolding events. Opposition to the movement may be expected to develop. Forces of social control include all people and groups
that operate against or inhibit the progress of the movement, for example, new laws passed by state legislatures to circumvent court decisions,
antiintegrationist organizations such as the White Citizens' Councils, and
hostile sheriffs.

Strategies and Tactics of Black Protest

Just as issues appear and reappear throughout black history, so do different strategies and tactics of protest. We saw how they surfaced in the
1950s and 1960s. Let us examine here the main strategies (long-run
plans) and tactics (day-by-day actions) that have been employed in the
black struggle for equality. Some tactics supplement one another, but
some run contrary to a competing group's ideology—such as the juxta-
position of armed self-defense with nonviolence. Strategies and tactics
may be grouped into the following broad categories:

Education
The legal approach
Nonviolent direct action
Use of the vote
Self-help schemes
Cultural identity and consciousness-raising programs
Self-defense, retaliatory violence
Urban rebellion

Naturally, these overlap; long-run objectives may be sought by a combination of tactics and indeed were during the civil rights movement.

Education is often thought of as the mildest of methods, relying as it does on persuasion rather than pressure. It is almost always a necessary supplement to other efforts. Education includes attempts to both inform and persuade outsiders of the justice of the cause, as well as to create awareness within the minority group. For years, moderate white organizations in the South engaged in data collection and the dissemination of information about inequality. Human relations groups were formed in many towns and cities of the nation to create dialogue between blacks and whites. School programs, debates, Brotherhood Week speakers, workshops, interracial weekends were all educational methods developed by human relations specialists who sought to affect people emotionally as well as intellectually.

Creative writers sometimes play a major role in developing empathy with those who are oppressed. In this case, major black novelists and poets communicated the feelings of their people to a wider audience. Occasionally a black artist, such as the singer and actor Paul Robeson, jeopardizes his or her career by using performances as a platform to speak out against discrimination.[2] As part of the counter-movement, a whole literature of scientific racism supported the posture of those who would slow down black advance. Television quickly became one more medium of mass communication tending to stereotype racial minorities. Protest arose against negative film and television portrayals that affected vast audiences. But television also became a significant vehicle in spreading news about civil rights demonstrations and in showing the contrast between nonviolent protesters and armed policemen.

The legal approach consists of every attempt to work through the official legal system—by test cases, pressure for the passage of specific laws or the repeal of others, challenges to the unfair operation of the courts or of police power, and the like. This tactic was most identified with the NAACP, founded in the aftermath of northern riots in which many black people were killed. The organization, we noted, attained a major victory in winning the landmark 1954 school desegregation case (and others leading up to it), an important precipitating factor bringing about the movement of the 1960s. The legal method and the organization that embodied it came under sharp attack when state legislatures successfully undermined attempts to enforce court decisions. The NAACP was for many years the only national protest organization with local branches in the South.

The use of nonviolent techniques was for some a limited tactic and for others a long-term strategy and philosophy. Those who argued for nonviolent direct action first saw it as a necessary supplement to legal action. Noncompliance and evasion often rendered legal victories virtually worthless. As we saw in chapter 5, the Freedom Rides of 1961 were an attempt to test desegregation decrees in interstate transportation. Segregation had been outlawed, but until these CORE-instigated test rides and the highly publicized violence against the riders occurred, the law was disregarded. Nonviolent demonstrations were often accompanied by singing and chanting, helping to create unity as well as a mood of defiance and persistence. Freedom songs were an important and inspiring part of the civil rights movement. Mass meetings served many purposes. Forbidden under slavery, they occurred secretly, becoming a means for sharing information, making joint decisions, planning escapes, and bolstering unity. In the movement of the 1960s, black churches became the site of frequent mass meetings and also the targets of terrorist bombs. The peaceful mass meeting was recognized as a dangerous tool.

The exercise of the vote is not only the sign and symbol of citizenship but, as suggested earlier, has often been viewed as essential for the attainment of other goals. The many devices invented by southern state legislatures—white primaries, the grandfather clause, difficult and unfair written or oral examinations for persons seeking to register—were often supplemented by threats of violence or economic reprisal against those who dared defy them. Against these odds, campaigns to register black voters became a central aim of the civil rights movement. The failure to break the power of the white primaries eventually—perhaps paradoxically—led black power advocates away from reform efforts toward more revolutionary postures.

Self-help efforts have always been extremely varied and accompanied many other strategies and tactics. Voter education became a necessary adjunct to registration attempts in the face of every kind of obstacle created by southern white registrars. But self-help was sometimes advocated as an accommodationist response to white hostility, as in the repressive period at the turn of the century. Structures were developed in the segregated black world through which networks of ties were built, within and between communities. These could be called upon in time of stress. Black churches, colleges, and fraternal organizations, despite their sometime conciliatory positions toward white power structures, were a source of community strength. Ministerial alliances, when acting in concerted fashion, could quickly communicate with a large proportion of black citizenry, especially in the South. Formal education was strongly valued, seen perhaps overoptimistically as the key to advancement. The predominantly black colleges provided a training ground for leadership, despite the varying postures of their presidents, who were almost always dependent on white funding and white sponsors. Through the college and fraternity system, sponsorship and aid could be provided to fellow blacks. Without a strong preexisting network of black organizations, the civil rights movement would not have taken place as it did (Morris 1981).

In the 1960s the Nation of Islam emphasized separation and self-development, a form of self-help, as its alternative to integrationist aims. Pride in black culture has sometimes but not always been tied to separatist movements. Consciousness-raising is the individual concomitant of pride in culture and community, an antidote to self-rejection and despair. A magnificent leader, Frederick Douglass, knew even in slavery that he ought to be free, but often the burden of racial stereotypes crippled the aspirations of other black individuals.

Finally, the normal human reaction of defense against assault has surfaced at various times throughout black history, sometimes as a conscious action and other times as spontaneous collective and unplanned human behavior. Individual acts of revolt by slaves resulted in dire physical punishment and death. Slave revolts and insurrections epitomized organized efforts to win goals through active personal struggle. The number of these has been debated but the several well-known major revolts were enough to bring about widespread fear of black violence. When slaves were finally allowed to join the Union Armies they demonstrated unusual valor, perhaps because they could, at last, openly fight for freedom.

Most of the time black people and their leaders have sought a peaceful redress of grievances. White mobs had attacked blacks many times before, but it was only in 1919, after many black servicemen had served overseas for their country, that the latter retaliated in kind. Even as Martin Luther King, Jr., was preaching nonviolence, others were in disagreement with his approach. Malcolm X maintained that self-defense was a basic right, and many heard him. Self-defense groups formed in some southern communities where the Ku Klux Klan actively pursued civil rights workers. Perhaps the most open expression of black anger occurred in the urban rebellions or riots of the 1960s (see chapter 9). In the second half of this decade, masses of urban blacks—their ongoing problems exacerbated by indifferent local governments and trigger-happy police—took to the streets, looting and destroying property in the ghettos. This collective action was understood by most black people as a form of protest. The urban-based Black Panthers openly espoused the carrying of guns for self-defense. Within a few years, their numbers were decimated by raids and shoot-outs and FBI-created dissension.

Riots, Revolutions, and Social Movements

Riots, one form of collective behavior, are hostile outbursts that express underlying tension and conflict that have not been satisfactorily channeled into more directed behavior. Riots, spontaneous mass marches, and the gathering of crowds are all types of elementary collective behavior that may be temporary or single-time occurrences. But when the same underlying dissatisfactions and discontents are channeled into organized, ongoing group actions, they are part of the formation of social movements. During a movement's history, incidents of collective behavior are prone to occur alongside more structured, planned actions. Opponents of the movement may also take part in spontaneous group action as well as organized campaigns.

When the aim is to overthrow an existing social order completely through the use of violence, a movement is revolutionary rather than reformist. As pointed out earlier, many have characterized the urban disorders of the 1960s as rebellion, action lying between these two types.

Despite the careful definitions of theorists, terms such as *revolution* (Killian, *The Impossible Revolution* 1968) and *revolt* (Lomax, *The Negro Revolt* 1963) have frequently been applied to both the nonviolent and black power phases of the movement. They dramatize the drastic nature of the changes sought, the massive mobilization of a large portion of the black population as well as of many whites, and the dramatic changes in consciousness that were a product of the 1960s decade. From the vantage point of nationally proclaimed values, Americans of African descent were asserting their right to be part of the accepted system. They were not challenging the ideals but the reality. In this sense, the civil rights movement was clearly reformist. Yet the South had never accepted the national system and even passed many laws contravening it. As most white southerners saw it, the movement sought to destroy their way of life.

Many have written of the dramatic revolution in black consciousness once people faced their oppressors head-on. The stigmatized identity and passive resistance were transmuted into pride and bravery. Later it became translated into expressions of cultural and political nationalism. Changes in white consciousness regarding blacks were less dramatic, but nonetheless many white persons were forced to confront their own racist images and come to terms with their prejudices. The changes in attitudes and behavior of certain national political figures, such as President Lyndon Johnson, were striking. Technically, the civil rights movement was a reform movement, dedicated to making the United States live up to its democratic ideals. The black power phase and the urban disorders constituted a rebellion, not a true revolution. Yet, if we define *revolution* in a less technical sense to mean creating a major change in behavior or consciousness, then the civil rights movement can be seen to have had many revolutionary aspects.

Chronology

1953   A successful ten-day boycott of buses takes place in Baton Rouge, Louisiana, in June. Led by Rev. T. J. Jemison, a former NAACP president, black citizens gain modifications in the segregation rules.

1954   On 17 May the U.S. Supreme Court (in *Brown* v. *Board of Education of Topeka Kansas*) declares segregation in the public schools to be inherently unequal, and mandates desegregation.

The first Citizens' Council is formed in Indianola, Mississippi, in July by whites determined to resist and nullify the school desegregation decision.

1955   The *"Brown II"* decision of the Supreme Court implements the 1954 ruling by requiring desegregation "with all deliberate speed."

The Interstate Commerce Commission outlaws segregated buses and waiting rooms for interstate passengers, but the order is generally ignored.

Emmett Till, a visiting teenage boy from Chicago, is viciously lynched in Mississippi on 28 August.

On 1 December Rosa Parks is arrested for violating the bus segregation ordinance in Montgomery, Alabama.

The Montgomery Bus Boycott begins on 5 December; the Reverend Martin Luther King, Jr., is elected president of the Montgomery Improvement Association.

The Supreme Court orders the University of Alabama to admit Autherine Lucy for graduate study.

1956 On 3 February, Autherine Lucy attempts to enter the University of Alabama, and white students riot for three days. First suspended "for her own safety," she is expelled permanently by the trustees. The university remains segregated for seven more years.

Southern senators, led by Harry Byrd of Virginia, sign a "Southern Manifesto" denouncing the Supreme Court's desegregation decision.

The Supreme Court upholds a favorable district court decision declaring Montgomery's bus segregation to be illegal. On 21 December, Montgomery's buses are integrated, and the bus boycott is called off after 381 days.

1957 In July Tuskegee, Alabama is redistricted in order to exclude most black voters from the city. This leads to a selective buying campaign against white merchants, lasting for four years. The vote is restored to black citizens in 1961.

The Southern Christian Leadership Conference (SCLC) is founded in January (at first under another name), and Martin Luther King, Jr., is chosen president. In February it acquires its permanent name.

Governor Orval Faubus of Arkansas calls out the National Guard to prevent nine black students from entering all-white Central High School in Little Rock. A court order requires Faubus to withdraw them. After threats of mob violence, President Eisenhower orders paratroopers to Little Rock to enforce integration and places 10,000 National Guardsmen on federal service. The troops remain the rest of the year to protect the students, who are guided by Daisy Bates, president of the state NAACP.

The first Civil Rights Act in 82 years is passed by Congress. Though weak, it has investigative and advisory functions and the power of subpoena. The Civil Rights Commission is established.

1958 A successful voter registration drive in Fayette and Haywood counties, Tennessee, leads to severe economic reprisals. Many black sharecroppers are evicted. In 1960 "Tent City" is set up and a national appeal for aid made.

1960 On 1 February, four black students—Ezell Blair, Jr., Joseph McNeil, David Richmond, and Franklin McClain—sit in at the

Woolworth's lunch counter in Greensboro, North Carolina. The action is repeated by college students throughout the South. Sympathetic picketing and boycotts occur in the North. Within a year and a half, demonstrations have been held in more than 100 cities and towns in every southern and border state.

The student demonstrators meet from 15 to 17 April at Shaw University in Raleigh, North Carolina. The Student Nonviolent Coordinating Committee (SNCC) is founded.

Dr. King is jailed in Atlanta on 19 October. Democratic presidential nominee John F. Kennedy telephones Coretta Scott King to express concern. This act is credited with gaining him the election in November.

1961 On 4 May Freedom Riders, led by James Farmer of the Congress of Racial Equality (CORE), leave Washington, D.C., by bus in order to expose illegal segregation practices in terminal accommodations. On 14 May a white mob burns a Freedom Riders' bus near Anniston, Alabama. Klansmen in Birmingham beat Riders aboard a second bus. The Freedom Rides continue. In September segregation in all interstate transportation facilities is declared illegal by the Interstate Commerce Commission.

Efforts to desegregate facilities in Albany, Georgia, are launched by local leaders (the Albany Movement). Students test terminal facilities and are jailed. The SCLC is called in. This campaign is viewed as relatively unsuccessful.

Voter registration campaigns are intensified. On 25 September Herbert Lee, a local activist, is killed in Amite County, Mississippi.

1962 The Council of Federated Organizations (COFO) is formed to coordinate voting registration activities.

On 1 October James Meredith becomes the first African American to attend class at the University of Mississippi after a weekend of riots, during which the National Guard is called in.

1963 On 3 April major demonstrations are launched in Birmingham by the SCLC to protest segregation. These continue throughout May. School children are recruited for marches and demonstrations. Police Commissioner Eugene ("Bull") Connor responds with police dogs, fire hoses, and mass arrests.

William Moore, a white CORE member who had planned a march from Chattanooga to Jackson to protest segregation is murdered in April. CORE takes up the march, joined by other organizations.

On 10 May Birmingham's white leaders agree to a desegregation plan. That night, Dr. King's motel headquarters and his brother's home are bombed and blacks riot until dawn.

Major demonstrations begin in Danville, Virginia, which are later joined by the SCLC.

On 11 June Alabama governor George Wallace tries to block integration at the University of Alabama by "standing in the door." The first student is admitted.

The next day, Medgar Evers, head of the Mississippi NAACP, is ambushed and shot to death at his home in Jackson, Mississippi.

The March on Washington, sponsored by a coalition of civil rights groups, churches, and some unions, attracts hundreds of thousands of peaceful demonstrators to the nation's capitol on 28 August.

September is marked by the death of four black girls and the injuring of many other people in the bombing of Birmingham's Sixteenth Street Baptist Church.

In November a slate of "freedom candidates" headed by Aaron Henry draws the votes of nearly 80,000 black Mississippians in a mock election paralleling the regular election for state governor from which they are excluded. To aid in the registration and organizing effort, SNCC imported about 100 northern white students.

An assassin kills President John F. Kennedy in Dallas, Texas, on 22 November.

1964 Hundreds of volunteers arrive to work in Freedom Summer, the Mississippi voter registration project organized by the combined civil rights organizations. Three civil rights workers, James Chaney, Mickey Schwerner, and Andrew Goodman, are abducted on 21 June while investigating an incidence of violence. Their bodies are found buried near Philadelphia, Mississippi, on 4 August.

The 1964 Civil Rights Act is passed by Congress on 2 July and signed by President Lyndon Johnson.

The Mississippi Freedom Democratic party challenges the seating of the "regular" (all-white) Democratic delegation at the party's September national convention. It rejects an unsatisfactory compromise, but black people overwhelmingly help reelect Johnson to the presidency in November.

Martin Luther King, Jr., receives the Nobel Peace prize.

1965 Lyndon Johnson outlines the Great Society program to attack poverty.

The desegregation campaign in Selma, Alabama, escalates between January and March. In nearby Marion, a local youth, Jimmie Lee Jackson, is shot by a trooper on 18 February and later dies.

Malcolm X is shot to death at the Audubon Ballroom in New York City on 21 February.

A planned march in Selma results in "Bloody Sunday," 7 March, when civil rights workers are charged by police on horses as they attempt to cross the Edmund Pettus Bridge. The next day, James Reeb, a Unitarian minister from Boston, dies of wounds inflicted by a club-wielding segregationist in Selma. King is criticized for agreeing to shorten a second march. On 17 March U.S. District Judge Frank M. Johnson, Jr., issues a court order, ruling that black protesters have the right to march from Selma to Montgomery. The massive march takes place from 21 to 25 March, drawing civil rights activists from all over the country. Viola Liuzzo, a white woman from Detroit, is killed on the last day of the march as she is transporting participants between Selma and Montgomery.

In August the Voting Rights Act is signed into law by Lyndon Johnson.

In the same month, the first major urban conflagration occurs in Watts, California, as black ghetto dwellers burn and loot following a police arrest of a black youth.

1966 James Meredith sets out on a one-man "March against Fear" in Mississippi in June and is gunned down by a sniper. Leaders of three major civil rights organizations continue the march, during which time Stokely Carmichael popularizes the slogan "black power."

The formation of the Black Panther party by Huey Newton and Bobby Seale takes place in Oakland, California, in October.

Martin Luther King, Jr., SNCC, and CORE take positions opposing the war in Vietnam.

SCLC begins a massive campaign in Chicago, which goes through spring and summer.

Urban rebellions take place in Chicago and Cleveland. Riots in major cities continue through 1967.

SNCC votes to exclude white members. CORE endorses the black power concept.

1967   The president appoints a National Advisory Commission on Civil Disorders to inquire into the causes of the urban rebellions. The report is published in 1968.

1968   Martin Luther King, Jr., is assassinated on 4 April while assisting striking sanitation workers in Memphis, Tennessee, in their quest for union recognition and improved wages. Massive riots take place throughout the nation.

Ralph Abernathy and the SCLC go ahead with the Poor People's campaign that had been planned by Dr. King. Thousands of the poor camp out in "Resurrection City" in Washington, D.C., in May and June.

Robert Kennedy, a candidate for the Democratic presidential nomination, is assassinated on 4 June as he leaves a rally.

Richard Nixon is elected president.

Notes

Chapter One

1. The general social movement seeking equal rights for black people has been in process since the earliest controversies over slavery, as shall be argued in the text, but it has had several distinct phases. At least one sociologist would have the civil rights movement include the litigation phase—the pursuit of desegregation and civil rights through the courts and legal system that culminated in the historic 1954 Supreme Court decision (Willie 1981). The choice here is to recognize that period as leading up to the period of nonviolent demonstrations here called the modern civil rights movement. Unless specified otherwise, further references to the civil rights movement in this text will mean its modern phase; the term had been used in earlier protest.

2. The nomenclature selected to refer to a people is often problematic. Minority groups tend to be "named" by the dominants; hence, liberation movements frequently seek a change of name. Group members themselves modify their preferences over time, and that has clearly occurred in the case of black Americans. While the first edition of this book was being written, two terms that appeared to be well accepted within the group were *black people* and *African Americans*. Both of these are still used in this edition, although a preference is growing for the latter term. Occasionally the term *Negro* will turn up in the writings of some of the boldest of the older protest leaders, but it came into disapprobation in the 1960s.

3. The virulent preoccupation of white males with black male–white female sexual relations has been explained psychoanalytically as projection or fear of reprisal for their own acts. See Dollard 1937 for a classical application of this theory to race relations. From the standpoint of power, the white male has traditionally tried to maintain control over both white and black women.

4. During this period, some white liberal voices in the South were speaking out against lynching. The Commission on Interracial Cooperation, formed in 1919, had as one of its central objectives the reduction of antiblack violence. Its

main weapons were conciliation, moral persuasion, and education. The Association of Southern Women for the Prevention of Lynching, a related group, collected thousands of signatures from southern white women who agreed with its aims (Myrdal 1944, 565, 846).

5. Du Bois, himself a prolific writer and activist, is probably better known for his emphasis on the "talented tenth," the group of educated persons whom he hoped would be the intellectual leaders of the race. His arguments for higher education to produce this group countered the prevailing belief in vocational education for blacks.

Chapter Two

1. Some analysts interpret Booker T. Washington as assuming different public and private postures, as acting out the "good nigger" role by agreeing with and flattering white people while secretly opposing some of their policies. See, for example, Meier and Rudwick 1966, 222.

2. By proving themselves in wartime, minority group members hope to influence the racial climate for the better. It is well known that Nisei—Japanese-American youth—volunteered for action during World War II and became a highly decorated unit. This occurred despite the wholesale removal of Japanese Americans from the West Coast to concentration camps, on the presumption of possible disloyalty. Ironically, some of the decorated soldiers had to visit parents still residing in the camps.

3. The full utilization of black men did not occur until the most recent wars, particularly the conflict in Vietnam. Not only was black participation disproportionately high, but so was the rate of black casualties.

4. As early as 1902, W. E. B. Du Bois presented a study of racial segregation in unions to Samuel Gompers, head of the AFL, only to be met with contempt. Du Bois found that 43 internationals had no black union members and only the United Mine Workers had a substantial number (1902).

5. Among the SCEF activists arrested and harassed were Anne and Carl Braden, whose home was bombed in retaliation for their integration efforts. In 1990, Anne Braden was honored by the American Civil Liberties Union for her distinguished lifetime contributions to civil liberties in the United States.

Chapter Three

1. A number of white civil rights activists interviewed by the author recalled the influence of early trips to the South. As children, they had been jarred or upset by the separate "colored" and "white" facilities and accompanying signs, sensing something "wrong."

2. An interpretation by Morris (1982; 1984) holds that King's very newness to the community made him a logical compromise choice for leadership over older, possibly competing, contenders.

3. As a matter of fact, she did lose her job at a department store and eventually had to relocate to find work. The myth of Rosa Parks being simply a tired worker returning from a job obfuscates her leadership qualities. Strategically, this image may have served the movement better than one of a long-term NAACP activist ready for the right opportunity to protest.

4. See Branch (1988, 132) for an interesting interpretation of the discrepancies in these accounts. Although women are often early leaders in social movements, they frequently move into background positions as men take over. Both internal movement dynamics, replicating society's patriarchy, and the pressures of the environment contribute to this transition. JoAnn Robinson's role in starting the boycott may also have been played down because of her vulnerable position as a state employee—a professor at a traditionally black college. (See also Blumberg 1988; West and Blumberg 1990, ch. 1.)

5. Dr. Falls was also active in the formation of the Committee to End Discrimination in Chicago Medical Institutions (of which the author was a member) in the 1950s. Many such local committees existed prior to the highly publicized nationwide organizations that became known in the 1960s. Their existence testified to the buildup of sentiments favorable to the later mass actions.

6. CORE first adopted the name the Committee of Racial Equality, later changing the first word to *Congress*.

7. The early Klan resorted to night riding in costumes, trying to scare blacks with the use of supernatural disguises, masks, and sheets. They believed blacks to be afraid of the supernatural—hence this effort at psychological control. According to one scholar, black people were truly frightened but often feigned ignorance. They knew there were murderous whites behind the masks (Fry 1977). The Klansmen chose white sheets in imitation of overseers who patrolled slave quarters to prevent them from running away.

8. A prizewinning author of an analysis of "the King years," Taylor Branch, writes:

Since 1984, I have sought the original FBI documents pertaining to the Bureau's steadfast contention that King's closest white friend was a top-level Communist agent. On this charge rested the FBI's King wiretaps and many collateral harassments against the civil rights movement. In opposing my request, the U.S. Department of Justice has argued in federal court that the release of thirty- to thirty-five year old informant reports on Levison would damage the national security even now . . . so far the logic of secrecy has been allowed to reach levels of royalist absurdity. . . .

Other evidence . . . has convinced me that Levison's character and historical contributions are established beyond significant doubt. (Branch 1988, xii)

Chapter Four

1. Ella Baker, who was a good deal older than the ministers of the SCLC, remained a key adviser to SNCC. The students' focus on grass-roots participa-

tion and democratic decision-making reflected her views; she was an open critic of top-down or pompous leadership.

2. Morris attaches much importance to the South's war against the NAACP. He states, "This attack against the NAACP greatly facilitated the emergence of the modern Civil Rights movement. The attack broke down the hegemony of the NAACP and the narrow bureaucratic and legalistic approach which it championed. Once this hegemony was broken, the way was cleared for other mass movement–oriented organizations and tactics to become widespread" (Morris 1984, 35).

3. At its 1948 convention, CORE had voted unanimously not to affiliate with "Communist controlled groups," reaffirming this position in 1949 and 1952 (Meier and Rudwick 1973). Communist delegates had proposed a number of resolutions to the 1949 NAACP national convention, but these were defeated. The next year, the convention adopted a resolution empowering the national office to expel any branch that came under communist control (Record 1964).

4. Later, when the school desegregation issue moved northward, the code word *busing* would be used by those who opposed integration in an oversimplification of the issues involved.

5. The Southern Manifesto was a statement circulated among southern congressmen which denounced the *Brown* decision as an abuse of judicial power. It pledged that the 101 senators and representatives from the eleven Confederate states who signed would "use all lawful means to bring about a reversal of this decision which is contrary to the Constitution" (Ashmore 1982, 231).

6. The author recalls being present at such a meeting in Somerset, New Jersey, in which face-to-face exchanges made vivid the economic plight of the sharecroppers and the daily dangers they faced.

Chapter Five

1. Some who dispute the size and extent of participation point out that demonstrations were not always large. This is true, for they became a day-by-day event, which took people away from jobs and schools. It is also true that black onlookers were usually supportive of demonstrators. Ann Moody, the author of the autobiographical excerpt at the beginning of this chapter, mentions that she stopped at a beauty parlor to have her hair washed after the sit-in session in which she was smeared with ketchup and mustard. The operator and patrons treated her like royalty, helping her to take off her dirty stockings and seeing that she had immediate attention.

2. The Southern Regional Council, organized in 1944, was an interracial human relations group that grew out of the Commission on Interracial Cooperation and the Durham-Atlanta-Richmond series of conferences. The Commission on Interracial Cooperation was formed in 1919 and tried to maintain some minimum amount of dialogue between blacks and whites even in the most difficult of

times. Interracial councils were created throughout the South and elsewhere in the nation to promote understanding. They represented the voice of white liberals. In 1942, a Durham conference of distinguished southern black leaders set forth a detailed statement of needed changes in the major institutional areas of the region—civil rights, agriculture, education, the military, and so on. Although the statement of black needs was forthright and comprehensive, it was couched in pre–civil rights movement rhetoric attuned to the conditions of the time. A group of liberal white southerners met in Atlanta in 1943 to consider the statement and found that it was "frank and courageous" and yet "free from any suggestion of threat and ultimatum" (Southern Regional Council 1944, 12). Further conferences followed in Richmond and Atlanta. At the latter, the nucleus of the Southern Regional Council was formed, and it included both black and white college presidents among its leaders. One of the more significant efforts at interracial cooperation in the South, the council sought to educate the public through its research on racial conditions, published in newsletters and reports.

3. Branch (1988), in an otherwise superlative version of the rides, calls the first group of Freedom Riders "a motley collection"—perhaps because they were diverse in age, race, sex, and background. In contrast, James Farmer writes of this group, "CORE recruited thirteen people with spotless reputations" (Williams 1987, 148).

4. This also held for the white female civil rights activists studied by the author, who considered the peace movement to be the one most closely linked to civil rights (Blumberg 1980a).

5. Strong protest centers, such as that in Birmingham, provided the organizational framework necessary for the emergence of the civil rights movement (Morris 1984, 74). Activists in movement centers often gave the public impression of being more spontaneous and less effective than they were, to throw off the opposition, but together they formed networks that could be mobilized when necessary. I observed the presence of movement centers in central New Jersey during this period. For example, in seeking white women civil rights activists to interview, I was deluged with an unusually large number of names of women who resided in the city of Plainfield. A few other centers provided more than a proportionate share of activists.

6. Many important details about the electronic surveillance of Martin Luther King, Jr., his associates, and the SCLC became public knowledge only in the 1970s. The Bureau's intervention in King's life by sending him an anonymous hate letter and what it felt to be a damaging tape in November 1964 made clear to him even then that the agency could not be counted upon for protection (see Garrow 1981, 9–18).

Chapter Six

1. Powell successfully guided 60 major laws to passage during his first five years as chair of the House Education and Labor Committee and helped push

through the 1964 and 1965 civil rights legislation. An outspoken challenger of segregation before such opposition became popular, Powell engendered animosity from many whites and a strong following among many blacks. Other congresspeople did not seem to undergo the kind of scrutiny to which Powell was subjected, and his natural flamboyance made him a target of criticism. Or probably more accurately, events in his personal life were used to countermand Powell's power and militancy. Further antagonism was aroused when Powell became an early supporter of Malcolm X, and in 1967 he was denied his seat in the House of Representatives pending examination of his "fitness." The Supreme Court ruled in July 1969 that Congress had acted unconstitutionally in barring him. For further details, see Haskins 1974.

2. A few southern whites, such as Virginia Durr, also flaunted southern custom by opening up their homes to civil rights workers. One such home was totally destroyed, and the owner almost lynched.

3. Allard Lowenstein and Bob Moses are credited as being important strategists in conceiving the idea of creating a nonsegregationist parallel Democratic party in Mississippi.

Chapter Seven

1. A 1963 public opinion poll of a nationwide sample of black people showed that King ranked highest as an individual leader.

2. One civil rights leader has been quoted as indicating that the press overplayed police violence in Birmingham. Many other firsthand accounts contest this point. Said Willie Bolden, an Alabama SCLC leader, "Even in filming, in many cases, they missed a lot of it because if the shit was gonna *really* go down, those folks tried to get those cameras out of the way first. And many times even after they were able to put the camera back into motion, much of the real *bloody* part of these marches was all over" (Raines 1977, 193).

3. King's speech, in which he repeatedly intoned the phrase, "I have a dream," has been reproduced many times on film and records. The films vividly reflect the overwhelming response of the audience, including those immediately surrounding him.

4. The Voting Rights Act was later renewed in 1970 and 1975. It was in danger of expiring on 6 August 1982, as the pro–states' rights president, Ronald Reagan, opposed further renewal. The outcry from civil rights groups forced him to modify his stance. In the interim, Brown Chapel had again become the scene of mass meetings. A commemorative, less publicized Selma-to-Montgomery march took place in February 1982, with some of the older leaders on hand. Among the marchers was a son of Viola Liuzzo.

5. "We Shall Overcome" was usually sung to conclude large meetings and rallies. Individuals stood with crossed arms, holding hands with the persons next to them. The basic verse was:

We shall overcome, We shall overcome
We shall overcome some day.
Oh, deep in my heart I do believe
We shall overcome some day

One of the variations was:

Black and white together
We shall overcome.

Chapter Eight

1. Only 4 percent of the responses to a survey of black studies programs at American colleges and universities indicated that some form of such a program had been initiated prior to 1966. "The figure became 7% by the long, hot summer of 1967, and rose to only 14% by the time Martin Luther King was assassinated in 1968. Eighty-six percent of the Black Studies offerings were established after this event" (Albert, Goldstein, and Slaughter 1974, 119).

2. Even the compromise offer made at the 1964 Democratic convention was claimed to be a temporary measure by Johnson supporters. Joseph Rauh, counsel for the MFDP, explains his reasoning in accepting the credentials committee offer to seat two delegates from the Mississippi Freedom Democratic party: "It wasn't a bad offer. Eventually, we accepted it, largely because of the promise that it would never happen again. A promise that, by the way, was carried out in Chicago in 1968 when the full inheritors of the Mississippi Freedom party were seated and the others were ousted. So we got in '68 what we should have got in '64, but we got it. That was the important thing" (Miller 1980, 393). It might be added that the southern bloc had defected to Goldwater in 1964, thus proving the compromise strategy rather ineffective.

3. The ultimate responsibility for the assassination of Malcolm X, as well as for that of King, has been a subject of controversy. Some authors allege FBI involvement (see Lane and Gregory 1977). Verified CIA plots to have certain foreign heads of state assassinated, as well as documentary evidence from the FBI's own files about its determination to harass civil rights leaders, lend some credence to such allegations. Typically, official explanations of the major assassinations of the 1960s call them the work of lone individuals. Were conspiracy involved, it would imply a group premeditated decision to eliminate a leader who was in disfavor, not very appropriate for a democratic country.

4. The advice to white people to modify their roles was repeated at many levels. Theodore Taylor, a black leader in Somerset, New Jersey, took the pains to visit the author at home in order to advise her that it would be wise to play a less prominent role in the township's civil rights activities. The memory of this scene is vivid.

5. West described the formation of "twin-track coalitions," black power groups joined with white support groups, in a number of localities. The understanding of these coalitions was that blacks were to be the leaders in setting policy.

6. The complicated relationship between black and Jewish people can only be touched upon briefly here and is still to receive definitive treatment in the literature. See Weisbord and Stein 1970 for one approach.

7. Some of the works written by participants in the black power movement express its ideas as well as its spirit in ways that cannot be captured in this account, which is, of course, written from the perspective of a white activist. See, for example, Brown 1969, Carmichael 1967 and 1971, Cleaver 1967, Malcolm X 1965.

Chapter Nine

1. The rise of the national unemployment rate to 10 percent in 1982 was a cause for massive concern, even influencing the Reagan administration to consider a jobs program. Yet such a rate for the black population arouses no special action.

2. The need for affirmative action was proclaimed in a presidential executive order in 1963, and regulations were gradually strengthened; in 1967 women were added to the groups protected.

3. For example, the Law Enforcement Assistance Administration in the Department of Justice paid 75 percent of the cost of local police riot programs.

Chapter Ten

1. "The purpose of Operation Breadbasket was to force companies doing business in the black community to hire blacks as employees; not just at the lowest levels, but throughout the corporate hierarchy" (Abernathy 1989, 400). If the process of negotiating with a business did not achieve results, black consumers would be urged to boycott the business or its products.

2. "The October 20, 1967, conviction of Deputy Sheriff Cecil Price and six of his codefendants marked the first successful jury conviction of white officials and Klansmen in the history of Mississippi for crimes against black people or civil rights workers," according to Cagin and Dray (1988, 451).

3. One of the best accounts of the Chicago effort is presented by Fairclough (1987, ch. 11, "Defeat in Chicago"). See also Abernathy 1989, ch. 11.

4. Edelman, in turn, attributes the general idea of bringing the poor to Washington to a conversation she had with Robert Kennedy (Hampton and Fayer 1990, 453).

5. In his own memoirs, Abernathy (1989) suggests that his close associa-tion with King gave them many opportunities for discussion and exchange. His agreement not to criticize King in public may have made his intellectual contri-butions less apparent.

6. The best known was probably the one at Cornell, where news photog-raphers captured the scene of black students moving out of a building in a disci-plined cadre, bearing firearms. It occurred in April 1969 during a weekend when parents were visiting the campus. Black students had held a number of demon-strations, and disciplinary action was being taken against some of those involved. On Friday, 18 April a flaming cross was thrown on the porch of a cooperative that housed black female students. The incident precipitated a decision to seize Willard Straight Hall, where the student union was located. Members of a white fraternity tried to enter it but were forced off the premises; whites in the radical SDS demonstrated in favor of the occupation. Rumors and tension abounded, and the black students had guns brought into the building. On Sunday, the college administration agreed to a number of the student demands and the occupation ended. Those who had been in the building filed out, with the scene recorded by cameras and flashbulbs. The immediate crisis was over, but the faculty and administration faced another when asked to ratify the conditions agreed upon. The campus was rent with disagreement, and resignations occurred. Cornell was not the only college to face black student revolt and serious faculty decisions, but it was the first one in which guns were displayed openly. See Edwards 1970 for a detailed account, sympathetic to the protesters.

7. Defense committees have been formed to come to the aid of persons considered political prisoners—that is, persons accused or convicted of crimes because of their political convictions or the need for a scapegoat—or when it is believed that a fair trial is unlikely to occur. There is little serious sociological literature that examines the consequences or significance of defense committees.

8. The reference is, of course, to a phase of temporary decline; the long-term movement for black liberation goes on.

Appendix

1. Fortunately, books have appeared on specific events in the movement that bring out some of its day-by-day intensity in particular communities. One, for example, traces the development of the struggle in the city of Greensboro, North Carolina, against the background of its early reputation as a relatively lib-eral southern city (Chafe 1981). This work is particularly important because Greensboro was the site of the first student sit-in demonstration that achieved national attention. Of course, Martin Luther King himself provided us with re-vealing personal accounts not only of the movement but of his own dilemmas as a leader (1958, 1963). In *My Soul is Rested,* Raines (1977) reports the colorful

reminiscences of individuals who were involved in the southern movement. More recently, the outstanding PBS television series *Eyes on the Prize* (parts 1 and 2) has been supplemented by companion volumes that present key events of the civil rights and black power movements from the eyes of the participants (Williams 1987; Hamptom and Fayer 1990). Taken as a whole, these and similar books tend to be vivid and detailed. They also provide correctives to one another and to secondhand accounts, for even the same event may be perceived differently by different observers.

2. Robeson's early speaking out severely limited his opportunities in the United States. Later, comedian Dick Gregory gave up a very lucrative career to devote full time to civil rights and other social causes.

Works Cited

Abernathy, Ralph D.
  1989   *And the walls came tumbling down.* New York: Harper & Row.

Albert, June, Rhoda L. Goldstein, and Thomas F. Slaughter, Jr.
  1974   The status of black studies programs at American colleges and universities. In *The black studies debate,* ed. J. V. Gordon and J. M. Rosser, pp. 111–60. Lawrence: University of Kansas.

Ashmore, Harry S.
  1982   *Hearts and minds: The anatomy of racism from Roosevelt to Reagan.* New York: McGraw-Hill.

Barbour, Floyd B., ed.
  1969   *The black power revolt.* Toronto: Collier Books.

Barkan, Steven E.
  1985   *Protesters on trial: Criminal justice in the southern civil rights and Vietnam antiwar movements.* New Brunswick: Rutgers University Press.

Bates, Daisy
  1962   *The long shadow of Little Rock; A memoir.* New York: David McKay Co.

Beardslie, William R.
  1977   *The way out must lead in: Life histories in the civil rights move-*
  1983   *ment.* Westport, Conn.: Lawrence Hill & Co.

Beifuss, Joan T.
  1985   *At the river I stand: Memphis, the 1968 strike, and Martin Luther King.* Memphis: B & W Books.

Bell, Inge Powell
  1968   *CORE and the strategy of non-violence.* New York: Random House.

Bennett, Lerone, Jr.
1966   *Confrontation: Black and white.* Baltimore: Penguin Books.

Berube, Maurice R., and Marilyn Gittell
1969   *Confrontation at Ocean Hill–Brownsville: The school strikes of 1968.* New York: Frederick A. Praeger.

Blackwelder, Julia Kirk
1979   Southern white fundamentalists and the civil rights movement. *Phylon* 40:334–41.

Blackwell, James E.
1982   Persistence and change in intergroup relations: The crisis upon us. *Social Problems* 29:325–46.

Blauner, Robert
1972   *Racial oppression in America.* New York: Harper & Row.

Bloom, Jack
1987   *Class, race, and the civil rights movement.* Bloomington: Indiana University Press.

Blumberg, Janice Rothschild
1985   *One voice: Rabbi Jacob M. Rothschild and the troubled South.* Macon, Ga.: Mercer University Press.

Blumberg, Rhoda Lois
1980a   Careers of women civil rights activists. *Journal of Sociology and Social Welfare* 7:708–29.
1980b   White mothers in the American civil rights movement. In *Research in the interweave of social roles: Women and men,* ed. Helena Z. Lopata, vol. 1, pp. 33–50. Greenwich, Conn.: JAI Press.
1982   Women as allies of other oppressed groups: Some hypothesized links between social activism and female consciousness. Paper read at Tenth World Congress of the International Sociological Association, 19 August 1982, in Mexico City.
1988   Progress in the historical reconstruction of the civil rights movement; Women leaders rediscovered. Paper presented at the "Dream and Reality" conference, Hofstra University, 19 February 1988.
1991   Rediscovering women leaders of the civil rights movement. In *Dream and reality: The modern black struggle for freedom and equality,* ed. Jeanine Swift. Westport, Conn.: Greenwood Press.

Blumer, Herbert
1951   Social movements. In *New outline of the principles of sociology,* ed. Alfred M. Lee, pp. 199–220. New York: Barnes & Noble.

Branch, Taylor
1988   *Parting the waters: America in the King years 1954–63.* New York: Simon & Schuster.

Brink, William, and Louis Harris
  1963   *The Negro revolution in America.* New York: Simon & Schuster.
  1966   *Black and white: A study of U.S. racial attitudes today.* New York: Simon & Schuster.

Broderick, Frances L., and August Meier, eds.
  1965   *Negro protest thought in the twentieth century.* New York: Bobbs-Merrill.

Brotz, Howard, ed.
  1966   *Negro social and political thought 1850–1920.* New York: Basic Books.

Brown, H. Rap
  1969   *Die, nigger, die.* New York: Dial Press.

Burns, W. Haywood
  1971   *The voices of Negro protest in America.* New York: Oxford University Press.

Caditz, Judith
  1976   Ethnic identification, interethnic contact, and belief in integration. *Social Forces* 54:632–45.

Cagin, Seth, and Philip Dray
  1988   *We are not afraid.* New York: Macmillan.

Carmichael, Stokely
  1967   *Stokely speaks.* New York: Random House.

Carmichael, Stokely, and Charles V. Hamilton
  1967   *Black power: the politics of liberation in America.* New York: Random House.

Carson, Clayborne
  1981   *In struggle: SNCC and the black awakening of the 1960s.* Cambridge, Mass.: Harvard University Press.

Carter, Dan T.
  1969   *Scottsboro: A tragedy of the American South.* Baton Rouge: Louisiana State University Press.

Chafe, William H.
  1981   *Civilities and civil rights: Greensboro, North Carolina, and the black struggle for freedom.* New York: Oxford University Press.

Clark, Septima, with Cynthia Stokes Brown
  1986   *Ready from within: Septima Clark and the civil rights movement.* Navarro, Calif.: Wild Trees Press.

Cleaver, Eldridge
  1968   *Soul on ice.* New York: Random House.

Cox, Oliver C.
  1948   *Caste, class, and race.* New York: Monthly Review Press.

Davis, James Chowning
1979   The J-curve of rising and declining satisfactions as a cause of revolution and rebellion. In *Violence in America,* rev. ed., ed. Hugh D. Graham and Ted R. Gurr, pp. 415–36. Beverly Hills, Calif.: Sage Publications.

Demerath, N. J., III, Gerald Marwell, and Michael T. Aiken
1971   *Dynamics of idealism: White activists in a black movement.* San Francisco: Jossey-Bass.

Den Hollander, A. N. J.
1953   The southern whites. In *Societies around the world.* vol. 2, ed. Irwin T. Sanders, Richard B. Woodbury, Frank J. Essene, Thomas P. Field, Joseph R. Schwendeman and Charles E. Snow, pp. 250–57. New York: Dryden Press.

Dollard, John
1937   *Caste and class in a southern town.* New Haven, Conn.: Yale University Press.

Downes, Bryan T., and Stephen W. Burks
1969   The historical development of the black protest movement. In *Blacks in the United States,* ed. Norvall D. Glenn and Charles M. Bonjean, pp. 322–44. San Francisco: Chandler Publishing Co.

Draper, Theodore
1970   *The rediscovery of black nationalism.* New York: Viking Compass.

Drewry, Cecelia Hodges
1971   Black theatre: An evolving force. In *Black life and culture in the United States,* ed. Rhoda L. Goldstein. New York: Thomas Y. Crowell.

Du Bois, W. E. B.
1902   *The Negro artisan.* Atlanta: Atlanta University Monograph.
1968   *The autobiography of W. E. B. Du Bois.* New York: International Publishers.
1969   *Black reconstruction in America.* 1935. New York: Atheneum.

Durr, Virginia Foster
1985   *Outside the magic circle: The autobiography of Virginia Foster Durr,* ed. Hollinger F. Barnard. University: University of Alabama Press.

Edwards, Harry
1970   *Black students.* New York: Free Press, Macmillan.

Evers, Myrlie, with William Peters
1967   *For us the living.* Garden City, N.Y.: Doubleday.

Exner, Judith
  1977   *My story.* New York: Grove Press.

Fairclough, Adam
  1987   *To redeem the soul of America: The Southern Christian Leader-
          ship Conference and Martin Luther King, Jr.* Athens: University
          of Georgia Press.

Farmer, James
  1985   *Lay bare the heart.* New York: Arbor House.

Feagin, Joe R., and Harlan Hahn
  1973   *Ghetto revolts.* New York: Macmillan.

Ferree, Myra Marx, and Beth B. Hess
  1985   *Controversy and coalition: The new feminist movement.* Boston:
          Twayne Publishers.

Fireman, Bruce, and William A. Gamson
  1979   Utilitarian logic in the resource mobilization perspective. In *The
          dynamics of social movements: Resource mobilization, social con-
          trol and tactics,* ed. Mayer N. Zald and John D. McCarthy, pp.
          8–44. Cambridge, Mass.: Winthrop Publishers.

Fogelson, Robert M.
  1968   From resentment to confrontation: The police, the Negroes, and
          the outbreak of the nineteen-sixties riots. *Political Science Quar-
          terly* 83:217–47.

Foner, Philip S.
  1955   *The life and writings of Frederick Douglass.* Vol. 4, *Reconstruc-
          tion and after.* New York: International Publishers.

Fry, Gladys-Marie
  1977   *Night riders in black folk history.* Knoxville: University of Ten-
          nessee Press.

Garfinkel, Herbert
  1969   *When Negroes march: The march on Washington movement in the
          organizational politics for FEPC.* 1959. New York: Atheneum.

Garrow, David J.
  1978   *Protest at Selma: Martin Luther King, Jr., and the Voting Rights
          Act of 1965.* New Haven, Conn.: Yale University Press.
  1981   *The FBI and Martin Luther King, Jr.* New York: Norton.
  1986   *Bearing the cross: Martin Luther King, Jr., and the Southern
          Christian Leadership Conference.* New York: William Morrow &
          Co.

Gerlach, Luther P., and Virginia H. Hine
  1970   *People, power, change: Movements of transformation.* Indianapo-
          lis: Bobbs-Merrill.

Geschwender, James A., ed.
1971   *The black revolt—the civil rights movement, ghetto uprisings and separation.* Englewood Cliffs, N.J.: Prentice-Hall.

Giddings, Paula
1984   *When and where I enter . . . The impact of black women on race and sex in America.* New York: William Morrow & Co.

Gitlin, Todd
1987   *The sixties: Years of hope, days of rage.* New York: Bantam Books.

Goffman, Erving
1967   *Interaction ritual.* Garden City, N.Y.: Doubleday.

Governor's Select Commission on Civil Disorder
1968   *Report for action.* State of New Jersey.

Graham, Hugh Davis, and Ted R. Gurr, eds.
1979   *Violence in America: Historical and comparative perspectives.* Rev. ed. Beverly Hills, Calif.: Sage Publications.

Gurr, Ted R.
1970   *Why men rebel.* Princeton, N.J.: Princeton University Press.

Hampton, Henry, and Steve Fayer
1990   *Voices of freedom: An oral history of the civil rights movement from the 1950s through the 1980s.* New York: Bantam Books.

Harding, Vincent
1981   *There is a river; the black struggle for freedom in America.* New York: Harcourt Brace Jovanovich.

Haskins, James
1974   *Adam Clayton Powell: Portrait of a marching black.* New York: Dial Press.

Holt, Len
1965   *The summer that didn't end.* New York: Morrow.

Isaacs, Harold R.
1963   *The new world of Negro Americans.* London: Phoenix House.

Jackson, Kenneth T.
1967   *The Ku Klux Klan in the city, 1915–30.* New York: Oxford University Press.

Jacobson, Julius, ed.
1968   *The Negro and the American labor movement.* Garden City, N.Y.: Anchor Books.

Janowitz, Morris
1979   Collective racial violence: A contemporary history. In *Violence in America: Historical and comparative perspectives,* ed. Hugh D.

Graham and Ted R. Gurr, pp. 262–86. Beverly Hills, Calif.: Sage Publications.

Johnson, James Weldon
1968   *Along this way; the autobiography of James Weldon Johnson.* 1933. New York: Viking Compass.

Jones, Le Roi, and Larry Neal
1968   *Black fire: An anthology of Afro-American writing.* New York: Apollo Books.

Karson, Marc, and Ronald Radosh
1968   The AFL and the Negro Worker, 1894–1949. In *The Negro and the American labor movement,* ed. Julius Jacobson. New York: Doubleday Anchor.

Kearns, Doris
1976   *Lyndon Johnson and the American dream.* New York: Signet.

Kennedy, Louise V.
1930   *The Negro peasant turns cityward.* New York: Columbia University Press.

Killian, Lewis M.
1975   *The impossible revolution, phase 2: Black power and the American dream.* New York: Random House.

King, Deborah
1988   Multiple jeopardies, multiple consciousness: The context of a black feminist ideology. *Signs* 4 (Autumn): 42–72.

King, Martin Luther, Jr.
1958   *Stride toward freedom: The Montgomery story.* New York: Harper & Row.
1963   *Why we can't wait.* New York: Harper & Row.
1967   *Where do we go from here: Chaos or community.* New York: Harper & Row.

King, Mary
1987   *Freedom song: A personal story of the 1960s civil rights movement.* New York: William Morrow & Co.

Kinoy, Arthur
1983   *Rights on trial: The odyssey of a people's lawyer.* Cambridge, Mass.: Harvard University Press.

Lane, Mark, and Dick Gregory
1977   *Code name "Zorro": The murder of Martin Luther King, Jr.* Englewood Cliffs, N.J.: Prentice Hall.

Levitan, Sar A., William B. Johnston, and Robert Taggart
1975   *Still a dream; The changing status of blacks since 1960.* Cambridge, Mass.: Harvard University Press.

Lewis, Anthony, and the *New York Times*
    1964   *Portrait of a decade: The second American Revolution.* New York: Random House.

Lewis, David Levering
    1978   *King, a biography.* 2d ed. Urbana: University of Illinois Press.

Litwack, Leon F.
    1980   *Been in the storm so long: The aftermath of slavery.* New York: Random House.

Lomax, Louis E.
    1962   *The Negro revolt.* New York: Signet Books.

Lynd, Staughton, ed.
    1966   *Nonviolence in America: A documentary history.* Indianapolis: Bobbs-Merrill.

Matthews, Donald R., and James W. Prothro
    1966   *Negroes and the new southern politics.* New York: Harcourt Brace Jovanovich.

McAdam, Doug
    1982   *Political process and the development of black insurgency 1930–70.* Chicago: University of Chicago Press.
    1988   *Freedom summer.* New York: Oxford University Press.

McCarthy, John D., and Mayer N. Zald
    1973   *The trend of social movements in America: Professionalization and resource mobilization.* Morristown, N.J.: General Learning Press.
    1977   Resource mobilization and social movements: A partial theory. *American Journal of Sociology* 82:1212–41.

McMillen, Neil R.
    1971   *The Citizens' Council: Organized resistance to the second reconstruction, 1954–64.* Urbana: University of Illinois Press.

Malcolm X
    1965   *The autobiography of Malcolm X.* New York: Grove Press.

Marx, Gary T., and Michael Useem
    1971   Majority involvement in minority movements: Civil rights, abolition, untouchability. *Journal of Social Issues* 27:81–104.

Marx, Gary T., and James Wood
    1975   Strands of theory and research in collective behavior. In *Annual review of sociology,* vol. 1, ed. Alex Inkeles et al., pp. 363–428. Palo Alto, Calif.: Annual Reviews.

Masotti, Louis H., Jeffrey K. Hadden, Kenneth F. Seminatore, and Jerome R. Corsi
    1969   *A time to burn? An evaluation of the present crisis in race relations.* Chicago: Rand McNally & Co.

Meier, August, and Elliott M. Rudwick
>1968   Attitudes of Negro leaders toward the American labor movement from the Civil War to World War I. In *The Negro and the American labor movement.* ed. Julius Jacobson, pp. 27–48. Garden City, N.Y.: Anchor Books.

>1969   The boycott movement against Jim Crow streetcars in the South, 1900–1906. *Journal of American History* 55:756–75.

>1973   *CORE: A study in the civil rights movement 1942–1968.* New York: Oxford University Press.

>1976   *From plantation to ghetto: An interpretative history of American Negroes.* 3d ed. New York: Hill & Wang.

Merton, Robert K.
>1972   Insiders and outsiders: A chapter in the sociology of knowledge. *American Journal of Sociology* 78:9–47.

Miller, Merle
>1980   *Lyndon: An oral biography.* New York: G. P. Putnam's Sons.

Moody, Ann
>1968   *Coming of age in Mississippi.* New York: Dell Publishing Co.

Morris, Aldon Douglas
>1979   The rise of the civil rights movement and its movement black power structure, 1953–1963. Ph.D. dissertation, State University of New York at Stony Brook.

>1981   Black southern sit-in movement. *American Sociological Review* 46:744–67.

>1982   Organization, mobilization and leadership in the civil rights movement. Paper read at the 77th Annual Meeting of the American Sociological Association, 6 September 1982, in San Francisco.

>1984   *The origins of the civil rights movement: Black communities organizing for change.* New York: Free Press.

Myrdal, Gunnar
>1944   *An American dilemma.* New York: Harper & Brothers.

National Advisory Commission on Civil Disorders
>1968   *Report.* With introduction by Tom Wicker. New York: Bantam.

Navasky, Victor S.
>1971   *Kennedy justice.* New York: Atheneum.

Nazel, Joseph
>1980   *Paul Robeson: A biography of a proud man.* Los Angeles: Holloway House Publishing Co.

Nelson, Harold A.
>1971   Leadership and change in an evolutionary movement: An analysis of change in the leadership structure of the southern civil rights movement. *Social Forces* 49:353–71.

Oberschall, Anthony
   1973   *Social conflict and social movements.* Englewood Cliffs, N.J.: Prentice-Hall.

O'Reilly, Kenneth
   1989   *"Racial matters": The FBI's secret file on black America, 1960–1972.* New York: Free Press.

Orum, Anthony M.
   1972   *Black students in protest: A study of the origins of the black student movement.* Arnold M. and Caroline Rose Monograph. Washington, D.C.: American Sociological Association.

Payne, Charles
   1990   "Men led, but women organized": Movement participation of women in the Mississippi delta. In *Women and social protest,* ed. Guida West and Rhoda Lois Blumberg, pp. 156–65. New York: Oxford University Press.

Perrow, Charles
   1979   The sixties observed. In *The dynamics of social movements: Resource mobilization, social control and tactics,* ed. Mayer N. Zald and John D. McCarthy, pp. 192–211. Cambridge, Mass.: Winthrop Publishers.

Pettigrew, Thomas F.
   1971   *Racially separate or together?* New York: McGraw-Hill.

Phillips, W.M., Jr., and Rhoda L. Blumberg
   1983   Tokenism and organizational change. *Integrateducation* 20:34–39.

Pinkney, Alphonso
   1968   *The committed: White activists in the civil rights movement.* New Haven, Conn.: College and University Press.
   1976   *Red, black and green: Black nationalism in the United States.* Cambridge: Cambridge University Press.

Piven, Frances Fox, and Richard A. Cloward
   1972   *Regulating the poor: The functions of public welfare.* New York: Vintage Books.
   1979   *Poor people's movements: Why they succeed, how they fail.* New York: Vintage Books.

Raab, Earl
   1966   A tale of three wars: What war and which poverty? *Public Interest* 3:45–56.

Raines, Howell
   1977   *My soul is rested.* New York: G. P. Putnam's Sons.

Rawick, George P.
1972   *From sundown to sunup: The making of the black community.* Westport, Conn.: Greenwood Press.

Record, Wilson
1964   *Race and radicalism: The NAACP and the Communist party in conflict.* Ithaca, N.Y.: Cornell University Press.

Reed, Adolph L., Jr.
1979   Black particularity reconsidered. *Telos* 39:71–93.

Revel, Jean-Francois
1971   *Without Marx or Jesus: The new American revolution has begun.* New York: Doubleday.

Rex, John
1973   *Race, colonialism and the city.* Boston: Routledge & Kegan Paul.

Robeson, Paul
1958   *Here I stand.* New York: Othello Associates.

Robinson, Jo Ann Gibson
1987   *The Montgomery bus boycott and the women who started it,* ed. David J. Garrow. Knoxville: University of Tennessee Press.

Rosen, Sumner M.
1968   The CIO era, 1935–55. In *The Negro and the American labor movement,* ed. Julius Jacobson, pp. 188–208. New York: Doubleday Anchor.

Rothschild, Mary Aickin
1979   White women volunteers in the freedom summers: Their life and work in a movement for social change. *Feminist Studies* 5:466–95.
1982   *A case of black and white: Northern volunteers and the southern freedom summers, 1964–65.* Westport, Conn.: Greenwood Press.

Saltman, Juliet
1971   *Open housing as a social movement.* Lexington, Mass.: D. C. Heath & Co.

Schaefer, Richard T.
1971   The Ku Klux Klan: Continuity and change. *Phylon* 32:143–57.
1979   *Racial and ethnic groups.* Boston: Little, Brown, & Co.

Seale, Bobby
1968   *Seize the time.* New York: Random House.

Sears, David O., and John B. McConahay
1973   *The politics of violence—the new urban blacks and the Watts riot.* Boston: Houghton Mifflin.

Sellers, Cleveland, with Robert Terrell
1973   *The river of no return.* New York: William Morrow & Co

Silver, James W.
1963   *Mississippi: The closed society.* New York: Harcourt, Brace & World.

Sitkoff, Harvard
1981   *The struggle for black equality, 1954–1980.* New York: Hill & Wang.

Smelser, Neil J.
1962   *Theory of collective behavior.* New York: Free Press.

Smith, Donald H.
1970   An exegesis of Martin Luther King's social philosophy. *Phylon* 31:89–97.

Southern Regional Council
1944   *The Southern Regional Council: Its origins and purpose.* Atlanta: Southern Regional Council.

Surace, Samuel J., and Melvin Seeman
1967   Some correlates of civil rights activism. *Social Forces* 46:197–207.

Taper, Bernard
1962   *Gomillion versus Lightfoot: The Tuskegee gerrymander case.* New York: McGraw-Hill.

Turner, John, with B. Stanton, M. Vahala, and R. Williams
1981   *The Ku Klux Klan: A history of racism and violence.* Montgomery, Ala.: Klanwatch, Southern Poverty Law Center.

van den Berghe, Pierre L.
1967   *Race and racism: A comparative perspective.* New York: John Wiley & Sons.

Vander Zanden, James W.
1965   *Race relations in transition.* New York: Random House.

Verba, S., B. Ahmed, and A. Bhatt
1971   *Caste, race and politics: A comparative study of India and the United States.* Beverly Hills, Calif.: Sage Publications.

Von Eschen, Donald, Jerome Kirk, and Maurice Pinard
1971   The organizational substructure of disorderly politics. *Social Forces* 49:529–43.
1967   The disintegration of the Negro non-violent movement. *Journal of Peace Research* 4:215–34.

Waskow, Arthur
1966   *From race riot to sit-in.* Garden City, N.Y.: Doubleday.

Weaver, Bill L.
    1979   The black press and the assault on professional baseball's "color line." *Phylon* 40:303–17.

Webb, Sheyann, and Rachel West Nelson, as told to Frank Sikora
    1980   *Selma, Lord, Selma: Childhood memories of the civil-rights days.* University: University of Alabama Press.

Weisbord, Robert G., and Arthur Stein
    1970   *Bittersweet encounter: The Afro-American and the American Jew.* Westport, Conn.: Negro Universities Press.

Weisbrot, Robert
    1990   *Freedom bound: A history of America's civil rights movement.* New York: W.W. Norton & Co.

Weiss, Robert Frank
    1978   Defection from social movements and subsequent recruitment to new movements. In *Collective behavior and social movements,* ed. Louis E. Genevie, pp. 228–38. Itasca, Ill.: F. E. Peacock Publishers.

West, Guida
    1979   Twin-track coalitions in the black power movement. In *Interracial bonds,* eds. Rhoda Goldstein Blumberg and Wendell James Roye, pp. 71–87. Bayside, N.Y.: General Hall.
    1981   *The national welfare rights movement; The social protest of poor women.* New York: Praeger Publishers.

———— **and Rhoda Lois Blumberg**
    1990   *Women and social protest.* New York: Oxford University Press.

Whalen, Charles, and Barbara Whalen
    1986   *The longest debate: A legislative history of the 1964 Civil Rights Act.* New York: Mentor.

White, E. Frances
    1984   "Listening to the voices of black feminism," *Radical America:* 7–25.

Wilkinson, Doris Y.
    1969   *Black revolt: Strategies of protest.* Berkeley, Calif.: McCutchan Publishing Corp.
    1970   Tactics of protest as media: the case of the black revolution. *Sociological Focus* 3:13–21.

Wilkinson, J. Harvie, III
    1979   *From Brown to Bakke: The Supreme Court and school integration: 1954–1978.* New York: Oxford University Press.

Williams, Juan
　1987　*Eyes on the prize: America's civil rights years, 1954–1965.* New York: Viking.

Williams, Robin M.
　1977　*Mutual accommodation: Ethnic conflict and accommodation.* Minneapolis: University of Minnesota Press.

Willie, Charles Vert, ed.
　1979　*Caste and class controversy.* Bayside, N.Y.: General Hall.
　1981　Social movements as innovation: The civil rights movement. Paper read at the 76th Annual Meeting of the American Sociological Association, 25 August 1981, in Toronto, Canada.

Wilson, William J.
　1973　*Power, racism and privilege.* New York: Macmillan.
　1978　*The declining significance of race.* Chicago: University of Chicago Press.
　1987　*The truly disadvantaged: The inner city, the underclass, and public policy.* Chicago: University of Chicago Press.

Wofford, Harris
　1980　*Of Kennedys and Kings: Making sense of the sixties.* New York: Farrar, Straus & Giroux.

Woodward, C. Vann
　1974　*The strange career of Jim Crow.* 3d rev. ed. New York: Oxford University Press.

Yinger, J. Milton
　1968　Recent developments in minority and race relations. *Annals of the American Academy of Political and Social Science* 378:130–45.

Zald, Mayer N., and Roberta Ash
　1966　Social movement organizations: Growth, decay and change. *Social Forces* 44:327–41.

Zald, Mayer N., and John D. McCarthy, eds.
　1979　*The dynamics of social movements: Resource mobilization, social control and tactics.* Cambridge, Mass.: Winthrop Publishers.

Zangrando, Robert L.
　1980　*The NAACP crusade against lynching, 1909–1950.* Philadelphia: Temple University Press.

Zinn, Howard
　1965　*SNCC: The new abolitionists.* Boston: Beacon Press.

Index

233

The Author

Rhoda Lois Blumberg, professor of sociology and a member of the graduate faculty at Rutgers University, was active in the civil rights movement in Illinois and New Jersey and in the development of black studies programs at Rutgers. Before receiving her doctorate at the University of Chicago, she spent a year as a Special Research Fellow at Fisk University. She is the editor of *Black Life and Culture in the United States* and co-editor of *Interracial Bonds* (with Wendell J. Roye) and *Women and Social Protest* (with Guida West). She was a Fulbright Research Scholar in India and has written two books on Indian women, one on organizations in contemporary society, and various articles on race relations, black studies, and women in social movements.